Herbert's Prayerful Art

Herbert's Prayerful Art

TERRY G. SHERWOOD

UNIVERSITY OF TORONTO PRESS
Toronto Buffalo London

© University of Toronto Press 1989
Toronto Buffalo London
Printed in Canada

ISBN 0-8020-2712-1

Printed on acid-free paper

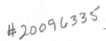

Canadian Cataloguing in Publication Data

Sherwood, Terry G. (Terry Grey), 1936–
Herbert's prayerful art

Bibliography: p.
Includes index.
ISBN 0-8020-2712-1

1. Herbert, George, 1593–1633. Temple.
2. Herbert, George, 1593–1633 – Criticism and interpretation.
3. Herbert, George, 1593–1633 – Religion.
4. Prayer in literature. I. Title.

PR3507.T43S48 1989   821'.3   C89-094550-0

Editions used: *The Works of George Herbert* ed F.E. Hutchinson
(Oxford: Clarendon Press 1941; corrected edition 1959);
the Bible: Authorized Version 1611.

The illustration on the jacket is taken from the title page of
Lewis Bayly's *The Practise of Pietie* (1620), and is reproduced
by permission of the Folger Shakespeare Library.

To Graham and Megan

Contents

Acknowledgments

Much of the research for this book was conducted at the Folger Shakespeare Library during a Study Leave from the University of Victoria. Like other Folger Readers, I remain grateful for the welcoming atmosphere at the library and for the help of its very competent staff. Also, during my year there I enjoyed the friendship of Professor Elliott Simon, who was on leave from the University of Haifa.

Three friends at the University of Victoria deserve special thanks. Edward Berry and Patrick Grant both read the entire manuscript and made detailed suggestions. The profits from their unselfish labours can be found throughout the final version. I am also grateful to Thomas Cleary for his wit, wisdom, and steady refusal to take the wrong things seriously.

At Victoria the manuscript was prepared at an early stage by Colleen Donnelly and Susan Mitchell. Later, Daniel Stewart assisted in proofreading and constructing the index. At the University of Toronto Press, Prudence Tracy showed great faith in the manuscript, while setting a wise course for its progress there. Final improvements were made by Judy Williams, who prepared the manuscript for publication.

Publication of this book has been made possible by a grant from the Canadian Federation for the Humanities, using funds provided by the Social Sciences and Humanities Research Council of Canada. Chapter three first appeared as 'Tasting and Telling Sweetness in George Herbert's Poetry' in *English Literary Renaissance* 12 (1982) 319–40.

I am happily indebted to Nancy for things great and small. The book is dedicated to Graham and Megan, who have come of age during its making.

Herbert's Prayerful Art

Introduction

'It was a surprise to me to realize, after going through the poems carefully, that a little more than half of these poems are actually in the form of prayer.'[1] This surprise expressed by one distinguished student of Renaissance literature points to a problem faced by many modern readers of George Herbert's *The Temple*. Those of us who approach it as a literary work may be surprised to discover the insistent demands of its prayerfulness. We may be unsettled further by imagining Herbert's own surprise at our approach. This primarily devotional work, which was written about his prayerful 'conflicts'[2] with God and hesitantly passed on to Nicholas Ferrar for him to assess its value for Christian readers, has become an important subject of literary criticism. Herbert hoped that the work would reflect the reader's prayerful communion with God. And, in fact, the spirituality of *The Temple* has had a continuing hold on Christian readers.

Not unexpectedly, more than one secular critic has been made uneasy by the need to interpret the spiritual experience expressed by Herbert's art. We wish to avoid rushing in where perhaps only the Christian should tread. Yet few Christian students of Herbert would deny that modern Herbert commentary has taught us all a great deal about the religious substance of *The Temple* and its lyrics. Paradoxically, our uneasiness as secular critics points to our limitations, while encouraging us to remove our blinders whenever we can. In regard to Herbert's spirituality, we can do so by attempting to comprehend more fully the nature of the prayerful communion embodied in the work.

The appearance of Herbert's works in the series the Classics of Western Spirituality[3] serves to remind us that *The Temple* is much more than a work of literature. The exact boundaries of any 'spirituality' can be elusive,[4] but the claim that spirituality is the 'life of prayer'[5] unequivocally locates the centre of Christian spiritual life. So, too, in *The Temple* the long devotional middle, 'The Church,' is dominated by works written in a prayerful mode. In orthodox Christianity prayer involving personal communion with God remains the centre of a life essentially, though not exclusively, interior. The individual believer's increasingly personal identification with Christ is the necessary condition for a sanctifying mutual communion inspired by his indwelling Spirit. The prayerful communion in this personal relationship between human and divine is the essential subject expressed in Herbert's art.

Herbert's admission that *The Temple* embodies his own relationship with God leads to inferences about both his art and his spirituality which are the subjects of this study. The art of *The Temple*, in expressing Herbert's communion with God, is a prayerful art which assumes, more generally, that the many practices of prayer are themselves artful. The special quality of self-consciousness that marks *The Temple* as a work of spirituality reflects this assumption. Even more generally, the prayerfulness that must fill all rooms of experience informs what can be called the arts of spirituality.

The burst of Herbert criticism in recent years has told us more about his theology than about his spirituality. By saying little about prayer, Gene Edward Veith's study of Herbert's 'reformation spirituality,' however useful, falls into the same pattern.[6] By no means has prayer been ignored in modern Herbert criticism. Louis Martz' pioneer work on the meditative poem underlined the importance of prayer in devotional poetry.[7] More recently, Anthony Nuttall has suggested some theological implications of Herbert's dialogue with God.[8] But the ways in which the prayerful mode enters into every aspect of *The Temple* need to be looked at more attentively, particularly by secular critics.

Chapter one in this study of Herbert's spirituality begins with the common ingredients in prayer which were taken for granted by Herbert and his contemporary readers. Many secular students of Herbert will find, as I did, that to discover these ingredients, however obvious they may seem to historians of spirituality, is to illuminate the poetry of *The Temple*. The poetry reflects the prayerful tenor of Herbert's life, which was established in the devout household of Magdalene Herbert and fulfilled at Bemerton in the regimen of private and communal prayer.[9] The ingredients in this prayerful existence are the natural building materials in Herbert's poetic temple.

The disciplines of prayer, which train the devotional poet in his art, become empty forms unless motivated by love that conforms the believer to Christ. Appropriately for a Christian poet, the psychology of Herbert's prayerfulness is rooted in love. His art of loving God, with its elements of holy parody drawing on the repertory of secular love conventions, defines his prayerfulness while expressing its basic motivation. However central in his spirituality, Herbert's experience of divine love continues to vex Herbert criticism, partly because *The Temple* questions how closely man can imitate Christ's love. Even more problematical is the fact that important commentators, in affirming the Reformation elements in Herbert's thought, slight man's love of God while stressing the importance of faith.[10] By addressing God's love, but not man's, these commentators present an unbalanced version of Herbert's spirituality. It is mutual love that generates prayerfulness; and to understand the prayerful 'traffick' ('The Odour,' 27) in love between God and man, however problematical it may seem, is to grasp the kernel of Herbert's spirituality. Herbert's understanding of this love is examined in chapter two.

The taste of sweetness, the fitness of experience properly formed, the abrasions of grief mollified by delight, the quickening of faculties slowed by sin's dullness – for Herbert these are central qualities of the prayerful life moved by the love of God. They are the respective subjects of the four chapters that follow. Herbert's own experience of these qualities variously colours his poetic struggle to express prayer and praise. The attempt to find the right words to discriminate these qualities, which emerge in his 'conflicts' with God, distinguishes his arts of spirituality.

The spirituality of any Christian writer is necessarily affected by his or her notion of the self and its powers. Appropriately, Herbert critics have examined the nature of the self in his poetry, although they have differed considerably in their judgments. The influence of Reformation thought on Herbert and his British contemporaries has encouraged the view that he believed in a debilitated self radically dependent on God. Yet much in Herbert's prayerful art moderates this influence. Herbert's notion of the self, which is the subject of the conclusion, expresses his conviction that it is inseparable from its artistic powers. The dialogue with God confers importance on the human partner, whose struggle to find the right words necessarily contributes to that dialogue. So, too, by rewarding this struggle to make prayerful art – with sweetness, fitness, delight, and quickness – God expresses his own delight in man's efforts. However temporary they may seem to the struggling believer, these rewards restore what has been lost in the created self. Herbert found in the struggle of his own prayerful art the evidence of his restoration.

1 *Sacrificing Prayer and Praise*

The constant interplay between prayer and praise in *The Temple* has deep roots in Christian spirituality. Unlike secular modern readers, Herbert's contemporaries would not have had to stop and note just how thoroughly the conventions of prayer and praise engrain *The Temple*. Instead, his contemporaries would have found in the emphatic role of 'The Sacrifice' the cues for understanding how Herbert conceived this poetic sacrifice of his lips.[1] That half of the lyrics are prayers and that the entire poem can be viewed as a work of praise alert us that Herbert is taking much for granted in his sacrifice that we might overlook.

One example is the relationship itself between prayer and praise. Herbert would not quarrel with the received notion that prayer is a conversation between man and God. Nor would he quarrel with John Damascene's widely quoted statement that prayer is 'raising the mind to God.'[2] At this point, however, we may find ourselves asking why Herbert, like his contemporaries, insists on distinguishing prayer from praise, since praise also involves such a conversation that raises the mind to God. After all, modern students of spirituality categorize praise as one form of prayer.[3] Still, Herbert is in good company; and statements pairing prayer with praise, while maintaining a biblical distinction between them, are everywhere in the religious literature of Herbert's time.

Augustine's famous claim that prayer is petition[4] helps us solve this apparent problem. Augustine is pointing to the essential context of prayer in which the sinful creature expresses his absolute need for the Creator's help. All other categories of prayer – contrition, confession, thanksgiving, adoration – are implicit in this petition for God's help: the sinner confesses and grieves for his sin, then thanks

and adores the God whose blessings in turn reclaim him. Also, here
we can resolve the difficulties in the apparent biblical separation
between prayer and praise: all praise is really thanksgiving and
adoration directed to God, who answers man's petitions for help.

Donne puts the relationship between petition and thanksgiving
more baldly when talking about the Psalter. 'Prayer and Praise is the
same thing,' he tells us. He is not equating prayer and praise, but is
saying that one cannot exist without the other: 'they doe not onely
consist together, but constitute one another.'[5] For Donne the bare
truth of the Psalter is that 'prayer' is petition; and 'praise,' thanksgiving. And just as petition assumes earlier praiseworthy blessings,
thanksgiving assumes the desire for subsequent blessings. And,
more, it expresses the expectation, more than mere hope, that God
will grant similar blessings later: 'God hath no law upon himselfe,
but yet God himselfe proceeds by precedent: And whensoever we
present to him with thanksgiving, what he hath done, he does the
same, and more againe.' God 'translates' praise as prayer, thanksgiving as petition. Thus, to praise a God who works by 'precedent' is
also to petition for more of the same, however implicitly. In that
sense praise is really prayer, that is, petition to God.[6]

Here we can return to Augustine's point that all modes of prayer are
inherent in petition. The longer we contemplate *The Temple*, the
more we find it dominated by the several modes of prayer and praise;
and the prayer of petition is the bass note, often immediate,
uncompromising, and complaining. In 'Sighs and Grones,' anguished, naked petition reverberates in the rhymed opening and
closing lines of each stanza:

> O do not use me
> After my sinnes! look not on my desert,
> But on thy glorie! then thou wilt reform
> And not refuse me: for thou onely art
> The mightie God, but I a sillie worm;
> O do not bruise me!   (1–6)

These reverberations ('do not urge ... scourge ... blinde ... grinde ... fill
... kill me') insist on a painful need that God must fill. Only the more
positive final request ('reprieve ... relieve me') hints at a release from
punishment. The speaker urgently requests release from pain; and,
although he confesses his sin as a cause of affliction and praises God
as the custodian of life and death, his petition is the creature's

anguished request for God's help. Here is the bare-bones relationship between a powerful though intimately loving God and his painfully inadequate creature, petitioning to be raised beyond his inadequacies.

Herbert plays this bass note throughout *The Temple*. Familiar Old Testament strains[7] in the yearning request that God 'Turn, and restore me' ('The Search,' 50) point to a recognizable helplessness and fear of God's absence. Only God, who turns away from sinful man, can repair the damage done to his sinful creature: 'Purge all my sinnes done heretofore' ('Trinitie Sunday,' 4). All the speaker's 'attendants,' especially his thoughts, are rebelliously destructive. Helplessness petitions God:

> Oh help, my God! let not their plot
> > Kill them and me,
> > And also thee,
> Who art my life: ...   ('Affliction (iv),' 19–22)

Yet these cries for help, tight with complaint, stand side by side with hope and knowledge that God will build and restore. There is a measure of assurance in the petition that God will identify the restored creature as his own: 'O be mine still! still make me thine! / Or rather make no Thine and Mine!' ('Clasping of Hands,' 19–20). But hope is inconstant, and assurance is affirmed only in the continual act of petition.

The insistent bass note of petition rarely sounds alone in *The Temple*. Although most forms of prayer look more to man's need than to God's gracious gifts, the habits of contrition and confession overrule more naked expressions of self. In 'The Altar' the concluding petition – that Christ's 'SACRIFICE be mine' and that God 'sanctifie this ALTAR' (that is, the poem that represents the contrite heart) – expresses both human weakness and adoration of God. His poem is a 'broken ALTAR' (1), the heart fully contrite and broken,[8] sorry for its sin. A humble, not a nakedly importunate voice makes the final petition that is simultaneously praise of God.

Yet even the confessing soul can play its wilful tricks, and its petitions may be suspect. In 'Confession' a meditation on affliction's role in exposing self-concealment modulates into a prayer of confession and petition. The heart builds its structures of deceit, although these ingenious closets and boxes cannot defend against the grief that exposes human sin. Only the breast 'open' (19) in confession can escape. In acknowledging the general problem of these deceitful structures, such 'fiction' (23), he makes a particular application to himself:

> Wherefore my faults and sinnes,
> Lord, I acknowledge; take thy plagues away:
> For since confession pardon winnes,
> I challenge here the brightest day,
> The clearest diamond: let them do their best,
> They shall be thick and cloudie to my breast.   (25–30)

Here meditation has shifted into confessional prayer and petition. But there is a half-possiblity, a remaining 'closet' of deceit, that the real motive of confession is less hatred of sin than self-serving desire to escape the pain of affliction. This possibility complicates this prayer of confession and petition.

Few poems in *The Temple* embody as many questions about the relationships between different modes of prayer as 'Gratefulnesse.' A direct petition immediately poses the crucial problem how to thank God for his blessings:

> Thou that hast giv'n so much to me,
> Give one thing more, a gratefull heart.
> See how thy beggar works on thee
>   By art.   ('Gratefulnesse,' 1–4)

All gifts come from God, even finding the right stance in thanking the Giver. And man's request for the gift requires 'art' that is uneasily self-conscious. But need enforces both petition and art; only then are thanks possible. Unfortunately, the need makes him clamorous, and distaste for his own noise only points out further his debt to God, who tolerates such a noisy 'beggar.' The biblical knocking at God's door[9] here becomes the obnoxious 'Perpetuall knockings' that petition for 'Gift upon gift.' Need is voracious: 'much would have more' (13–15). Self-loathing and confession must acknowledge the necessity for his noisy petition. But the flawed creature can work to shift the heart's gaze to God:

> Wherefore I crie, and crie again;
> And in no quiet canst thou be,
> Till I a thankfull heart obtain
>   Of thee:

> Not thankfull, when it pleaseth me;
> As if thy blessings had spare dayes:
> But such a heart, whose pulse may be
> Thy praise.   ('Gratefulnesse,' 25–32)

In that very desire to look to God, even amidst his own clamour, the speaker recognizes a proper thanks in praise of God's goodness. Confession, petition, thanksgiving, and praise here merge.

Petition leads necessarily to thanksgiving and praising. And there is arguably a refined praise that looks beyond God's blessings to God himself. For Donne a tough spiritual realism makes him doubtful that man can free praise from the memory of blessings received. But his contemporary John Preston wishes to distinguish thanksgiving grounded in human need from pure thanks that concentrate on the Giver and work free from 'desire' that is the voice of need.[10] In *The Temple* adoration does struggle upward, even if not completely forgetful of self, propelled by love to praise God. That struggle distinguishes Herbert's poem. John Booty finds an Anglican 'rhythm' of contrition and praise revealed at the outset in 'The Altar.'[11] The 'stones' of the broken altar, cemented by contritional tears, meet to 'praise thy Name' (12). This same instinct to praise struggles throughout *The Temple*, even amidst clamorous petition, as in 'Gratefulnesse.' There, the very request for thankfulness to transform the heart's lifebeat into a pulse of praise is itself struggle to praise.

As we have already seen, noting the major categories of prayer – petition, contrition, confession, thanksgiving, adoration[12] – and their relationship to praise contributes to a rudimentary understanding of prayer in *The Temple*. Other recognizable traditional elements, such as Augustine's equation of prayer and petition, are also essential. Another of these is the biblical notion that prayer is calling on God. David, in danger, prays to God: 'Hear me when I call, O God of my righteousness: thou has enlarged me when I was in distress; have mercy upon me, and hear my prayer' (Psalm 4:1). Whereas David's call is a somewhat crude petition to escape a pressing earthly threat, Peter speaks of a dutiful call for spiritual fulfilment: 'whosoever shall call on the name of the Lord shall be saved' (Acts 2:21). But this prayerful calling is a response to God's own call: 'For the promise is unto you, and to your children, and to all that are afar off, even as many as the Lord our God shall call' (Acts 2:39). Thus, calling to God in prayer answers that earlier call, which, as we will see in chapter four, is a continuous event that opens to man the promise of salvation. Man's prayerful call to God is his answer, an invocation of God's transforming help and presence.

This 'call,' this invocation of God, has several broader meanings. Herbert's 'thy dust that calls' ('Complaining,' 5), like the distressed David, first seeks God's attention, apparently turned away by man's sin. In fact, man and not God is inattentive; and distress turns his attention to God as the fulfilment of his need. This renewed attention becomes translated into a linguistic form – 'calling' to God – and into a ready fiction that God, who always listens, must nonetheless be made to hear. A further shade to 'calling' is the idea of addressing, hence acknowledging his identity ('Consider, Lord; Lord, bow thine eare, / And heare!' 'Longing,' 29–30), and recognizing in the divine name the power and goodness sustaining all being. Thus, the narrower sense of invocation contains the germ of the broader meaning – of linguistically expressed attention to God, the source of all being.

For Lancelot Andrewes this broader sense of calling describes all prayer. 'Prayer or invocation consists of confession and petition.'[13] His carefully dissected 'invocation' includes all the categories of prayer we have noted. Reflecting a traditional breakdown of con-fiteri,[14] he divides confession into 'confessio fraudis ... confession of sins' and 'confessio laudis, that is, thanksgiving to God for His goodness in pardoning our sins, and bestowing His benefits upon us.'[15] Praise, as we have already noted, is a necessary component in thanksgiving. As to petition, it consists of prayer either that 'evil be removed' or that 'our want be supplied with good things.' The upshot is that for Andrewes, as for Job, 'it is our duty invocare Deum omni tempore, "always to call upon God"' in prayer.[16]

This 'calling,' seen as prayerful attention to God in answer to God's continuing call to man, is one essential linguistic conception of prayer. Another linguistic conception of this two-way relationship between man and God is expressed by Joseph Hall: 'What do we in our prayers, but converse with the Almighty ... ?'[17] Other variations include colloquy, dialogue, speaking with God. The demur, that the believer speaks 'to' not 'with' God and that he hears without always answering directly, denies neither the two-way essence of prayer nor its linguistic form. For Herbert the traditional, linguistic character-ization of this two-way relationship is strongly stamped by mutual calling:

> For when *My Master*, which alone is sweet,
>> And ev'n in my unworthinesse pleasing,
>>> Shall call and meet,
>> *My servant*, as thee not displeasing,
> That call is but the breathing of the sweet.   ('The Odour,' 21–5)

This commerce through prayer, which expresses conformity by lovingly calling and identifying man and God, suggests the active intercourse. So, too, do Herbert's other expressions of the linguistic relationship between man and God. In 'Dialogue' the two-way relationship is expressed in stanzas, alternating human and divine voices, the believer talking directly with God. Hall would say that this speaker does 'converse with' God. In *The Temple* the divine voice in prayer can be intrusive, direct, conversational. Often Herbert leaves the human speaker only speaking 'to' the listening God. But, whichever expression of this two-way relationship prevails, it is conceived linguistically. Herbert does not attempt to describe the wordless prayer of pure contemplation. Prayer is expressed as words.

So far we have said little about the basic motivation of man's prayerful conversation with God. The Psalmist's distressed complaint or the pain of the afflicted ('Kill me not ev'ry day,' 'Affliction (ii),' 1) creates immediate needs. And certainly need that inspires blunt petition is motive enough. But the fact of spiritual affliction suggests the more complicated motivation of thwarted desire for happiness. Not all desire is thwarted, but all desire does express unsatisfied need; and prayer is a means to satisfy it. Richard Hooker's understanding of these relationships provides a clear norm in early Anglican thought about prayer:

> Everie good and holie desire though it lacke the forme, hath notwithstandinge in it selfe the substance, and with him the force of a prayer, who regardeth the verie moaninges grones and sighes of the harte of man. Petitionarie prayer belongeth only to such as are in them selves impotent and stand in neede of reliefe from others. Wee thereby declare unto God what our own desire is that he by his power should effect. It presupposeth therefore in us, first the want of that which wee pray for; secondly, a feeling of that want; thirdly, an earnest willingnes of minde to be eased therein; fourthly, a declaration of this our desire in the sight of God ...[18]

Such 'holie desire' in itself has the force of prayer, but it remains inchoate, lacking form; for prayer is the 'meane to expresse our lawfull desires.'[19] The connection between heart and word, between motivation and necessary experience, is crucial.

Hooker here progresses along a line of thought running through Thomas Aquinas and emerging even in Herbert's left-of-centre Protestant contemporary at Cambridge, John Preston. For Aquinas prayer and desire are 'synonymous';[20] and his amplification, that prayer is the 'expression' or 'interpreter of desire,'[21] can be heard running through later discussions of prayer, both Catholic and Protestant. What Aquinas means is that the root action is appetite, the movement of the will, that is, desire, toward an object. To say that prayer expresses or interprets desire is to say that the intellect takes a hand in understanding and disposing the motions of desire. Hooker's claim that prayer 'expresses' desire stands in Aquinas' lengthened shadow; for it is the understanding that arbitrates the will's desires, in prayer and otherwise.[22] Andrewes in examining the Spirit's role in prayer is likewise the disciple of Aquinas. The Spirit works on the understanding through the light of faith and on the will by inspiring 'holy desires.' Prayer, the 'interpreter' of desire, performs a 'reasonable' service, again exercising the intellect to acknowledge human weakness and need, and requesting blessings from God.[23] The strength of this main line in Anglican thought can be measured by its appearance in a more extreme Protestant like Preston.[24] His succinct definition, that prayer 'is an expression of holy and good dispositions,'[25] follows Hooker's emphasis on prayer as expression. Even his substitution of 'disposition' for 'desire' on the grounds that in some 'thanksgiving ... you desire nothing at *Gods* hands'[26] grants the legitimacy of the near synonym 'desire' in the other modes of prayer.

Desire has many faces, natural and supernatural, but prayer expresses and interprets that desire which Hooker alternately calls 'lawfull' and, with Andrewes, 'holy.' This desire to do God's will[27] competes with the will's selfish desires. Andrewes follows this true desire, which is the motivation of prayer, to its traditional root:

> For from the love of God proceeds this love and affection in us that we desire Him and all His blessings, and therefore make our prayer to Him to that end, which is nothing else but *explicatio desiderii*; so that we do not so soon desire any good thing, but we are ready to pray for it. So saith the Prophet, 'Lord, Thou knowest my desire, and my groaning is not hid from Thee' [Ps. 38:9].[28]

The believer loves the true good that lies in God's own desires, then seeks through prayer to enjoy the blessings of that goodness. So, too, in Herbert's 'Love (II),' the love-sonnet form conveys its basic motivation. The speaker petitions the God of power and love, the 'Immortall Heat,' who must 'kindle in our hearts such true desires, / As may consume our lusts, and make thee way' (4–5). Donne exploits this same competition between love of God and of his creatures in the penitential love sonnet, 'Batter my heart three-person'd God.' Herbert's petition, like Donne's, expresses love's desire to be empowered by divine love. True desire warmed by a loving God burns away sinful debility, returning love's warmth to God through praise, the 'hymnes,' the 'invention' of 'our brain' ('Love (II),' 6–8). The poem captures a chain of motivations: love's desire petitions for further desire. And there is a chain of prayer: the poem itself, which is the brain's invention, expressing, interpreting the desire for further prayer, that is, the hymns of praise to come. Thus, in love's desire, interpreted and expressed, we find in Herbert the familiar vein we have been tracing.

The concluding couplet of 'Love (II)' brings together in terms of falling and rising much that we have been describing. 'All knees shall bow to thee; all wits shall rise, / And praise him who did make and mend our eies' (13–14). The opening petition for God's aid, if answered in full, would bring all to their knees, not just those already praying humbly like the speaker. Just as the sonnet form emphasizes that love motivates this petition, so does this couplet remind us that the sonnet is a prayer. The spatial paradox that lowering is also rising conveys the humility and love necessary for the petition as well as for true hymns to God. While identifying the poem as both humble petition and elevating praise, the paradox also implicitly characterizes the speaker as a sinner humbled and elevated by his conviction that God will move men to love and praise him. The poem's intent is that the reader join the speaker, knees bowed in prayer, heart warmly desiring God in love, and wits rising in praise to God. As we will see more fully in chapter two, the role played by love in motivating spirituality has far-reaching effects on Herbert's art in *The Temple*.

The paradox of humility and elevation expresses the sacrificial pattern of Christ's experience that is the centre of *The Temple* as a poem of prayer and praise. In 'Mattens' Herbert expresses one of the deepest assumptions of *The Temple* as a work of sacrifice:

> I cannot ope mine eyes,
> But thou art ready there to catch
> My morning-soul and sacrifice: (1–3)

The doubleness of 'sacrifice' here involves both the morning prayer that is the poem and also the heart offering the prayer itself. The commonplace Christian notion that prayer is a sacrifice points to one of Herbert's emphases in *The Temple*, which is expressed most obviously in the pivotal role of 'The Sacrifice.' The power that Herbert finds in that commonplace notion is central to his understanding of prayer and praise.

The full commonplace, so self-consciously repeated by British Reformation writers,[29] includes two kinds of sacrifice. The first, a propitiatory blood sacrifice offered by Christ to the Father to satisfy divine justice, is compellingly dramatized in 'The Sacrifice.' The second, an honorific and dutiful sacrifice offered by the believer, for whom Christ has performed a lasting act of expiation, can be expressed, in particular, as prayer and praise. Calvin gives one of the most articulate, coherent expressions of this Reformation commonplace. In his biblical orthodoxy Old Testament sacrifices merely prefigure Christ's actions, the only true 'sacrifice of propitiation or of expiation.' Only Christ's sacrifice could 'appease God's wrath ... satisfy his judgment, and so ... wash sins and cleanse them that the sinner, purged of their filth and restored to the purity of righteousness, may return into favor with God.'[30] The second kind of sacrifice is a 'method' which God 'instituted' for man 'to transmit to the believing folk the benefit of the sacrifice offered to himself by his Son.'[31] And this is a '"sacrifice of praise and reverence,"' or in other words, a '"sacrifice of thanksgiving."' By means of this sacrifice, believers 'pay back' to God 'their whole selves and all their acts' in return for his many 'benefits.'[32]

The larger truth of the sacrifice of duty or honour paid to God is that all righteousness and all varieties of worshipful attention to God are sacrifices. Herbert's intention that devotional poetry 'turn delight into a sacrifice' ('The Church-porch,' 6), an experiencing of pleasure by reading a work centred in Christ's own sacrifice, subtly embodies this truth. So does the petition in 'The Altar' to embody Christ's sacrifice, a request that, as well as alluding to David's sacrifice of the 'broken and contrite heart' (Psalm 51:17), also implicitly praises God as the source of divine aid by requesting that aid. The request to embody Christ's sacrifice in praise is itself implicitly a sacrifice of praise. Here we have natural pairing of contrition and praise,[33] expressed as a poetic petition that is intended as sacrificial delight. Calvin would say that in this way Herbert can 'pay back' God for Christ's expiatory sacrifice, which is the enlivening centre.

While 'The Altar' draws upon the full power of the commonplace two sacrifices, 'The Sacrifice' establishes Herbert's emphasis on sacrifice itself. Its title, in underlining the principle of sacrifice, points to one of its crucial differences from its precursors in the *Improperia* and *O vos omnes qui transitis* traditions.[34] Whatever we say about the poem and its importance in *The Temple* must refer to that principle in Herbert's thought. Necessarily involved is the conformity between Christ and the believer, the nexus between the two kinds of sacrifice. The key to understanding that conformity between God and man is to be found in 'The Sacrifice,' dramatically unique in 'The Church' since it is spoken exclusively by a divine voice, while describing the events of the Passion. We hear the person of Christ, obedient to his calling, grieved at man's inhumanity, and shocked by the bloody insult to his person. This voice that expresses Christ's sacrificial surrender is recalled repeatedly in the blood imagery throughout *The Temple*. Conformity lies in trying to imitate this sacrifice.

When sacrificing the broken and contrite heart ('Lord, I adjudge my self to tears and grief,' 25), the speaker in 'Ephes. 4.30' expresses man's self-sacrifice that conforms to Christ's. These common Reformed roots are fully articulated in Calvin's notion of the 'wholehearted sacrifice of heart and life to God'[35] in conformity to Christ. At every turn Calvin's conception of this sacrifice admits its Old Testament and New Testament heritage. This sacrificial offering of the self replaces the offering of sacrificial animals[36] and involves a self-immolation that fulfils the Old Testament immolation of the sacrificial victim. For Calvin this self-denial mortifies our 'natural concupiscence.'[37] The model of self-denial is Christ,[38] offered as a sacrifice to God, to be followed by the believer as the true imitation of Christ.[39] Christ acts as the priest sacrificing on the believer's behalf, like the royal Melchizedek mediating between God and man (Genesis 14:18). The self-sacrificing Christ fulfils the Old Testament priest offering the victim and sprinkling himself with its blood in performing the sacrifice for sin. Christ is also the priest performing a Covenant sacrifice, sprinkling the whole temple, that is, his own body, in sacrificing the victim to God.[40] In imitation the believer must offer himself, a temple of God cleansed in Christ's blood.

Man's self-offering informs his service to God, involving prayer, praise, work – all are actions of sacrifice. Though not bloody themselves, these sacrifices recall the meaning of Christ's sacrifice in blood.

Herbert's *The Temple* admits its Reformed background. His Christ is also a Melchizedek, a 'Prince' of peace ('Peace,' 22) offering a mediator's sacrifice to God. He, too, is a sacrifical victim, a 'Paschal Lambe' ('The Sacrifice,' 59); and his body, too, is the 'Temple' bloodied by his sacrifice, then 'raz'd, and raised' ('The Sacrifice,' 65–6). Herbert's Christ is the priest of the New Covenant, his '*bloud*' ironically sprinkled on his persecutors, '*on them and theirs*' (107), for whom he performed his sacrifice. And Herbert sees the believer, who can imitate even if not repay in blood, as one who must offer himself – his heart an offering, a sacrificial 'oblation' ('An Offering,' 39), a 'gift' (1). With God's 'favour' (37) both his sacrifice of self and his hymn of praise can resemble David's sacrifice of a broken and contrite heart, and of praise, which are the 'sacrifices of righteousness'; these are the true 'burnt offering' (Psalm 51:18–19) whose 'savour' ('An Offering,' 38) of sweetness will rise to God.[41] In Herbert, as in Calvin, that self-offering is the 'whole hearted sacrifice of heart and life to God'; and in that sacrifice we can include *The Temple* itself, its prayer and praise constantly recalling Christ's sacrifice in blood while reminding us that our sacrifice lies in words and deeds. In that offer of self can be found how Herbert understands the true meaning of sacrifice – to draw near to God.[42]

To speak of this conformity between man's sacrifice and Christ's is to find the centre of Herbert's conception of prayer and praise. The next step is to examine his psychology of prayer and praise in light of this conformity. But, first, there is the relationship in Herbert's thought between sacrifice and the Eucharist, since it bears clearly on his notion of prayer. The importance of this relationship comes as no surprise at a time when the theological battle lines are so clearly drawn on the matter. Like British Reformers, such as Cranmer,[43] Herbert denies that Christ's propitiatory sacrifice is repeated each time in the Eucharist; at the same time he fully understands the problem inherent in the Protestant position. The Reformers want it both ways: to retain the Eucharist at the centre without granting its unique power as repeated propitiation. But a Eucharist no longer propitiatory, only commemorative, surrenders its uniqueness, granting equality to other sacrifices, such as prayer, praise, righteousness, the Christian life in general. Herbert's solution to this problem is to mingle the identities of the Eucharist and prayer. By treating them as inextricable expressions of the same truth, he reveals a subtle grasp of both biblical sacrifice and the Reformed position.

The key lies in his characterization of prayer as the 'Churches banquet' and 'Exalted Manna' ('Prayer (I),' 1, 10). In an obvious sense the notion of Eucharist, literally meaning thanksgiving, can allude to prayer as thanksgiving. But Herbert's tendency throughout *The Temple* to merge prayer and the Eucharist goes beyond the more limited meaning. Sacrifice is the pivot. The typology of manna draws us back to 'The Sacrifice' and the Christ who feeds us: 'yet, when they did call, / With Manna, Angels food, I fed them all' (238–9). Throughout the earlier poem Herbert plays hard on the typology that links sacrifice and the Eucharist. God first gave manna, then the Eucharist; and Moses, the intermediary who pointed to the manna (Exodus 16:15–19),[44] also struck the rock (122)[45] from which the water flowed, typologically like Christ from whose bloody side the sacraments flowed (246). The Moses typology serves Herbert's characterization of Christ's sacrifice and its necessary connection to Christ, who feeds man ('I give them bread,' 7) with himself, the 'Paschal Lambe' (59). We recall Moses, on whose advice the sprinkled blood of the Passover, typologically Christ's bloody sacrifice, saved the Israelites from death (Exodus 12:21–7). Herbert's understanding of that Passover meal reveals his sense of Christ's sacrifice as a spiritual food that necessarily feeds the life of prayer.

Several other elements in biblical sacrifice are informative here. The first is the necessary modulation between prayer and sacrifice in the Bible. They both have the same goal, to establish union with God and to serve him. Since sacrifice was necessarily accompanied by prayer, it followed naturally that biblical reformers, looking hard at the materialism in sacrificial practices, should emphasize the efficacy of prayer instead. Prayer viewed as a sacrifice is a half turn in that approach. Hosea exhorts his listeners: 'Take with you words, and turn to the Lord: say unto him, Take away all iniquity, and receive us graciously; so will we render the calves of our lips' (Hosea 14:2). Against this background, Calvin repeatedly draws the attention of his readers to the close ties between sacrifice and prayer. When discussing the burnt sacrifice of Psalm 20:3, he observes:

> But under these two kinds David intended to comprehend, by synecdoche, all sacrifices; and under sacrifices he comprehends requests and prayers. We know that whenever the fathers prayed under the law, their hope of obtaining what they asked was founded

upon their sacrifices; and, in like manner, at this day our prayers
are acceptable to God only in so far as Christ sprinkles and sanctifies
them with the perfume of his own sacrifice.[46]

Herbert's 'morning-soul and sacrifice' in 'Mattens' (3) comes easily to
mind as an analogue.

But prayer itself as a Eucharistic experience draws even more
exactly on the biblical conception of sacrifice. One form of sacrifice, a
feast shared between God and man, culminates in the Last Supper.
Either a sacrificial animal, its blood spread about the altar as a sin
sacrifice and some parts reserved for God as well as man, or a
bread-offering shared by all believers, is the centre of the meal. The
offering is consumed in a communal act binding man and God. The
Passover meal is an example of this form of sacrifice, and the Last
Supper is its fulfilment.[47] Christ's offer of himself, his body as bread
and his blood as wine, is the centre of Herbert's profound sense of the
sacrifice in terms of food; and here also is the centre in his conception
of prayer as sacrificial and Eucharistic. But we lack one last term, the
broad notion of Christ as one who feeds others. The force of the Last
Supper, then the Eucharist in turn, lies in the Johannine sense that
Christ is the Bread of Life (John 6:35) fed to the believer. Alternately,
he is the Good Shepherd, who surrenders his life for his sheep (John
10:11) and who commands Peter to feed them (John 21:15–17).
Earlier, he had literally fed the multitude, sustaining their physical
lives in order to feed them spiritually (John 6:5–13). Christ's person,
his message, his sacrifice, and their assimilation by the believer all
work through each other in numerous variations that offer his
teaching and sacrificial self-surrender as food. To call prayer a
'banquet' is to show a way to consume, hence assimilate to the god
who sacrificed himself.

Thus, the identities of prayer and the Eucharist become blurred.
Herbert would see that same truth in the *Book of Common Prayer*
when the priest offers the wine 'in remembrance that Christ's blood
was shed for thee,' with the admonition to be thankful. The prayer to
the Father, which follows, with its petition that God 'accept this our
sacrifice of praise and thanksgiving,' involves both the prayer and the
believer's Eucharistic actions. Herbert would appreciate the wisdom
of this prayer when it dedicates the whole person: 'And here we offer
and present unto thee, O Lord, ourselves, our souls and bodies, to be a
reasonable, holy, and lively sacrifice unto thee, humbly beseeching
thee, that all we which be partakers of this Holy Communion, may

be fulfilled with thy grace, and heavenly benediction.'[48] Both in the Eucharist and in prayer, body and soul together sacrifice the self in the offer of thanks and praise. Herbert would see with a clear 'Anglican'[49] eye how the boundaries between prayer and Eucharist tend to blur in this experience of conforming to Christ's sacrifice.[50]

Prayer and the Eucharist share the same psychology of conformity. We have already discussed much of this psychology in prayer: the motive of love, the faithful conviction based on humility and trust in Christ, the surrender of self that embodies these elements. But more needs to be said about Herbert's sense that prayer is lifting the heart to God. In *The Country Parson* we hear the echo of biblical tradition: 'The Countrey Parson, when he is to read divine services, composeth himselfe to all possible reverence; lifting up his heart and hands, and eyes, and using all other gestures which may expresse a hearty, and unfeyned devotion' ('The Parson praying,' p 231). The heart lifted in prayer carries echoes of familiar Old Testament voices: David,[51] Hezekiah,[52] Jeremiah,[53] and others. The work of Herbert's contemporaries carries the same echoes: Andrewes urges that 'we should lift up our hearts and affections from earth to heaven';[54] Bishop Hall rhetorically asks, 'What do we in our prayers, but converse with the Almighty; and either carry our souls up to him, or bring him down to us ... ?'[55] Herbert's country parson with hands, eyes, and heart uplifted embodies publicly what is experienced privately in prayer as well. Like his biblical masters Herbert raises in prayer not only the eyes of the body, but those of the soul as well: 'If I but lift mine eyes, my suit is made: / Thou canst no more not heare, then thou canst die' ('Prayer (II),' 5–6). In this prayer one feels the assurance of the Psalmist: 'I will lift up mine eyes unto the hills, from whence cometh my help' (Psalm 121:1).

Through lifting or raising the soul, through rising, man conforms himself to Christ's sacrifice. Falling cannot be separated from rising; the crucifixion cannot be separated from the resurrection; humility and repentance cannot be separated from love, joy, and adoration. This is the full truth suggested by the intoxication of Christ's blood, the elevating 'wine' ('The Agonie,' 18) that through Christ's death ironically 'did put some bloud' in death's own face ('Death,' 13). Herbert appreciated the essential paradox of primitive blood sacrifice, which both costs and gives life. Accordingly, the problem of imitating Christ's sacrifice is solved by surrendering not only in humility, but in exhilaration. The sacrificial blood of Christ recalled throughout *The Temple* gives it life, just as primitive blood sacrifice gave life to its participants.[56] The believer who imitates Christ's sacrifice must imp his wing on the risen Christ, fulfilling the sacrifice of self by rising to God, primarily in prayer.

But rising is not reserved for prayer alone. In the Eucharist the soul is 'rais'd ... up,' flying skyward on a 'wing' ('The Banquet,' 37, 42). And in religious music the soul moves 'without a bodie ... Rising and falling' on the 'wings' of music 'to heavens doore' ('Church-musick,' 5–6, 12). Uplifting the soul by imping its wing on the risen Christ's is the central motion in *The Temple*, the measure of all other motions. Here is the soul's keen longing for exhilaration in God, naturally seeking to express itself, linguistically, musically, devotionally, sacramentally. But soul is cross-biased by falling through its own limitations. That burden of man's fallen nature is felt as the countermotions that harden, scatter, frustrate, and encumber the natural upward movement of a loving soul. Conformity to the broken and risen Christ breaks that hardness and concentrates the powers of the soul, freeing its movement upward like the savour of burnt sacrifice. The means of this conformity are embodied in scriptural truth, devotional and liturgical forms, the sacraments, church music, and above all prayer. But only prayer and praise lift man to God by exercising his essential linguistic nature.

To say that prayer lifts the heart to God through conformity to the Sacrifice is to express, in particular, the more general truth that in this way the believer can participate in the qualities of the godhead. Herbert explicates this more general truth in 'Prayer (II).' An obvious structure lays out how, if the speaker will just lift the eyes of his soul, he can participate in God's ease, power, and love, introduced respectively in the first three stanzas. The final stanza underlines this structural point:

> Since then these three wait on thy throne,
>   *Ease, Power,* and *Love;* I value prayer so,
>   That were I to leave all but one,
>   Wealth, fame, endowments, vertues, all should go;
> I and deare prayer would together dwell,
> And quickly gain, for each inch lost, an ell.   (19–24)

Rising to petition in prayer completes the fortunate fall and makes possible a quick 'gain' in ease, power, and love.

At the outset the poem readies us explicitly to understand how man can participate in these qualities.

> Of what an easie quick accesse,
> My blessed Lord, art thou! how suddenly
>   May our requests thine eare invade!
> To shew that state dislikes not easinesse,
> If I but lift mine eyes, my suit is made:
> Thou canst no more not heare, then thou canst die.   (1–6)

God's inherent ease naturally encourages man's easy, quick petition. And the necessary logic that God must hear assumes that man, who participates in God's ease through prayer, likewise participates in his power and love. That is, just as man is empowered to reach upward and invade the attention of the all-powerful God, so also the love motivating his prayer and conforming him to Christ participates in the immortal Love that guarantees him a continuous hearing. The poem never stops to explicate its supporting assumption that all motions of prayer, in ease, power, and love, are initiated by the indwelling Spirit.

But the poem does explicitly examine these qualities of God that inform man's experience of prayer. God's ease, which is achievement without impediment or care, is a function of his power; and power is the unhindered ability to work with and give all things their 'measur'd houre.' That wondrous 'great arm, which spans the east and west' ('Prayer (II),' 8–10) established the vast scope that Herbert manipulates so strikingly in 'distances' of 'vast extent' of 'fourtie heav'ns, or more' ('The Temper (I),' 5–10). Consciousness empowered to rise easily by prayer to God's throne experiences the scope of that 'almightie power' ('Prayer (II),' 7). That scope also informs our understanding of Christ's Sacrifice, that 'unmeasurable love' (13) of the immortal God who took 'our flesh and curse' (15). To pray is to imitate that loving Sacrifice, who as one expression of his love, taught man how to raise the heart to God in prayer.[57]

The ease in rising to God is a more vexing matter to understand than power and love, since prayer in *The Temple* often seems more struggle than ease. Too often the prayerful soul seems more grounded in hoarse longing and broken efforts than raised in exhilaration. The soul's natural movement upward to God is restricted by depression, weariness, dullness, and care – sin's legacy. The orthodox solution to the problem can be found in the poem 'Jesu,' which relates affliction to 'ease.' Before affliction the speaker finds the 'sacred name' (1) of Jesus in his heart, then afterwards in the heart's broken pieces. He discovers '*J*' '*ES*,' and '*U*': that is, '*I ease you*' (9). Here is the relief, comfort, and ease paradoxically through suffering itself, with Christ as the model of breaking that frees the will from sin's impediments. This ready Christian orthodoxy offers right struggle and suffering as the means of rising by breaking sin's hardness. Such paradoxical, suffering ease is the means of participating in the heavenly peace or 'leisure' that is opposed to 'cares and businesse' ('Heaven,' 17, 19); only there is cessation of work, effort, and worry impeding the soul's enjoyment. In heaven the earthly soul will no longer have its natural movement encumbered by worldly motions and by its congenital earthly 'restlesnesse' ('The Pulley,' 17). These impediments can be totally removed only in the state of satisfied rest and leisure in heaven. Conformity with Christ assumes that earthly participation in this ease paradoxically implicates man in penitential grief and corrective affliction. Prayer as conformity to the Sacrifice offers just such paradoxical ease.

Ease, love, and power do not exhaust those heavenly qualities experienced by the heart lifted in prayer. But, when Herbert speaks more generally of the 'Softnesse, and peace, and joy, and love, and blisse' in prayer ('Prayer (I),' 9), it is praise more particularly that must be examined; for in praise the soul, by concentrating upon God and not its own motions, rises closest to its fruition. The final stage in rising through prayer is to express enjoyment and adoration of God. Clearly, in the manner of the Psalms, Herbert's praise is leavened by delight. Although Herbert does not follow the Psalmist in shouts of gladness, his praise is buoyed by enjoyment. This is the earthly equivalent of the weightless, pure praise of angels and glorified souls in joyful, direct communion with their Creator. There, no contrary motions encumber linguistic beings joyously, harmoniously, sweetly singing praise of God.

The earthly mode of this harmony is the primary truth in 'Providence.' Herbert steps back here, disentangled from the task of making praise, to examine the idea of praise. Significantly, this is a poem about nature, including man's role in it. All creatures praise God by fulfilling their natures; for, so doing, they reveal the goodness that created them as necessary parts in a benign universe that serves and hence fulfils man. Only man can 'expresse thy works' (142), since he alone 'knows,' comprehends the goodness of creation. As 'Secretarie of thy praise' (8), as a special confidant entrusted both with God's secrets (OED) and also the task of using language to honour God, man fulfils nature itself by fulfilling his own nature. Man's praise both is and is not different in kind from other creatures:

different as a linguistic fulfilment; the same, as a fulfilment of his nature. In its regularity of metre and stanzaic form, this hymn (148) of adoration reflects the harmony of the created world and of the human soul fulfilling its created nature by rising to praise God. In these terms Herbert comprehends praise as song.

The personal and the traditional coalesce here. A lyric poet, a lutenist, a lover of church music – Herbert sees in his own poetic attempts to praise God the same connection between praise and song of the Psalms. When Herbert commits his 'utmost art' to 'sing' thee ('Praise (II),' 9–10) or commands his heart to 'rise' and his lute to 'Awake' ('Easter,' 7), we hear David in the background:

> I will sing and give praise. Awake up, my glory; awake, psaltery and harp: I myself will awake early. I will praise thee, o LORD, among the people: I will sing unto thee among the nations.   (Psalm 57:7–9)

But we hear more as well. Parody absorbs and transforms the voice of the courtly love poet expressing love and praise near a throne. His instruments awakened, the lyric devotional poet motivated by love joyously praises God in song:

> Blessed be the God of Heaven and Earth! who only doth wondrous things. Awake therefore, my Lute, and my Viol! awake all my powers to glorifie thee! We praise thee! we blesse thee! we magnifie thee for ever!   (The Country Parson, p 289)

He commits all his powers, all his gifts to bless God in praise.[58] His lute and viol, more than mere instruments, represent man's created physical and psychological instrumentality, which, committed to God, can work to achieve the harmony of being brought in measure, of rising in song, to bless God in conformity to Christ.

Not the enjoyment of this harmony, however, but nagging grief in its absence more often rules The Temple. John Booty quite rightly points to the countermotions that balance rising with falling.[59] But in Herbert there is less joy in the falling of contrition and affliction than in Donne, and less satisfied acceptance that God's power enables him to raise man by various means – joy, grief, love, and, as we learn in 'The Pulley,' restlessness, the dissatisfaction in the earthly life itself. The ironies here lie less in the contradiction that falling can raise him than in his knowing resistance to what he takes to be true. Thus, we hear urgent frustration in his very attempt to praise: 'To write a verse or two is all the praise, / That I can raise' ('Praise (I),' 1–2). His petition – 'O raise me then!' (17) – admits that his meagre praise is earthbound. We only underline his frustration by noting his contrast to Andrewes and Donne, who subordinate praise to thanksgiving, thus admitting that praise cannot free itself from man's need. But Herbert's desire to free praise from this self-consciousness plus his frustration at not being able to do so are all the greater given this desire. Herbert's instinct to avoid pain competes with his orthodox conviction that suffering is necessary. The ironies compound themselves, beginning with the contradiction that falling, the purifying grief through humble confession and contrition, elevates the believer; and that his frustrating inability to express praise of God is itself a grief that elevates him. Nonetheless, Herbert never frees himself from the desire to escape this elevating suffering, the conformity with Christ's Sacrifice that is the only true means to rise. The struggle to praise God is the necessary mode of rising; and he can only truly 'raise' God in his 'heart' ('Praise (II),' 18–20) through the struggle in love that conforms and leads him to Christ. But Herbert yearns to have what he can achieve only infrequently, the sense of the soul unencumbered, unself-consciously and harmoniously rising joyously to bless God.

The difficult question about the status of prayer and praise in *The Temple* remains. We must ask how much of 'The Church' can be regarded as actual prayer and praise with affinities to the Psalms or to Donne's expostulations and prayers in *Devotions upon Emergent Occasions*. Much is at stake here: Herbert's relationship to his audience, the role of his speakers, the nature of prayer and praise, his basic literary intentions.

Anthony Nuttall speaks problematically of one possible solution when he says that 'What we have been treating as prayer in poetic form are really poems which imitate or represent prayer.' These poems might be regarded as 'fictions,'[60] like other poetic imitations. Herbert himself would seem to encourage this line when communicating to Nicholas Ferrar that *The Temple* gave a 'picture of the many spiritual Conflicts that have past betwixt God and my Soul. ...'[61] The inference can follow that these 'pictures' are literary artifices, not experiences but self-conscious imaginative representations of them. From such an argument it seems to follow that we have something different in kind from the Psalms, which are actually prayer and praise offered directly to God. Unfortunately, the matter does not fall into place so cleanly. Too often we hear Herbert's own naked voice praying:

> Bowels of pitie, heare!
> Lord of my soul, love of my minde,
>   Bow down thine eare!
>   Let not the winde
>   Scatter my words, and in the same
>   Thy name!   ('Longing,' 19–24)

Such lyrics are akin to the Psalms; they are prayers in lyric form, artifacts that can be said to give 'pictures,' though not self-conscious, imaginative 'fictions' of the heart at prayer. That is, Nuttall's useful distinction can account for some, but not all, of Herbert's lyrics. Only some pictures are 'fictions.'

Moreover, the troublesome fact remains that the 'fictions' are not necessarily less 'true' representations of Herbert's experience. The categories begin to invade each other when we admit that both can give accurate pictures of the 'spiritual conflicts' in prayer that passed between him and God. Donne's works offer a parallel. Helen Gardner is right in saying that the *Holy Sonnets* give us an 'image of a soul working out its salvation in fear and trembling.'[62] Few readers question that this is an image of Donne's own experience. But these sonnets are self-conscious 'fictions' unlike the picture of his experience in the *Devotions upon Emergent Occasions*. There, like the Psalmist, Donne speaks in his own voice, not distanced self-consciously from the speaking voice by irony, as in sonnet 5 ('If poysonous mineralls'). In this poem the speaker's sinful logic, delimited by assuming that non-rational goats and human beings should be categorized together, reflects this sinful self-concern. The irony separates the speaker from Donne himself, who thus gives an accurate fictional image of his own impulse to self-delusion while praying. In contrast, Donne himself speaks directly in the expostulations and prayers in the *Devotions*. We have a clear distinction between two kinds of pictures here, one prayer, and one merely its image.

But do we? Confidence in the usefulness of these categories in understanding *The Temple* is eroded by the consideration that God is the primary audience. Herbert's dedication is explicit:

> Lord, my first fruits present themselves to thee;
> Yet not mine neither: for from them they came,

And must return. Accept of them and me,
And make us strive, who shall sing best thy name.
  Turn their eyes hither, who shall make a gain:
  Theirs, who shall hurt themselves or me, refrain.

('The Dedication')

One approach would be to view God as a 'fictional addressee' inside
the poem, which is written for man and not God, and the reader as the
real addressee outside the poem.[63] But Herbert's own admission that
The Temple embodies his own prayerful 'conflicts' with God, added
to the unshakeable conviction of many readers that Herbert is
writing to God, makes us question this solution. If prayer is lifting the
heart and mind in conversation with God, then not only some lyrics
but all of 'The Church' is in some sense prayer. After all, Herbert can
be said to be communing directly with the God who dwells in his
consciousness.

To ask if 'The Church' can 'in some sense' be regarded as prayer is,
first, to engage some of the obvious problems arising from artifice in
prayer. They range from the making of artifacts as prayer, to their use
as ready-made forms in both private devotions and public worship.
Whenever a believer self-consciously embodies his own prayer in
literary form or whenever that artifact is self-consciously used by
others, it becomes a potential diversion. Some modern believers may
think that the very presence of artifice compromises the internal
colloquy between the human heart and God. In turn, the communal
use of these artifacts removes them from the intimate experience of
their makers. This distance is further increased in the conditions that
prevail in public worship. Ready-made prayers, whether in private or
public use, too easily harden into formulae that can idolatrously
divert the heart from God.

Significantly, artifice in prayer was not generally an urgent
problem in Herbert's time. The legitimacy of artifacts in prayer can
be measured by imagining the response of Herbert's contemporaries
if told that the Psalms are not true prayer and praise. Probably Herbert
intended that some prayers in *The Temple* be used in the devotions of
his readers. The ready entry of some Herbert lyrics into British
Protestant use attests to a willingness to adapt the prayers of others.
And Henri Bremond's observations on public prayer in the sixteenth
and seventeenth centuries are telling. He briskly disposes of the
argument against set public prayers in terms of the standardized
elements prevailing in private devotions as well. Both kinds of prayer
are defensible on the same grounds:

> L'une et l'autre de ces deux prières répondent également à la défini-
> tion de la prière en soi, ou prière pure; l'une et l'autre réalisent une
> seule et même expérience, à savoir un certain contact avec le
> divin, une certaine 'élévation de l'âme vers Dieu.'[64]

His defence of standardized forms in private devotions can apply to
the Anglican as well as the Catholic context. *Preces Privatae*, the
private devotions of Lancelot Andrewes, which set out a lengthy
standardized program as a backbone for his own spiritual exercises,
are a good case in point. These are as much artifacts as prayers. The
same holds true for public prayers as well. The true measure is
whether or not they can be used to raise the heart to God.

What is and what is not prayer can be a vexed matter anyway, as
Christians soon discover when trying to understand Paul's injunction to 'Pray without ceasing' (1 Thessalonians 5:17). Any devout
seventeenth-century Christian humbly falling to his knees on a busy
London street would soon discover the dangers of literal interpretation. But to say that 'without ceasing' means 'regularly' would not
satisfy those believers working toward continual awareness of God.
A more satisfying explanation is that Paul means a continuing
disposition to lift the heart to God. This ready disposition denies
neither the private nor the public practices of prayer; but it does
tend to weaken the compartmentalization between mundane real
life and the practices of prayer. The constant is 'prayerfulness,'[65]
the unbroken disposition to be attentive to God; this disposition
would be expressed not only in the formal habits of private and
public prayer, but also in less formal awareness of God whenever
possible.

For Herbert, like Hooker earlier, set forms of prayer necessarily
frame spiritual attention, but a prayerful disposition is the grounds-
well working to lift the heart to God. This disposition can modulate
in and out of various dimensions in Christian existence. Hooker
measures its breadth:

> Is not the name of prayer usuall to signifie even all the service
> that ever wee doe unto God? And that for no other cause, as I
> suppose, but to show that there is in religion no acceptable dutie
> which devoute invocation of the name of God doth not either
> presuppose or inferre.[66]

According to Hooker, the motion of prayerfulness, 'Everie good and
holie desire,' has the 'force of a prayer,' though it 'lacke the forme.'[67]

For both him and Herbert, these motions run through all the various ways of man's Christian existence.

But the natural embodiment and discipline of prayerfulness are the set forms of private and public prayer. Joseph Summers stresses Herbert's 'meticulous explanation of Anglican formal practice' to his Bemerton parishioners as evidence of his commitment to existing forms.[68] Walton finds the centre of life at Bemerton in the set forms of prayer. Twice daily, 'at the Canonical hours of 10 and 4,' Herbert was joined in the chapel not only by his whole family, but by most of 'his Parishioners, and many Gentlemen in the Neighbourhood.' And some of 'the meaner sort' of his parish 'would let their Plow rest when Mr. *Herberts Saints-Bell* rung to Prayer,' afterwards to return 'back to their Plow.' Walton's summation points both to Herbert's motive and his influence: 'Thus powerful was his reason, and example, to perswade others to a practical piety, and devotion.'[69] This persuasion, we can say, follows from the lifelong discipline of his own private devotions and the habits of set family devotions. The larger truth remains, however, that such disciplines of prayer reveal a prayerfulness working through existence at Bemerton, just as it does *The Temple* with its modulations from self-examination to direct communion with God. This prayerfulness is the 'sense' in which 'The Church' can be regarded as prayer.

The question of Herbert's primary audience obtrudes here. We recall Rosemond Tuve's reprimand of George Herbert Palmer's criticism that Herbert in *The Temple* was self-absorbed, that the work was not really written with much awareness of other humans.[70] Her counter-claim, that Herbert was motivated by basic Christian charity, that the contents of *The Temple* were written to edify other readers, however, could not in itself satisfy readers who hear a basic voice concentrating there upon its own inner experience at the expense, it would seem, of other human readers. Both sides in this argument tended to ignore the implications of Herbert's divine hearer. The link between these two extremes is the sense of calling to serve man and God expressed in his own prayerful sacrifice. Herbert's invitation that the reader 'taste / The churches mysticall repast' ('Superliminare,' 3–4) allows the human reader to participate in Herbert's own colloquy with God. And that colloquy is the stuff of his own service as a devotional poet.

Herbert's Protestant emphasis upon calling defines the prayerfulness of *The Temple*. Protestant belief in the sanctity of work loosens any rigid separation between secular and religious activities. The natural prayerfulness that would pervade the life of any committed believer would increase naturally in this broadened notion of vocational service. Work performed as service to God, as part of communion with God and man, is a form of worship.[71] And for Herbert, the habits and duties of prayer are the stuff of his priestly calling. This vocation is calling on God from the pulpit, from the reading-pew while reading prayers from the *Book of Common Prayer*, and from the family table during devotions. Even more, his calling as a devotional poet tends to break down the boundaries between what he did as 'work' and how he communed with God in his own personal prayer. To write a poem that is a prayer or a 'fiction' of a prayer, that is, a literary work, is to call upon God in writing, thus answering the obligations of his poetic calling while also satisfying the intimate spiritual needs of his own heart. Working, praying, being become the same sacrificial actions performed with the heart lifted to God. God is the primary audience, but the human reader is intended to listen in.

2 *The Problem of Love*

For Herbert, as we have just seen, the prayerfulness expressed in the
formal disciplines of prayer also guides the skills necessary in a
Christian vocation. These disciplines and skills are arts of spirituality that edify the temple of the human heart. They also edify Herbert's
poetic temple. But it is not enough to say that prayerfulness
stimulates the building of temples without searching at the same
time for its deepest motivation in the relationship between love and
faith. This search, which is complicated by Herbert's questions about
imitating God's love, has been made even more problematical by the
tendency in some recent Herbert criticism to ignore the love of God
in his spirituality. But for Herbert there is no prayerfulness without
this love.

One modern student of spirituality usefully pinpoints the basic
motivation of the prayerful Christian life. 'Christian spirituality
begins when God's word is accepted in faith. It manifests itself in the
expression and the development of the love of God in prayer and
action.'[1] Herbert puts the matter of motivation in a nutshell: 'Thy
power and love, my love and trust / Make one place ev'ry where' ('The
Temper (I),' 27–8). This essential tie between divine and human
recalls the private love that makes 'one little roome, an every where'
in Donne's 'The Good-morrow' (11).[2] Herbert transforms Donne's
'every where,' which contracts all into a private enclosure, into a
sense of vast space expressing the power and greatness of a loving
God. At the same time Herbert's syntax, in holding God's and man's
love side by side, expresses the most immediate contact between God
and man. This love is defined by God's power, understandable as an
expression of a loving nature and, in turn, man's faithful trust in that
powerful love. But the primary point of contact, expressed syntacti-

cally, is the mutual love of Christ and the believer, between the divine and human persons through the agency of the Holy Ghost. Thus, the syntax captures the primary truth in Herbert's spirituality.

But here we encounter difficulties in defining his spirituality if we wish to profit from recent 'Protestant' interpretations of his work. Unfortunately, such interpretation says too little about Herbert's problematical treatment of man's love for God. Barbara Lewalski finds in *The Temple* a 'Protestant-Pauline paradigm of salvation' supported by Calvinist theology.[3] Love plays only a minimal role in her scheme constructed of 'election, calling, justification, adoption, sanctification, glorification.'[4] Richard Strier sets the centre of *The Temple* in the Reformation emphasis on justification by faith, specifically in Lutheran terms.[5] Strier's analysis boldly opens up a Lutheran window that modifies Lewalski's Calvinist perspective, but he slights the problem of man's love for God. The truth embodied in Herbert's syntax, the juxtaposed human and divine loves, must be taken more seriously, for it points unavoidably to prayerful communion in love as the heart of Herbert's spirituality. Ironically, Strier does not investigate the other side to his own title, *Love Known*. The love in *The Temple* is not just God's love for man, but also man's answering love for God. Gene Edward Veith's informative study of Herbert's 'Reformation' spirituality suffers from a different but no less overriding irony in that he says little about love (and even less about prayer) in *The Temple*.[6] Admittedly, such ironies naturally emerge when attempts are made to fit Herbert into his theological context, in which the fellow doctrines of justification by faith and sanctification necessarily occupy the centre of attention. Also, Calvinist thought, with its austere, majestic God and its concentration on faith depicted by intellectualized language,[7] dramatically turns away from mutual love between man and God in medieval Augustinian thought. More than Calvin, Luther emphasizes God's love for man, but his spirituality also concentrates on man's faith, not his direct love of God.

This strong Reformation tendency is deeply anchored in Pauline *agape*, the unmerited, freely given divine love expressed through Christ. Man responds not in love, but in faith. One modern biblical scholar specifies just how little Paul does say about love for God: 'Excluding absolute uses and Eph. 6:24, there are at most five places where love toward God or Christ is mentioned.'[8] Anders Nygren provides a familiar perspective on the matter, since his analysis of Christian *agape* has become almost a staple in discussion of *The*

Temple, having been enlisted first by Rosemond Tuve, then later by Strier and others.[9] Questionably, Nygren argues that Paul's 'faith' really means 'love.' The reason lies in Paul's concept of *agape*, God's love to man: 'For if Agape is a love so utterly spontaneous and uncaused as the love which is manifested in the Cross of Christ, then the name Agape cannot fittingly be used to denote man's attitude towards God.'[10] Nygren would have it that the term 'faith' is actually a 'love to God that is receptive, not spontaneous.'[11] One intention of this sleight-of-hand is to remain consistent with Paul's general emphasis upon the importance of love, while bringing him neatly into line with the command to love God with 'all thy heart, and with all thy soul, and with all thy mind and with all thy strength' (Mark 12:30). Predictably, however, Nygren's arbitrary interpretation of Paul's 'faith' as love has not pleased all readers.

The important point is that New Testament texts allow more than one solution to the problem of loving God, as two later developments make clear. One is a mystical Augustinian and Bernardine tradition, which develops the notion of mutual love between man and God. For Bernard of Clairvaux, whose commentary was influential well into Herbert's century, the Song of Songs, with its powerful language of heterosexual love, betrothal, and marriage between the Bride and Bridegroom, expresses the essential relationship in love between the believer and Christ. A second major development is the return to Paul in the Reformation to support an aggressive doctrine of justification by faith. The general thrust of this major development is to keep love and faith distinct: faith in God and love to man. Love is expressed to God only in an undeveloped way, since *sola fides* encouraged it to atrophy.

Admittedly, there is a danger in caricaturing Luther and Calvin on this subject, particularly Luther, whose theology emphasizes love. But the Pauline lineaments, of faith in God and love for man, mark Luther's increasingly reiterated claim that man's love for God is really shown indirectly through other men, just as God shows his love for man through Christ. When discussing Christ's question put three times to Peter, whether he loved Christ or not, Luther expresses his sense of how man loves God in this roundabout way:

> But how can a person have such love for Christ unless he first believes firmly that he has everything in Him, unless he is convinced beyond a doubt that Christ is his Treasure and Savior, his Life and Comfort? When this conviction is rooted in the heart, love

will flow and follow in its wake. And where there is that love, it
cannot rest and be idle. It goes forth, preaches to, and teaches every-
one. It is eager to plant Christ in every heart and to bring every-
body to Him.[12]

Luther scholar Paul Althaus explains that Luther saw both parts of
the Great Commandment fulfilled in charitable actions:

> The commandment to love our neighbor stands beside the com-
> mandment to love God. Basically these are not two commandments
> but one and the same. God directs me to my neighbor. He wants
> nothing from us for himself, only that we believe in him. He does
> not need our work for himself. He does need it, however, for our
> neighbor. Loving the neighbor becomes the way in which we love
> God; and in serving the neighbor we serve God himself. God is
> present for me in my neighbor.[13]

Man's relationship to God is, first, through faith; then, second,
through love of man. This sequence was the rock on which Luther
stood to battle Rome on the faith-works question. Love followed
necessarily from faith, but after it. And, conversely, if there is no love
of man, there is no faith in God.

Although Calvin falls in step with Luther, restricting man's direct
relationship to God to faith, then verifying faith through love to other
men, love is in general far less central in his thought than Luther's.
Whether or not it is fair to accuse him of a 'betrayal of the God of
love,'[14] it must be said that the fires of love are considerably cooled
and dampened in his thought. The deeply influential *Institutes of the
Christian Religion*, which was offered as a condensed version of
religious truth, is especially revealing in this regard in saying little
about loving God. Calvin affirms the familiar sequence: Christ's
sacrifice in love generates faith leading to love: 'But how can the
mind be aroused to taste the divine goodness without at the same
time being wholly kindled to love God in return?' Significantly, this
statement of love for God, rare in the *Institutes*, is introduced to
buttress his argument against the Roman Catholic claim that faith
depends upon prior good works expressing love: 'For the teaching of
the Schoolmen, that love is prior to faith and hope, is mere madness;
for it is faith alone that first engenders love in us.'[15] Such love is the
'good works toward our neighbor' that fulfil the Law.[16] For Calvin as
for Luther, love resulting from faith in Christ is directed primarily to

other men, not God. And when, elsewhere, he does talk about loving
God, it is often really faith that he has in mind, as in this discussion of
John 16:27 ('for the Father himself loveth you, because ye have loved
me'):

> These words remind us that the only bond of our union with God
> is, to be united to Christ; and we are united to him by a faith which
> is not feigned, but which springs from sincere affection, which he
> describes by the name of *love*; for no man believes purely in Christ
> who does not cordially embrace him, and, therefore, by this word
> he has well expressed the power and nature of faith. But if it is only
> when we have loved Christ that God begins to love us, it follows
> that the commencement of salvation is from ourselves, because we
> have anticipated the grace of God. Numerous passages of Scrip-
> ture, on the other hand, are opposed to this statement.[17]

Calvin here reveals his true colours, solving the problem of a
troublesome text by telling us that 'love' really means 'faith.'[18] What
happens here is what happens generally in Reformed thought: the
importance of faith simply crowds out direct love of God.

And this is precisely what happens in 'Protestant' interpretations
of Herbert. These necessary attempts to put Herbert in his theological place, first by William Halewood,[19] later by Lewalski, Strier, and
Veith, express an important development in Herbert criticism. The
'medieval' approach of Rosemond Tuve[20] and the 'Anglican' approach of Joseph Summers[21] have been revised in ways that have
taught us to consider Herbert and *The Temple* more accurately in
their theological and spiritual contexts. Such attempts, I think it fair
to say, have become a mainstream in Herbert criticism, making their
shared failure to engage man's love for God in *The Temple* all the
more critical. In sharp contrast, Diana Benet has seen with a clear eye
that 'the spirit of charity pervades *The Temple*.'[22] In charity there is
'God's love to man and man's love to God and to his neighbor.'[23] More
important, she accepts as true what Tuve said before her: that 'the
place to fix our attention in Herbert's poems is upon their revelation
of man's love of God.'[24] A considerable gap yawns between this view
of *The Temple* and mainstream 'Protestant' views with their emphasis on justification by faith.

We need to close that gap, bearing in mind that for Herbert it is both
'love and trust' that can, with God's 'power and love,' make 'one place
ev'rywhere.' The precise connection in Herbert's spirituality be-

tween man's love and faith requires further attention. But at the same time we need to admit Tuve's argument that 'all but some twenty of the hundred and seventy odd poems raise one or more of the many traditional questions which surround the problem of the nature of Christian love.'[25] The force of numbers here suggests that love is the true centre of Herbert's concern and that consideration surrounding justification by faith should be referred to love, not vice versa. But we must also note Tuve's own nervous admission that 'Herbert seems to write much more of God's love for man than of what man's love to God should be.'[26] She leaves unexamined, moreover, some of the primary, startling facts about love for God that characterize *The Temple*.

For example, Herbert's conception of man's love for God can be defined as much by what it is not as by what it is. In this regard the severely curtailed allusions to the Song of Songs, the absence of interest in sexual embrace as a figure for union, and, in general, the scarcity of allusions to sexual love – these are striking when we consider that embrace, betrothal, and marriage between the Bride and Bridegroom are primary, traditional expressions of the union between the believer and Christ. Donne's calculated shock in inviting a divine rape, for example, is merely a flamboyant variation of heterosexual embrace to express union. If, as Tuve convincingly claims, Herbert is investigating various elements in Christian love with an almost surgical, even programmatic care,[27] the absence of love embrace is surprising. It follows that we need to pay particular attention to just how Herbert did conceive the union between man and God. We find that his repeated interest in spiritual taste, sweetness, and the Eucharist suggests a much different sense of man's essential love experience of God. In Herbert the centre is much different than in many other contemporary Christian writers.

This contrast can be made more clear in terms of some useful measuring sticks in Herbert's Calvinist ambience at Cambridge. Historians have demonstrated that the influence of Calvinistic thought in the British church was pervasive and varied in Herbert's time, particularly in Cambridge.[28] British divines can be distinguished from each other by the differing ways in which they absorbed various elements in Calvinistic thought. However divided on ecclesiastical matters such as church government, Christians might share Calvinistic theological assumptions such as predestination and election. A particularly useful way of measuring the love of God in Herbert's *The Temple* is in relation to the notions of two influential

Cambridge contemporaries, John Preston and Richard Sibbes, who like Herbert have been characterized as 'Calvinist.'[29] Like Herbert, but unlike Calvin and, more important, William Perkins, the dominant Calvinist presence in the immediately preceding Cambridge generation,[30] Preston and Sibbes develop notions of loving God that amend their received Calvinism. With Herbert they are making a Calvinist's attempt to change the emphasis on justification by faith that ignores love of God. As measuring sticks, their notions provide us with informative differences as well. It is equally crucial to note that, unlike both these Calvinist writers and Donne, for whom loving God is likewise central, Herbert rejects the notion of love embrace and downplays the Song of Songs as a means of defining his union with God.

Preston's *The Breastplate of Faith and Love* offers a useful, contemporary foil for understanding *The Temple* in this regard. By invoking Paul's Christian warrior in his title, Preston throws down his own gauntlet, for he chooses the broader 1 Thessalonians 5:8 and not the narrower rendition of the 'breastplate of righteousness' of Ephesians 5:14. He thus pointedly expands the centre of belief to include the direct love of God, not just the more restrictive justification by faith. Significantly, Preston's 'love' goes beyond the standard Reformation emphasis – faith in God and love to others – to emphasize love for God. Thus, the title expresses a necessary sequence – first faith, then love of God, then love of other men – which determines the actual structure of this work. How Preston treats this love that completes faith is arresting.

His Galatians text for the several sermons on love bears a special Reformation burden: 'For in Jesus Christ neither circumcision availeth any thing, nor uncircumcision; but faith which worketh by love' (Galatians 5:6). Luther and others after him, including Calvin, repeatedly used this text in mounting the argument for justification by faith against the Roman counterattack on the *sola fides* argument. Thus, the implications of this Galatians text were at the centre of the battle between the Reformers and the Church of Rome. On one side, the Reformers, in denying human merit and surrendering all power to God, who inspires faith, downplayed good works in the balance sheet of salvation. Only faith really mattered. On the other side, the Roman position granted more freedom of choice to sinful man and, hence, allowed merit and reward for good works. Whereas the Reformers were trying to avoid rewarding external actions at the expense of internal truth, the Catholics were trying to avoid social irresponsibility and self-deluding narcissicism. Luther's Pauline offence against the Catholic position was supported by Galatians 5:6, interpreted to mean that charitable works were the necessary consequence of faith, not a contributing cause:

> He [Paul] says that works are done on the basis of faith through
> love, not that a man is justified through love. And who is such an
> uneducated grammarian that he cannot understand from the force of
> the words that being justified is one thing and working is another?
> For Paul's words are clear and plain: 'faith *working* through love.'
> Therefore it is an obvious trick when they suppress the true and
> genuine meaning of Paul and interpret 'working' to mean 'justifying'
> and 'works' to mean 'righteousness,' although even in moral phi-
> losophy they are forced to admit that works are not righteousness,
> but that works are done by righteousness.[31]

Roman Catholics interpreted this text to mean that faith in God is informed and developed by such charitable actions and is dependent on them: 'The scholastic doctrine of "faith formed by charity," ... was often documented by Scripture passages such as Galatians 5:6: "*fides quae per charitatem operatur.*" '[32] In sum, this text from Galatians stands right on the edge of one of the great historical divides in Western thought.

Preston's different use of the Galatians text should be seen against this historical backdrop. By his time the effects of the Reformed constriction and hardening of the medieval Christian emphasis on conformity between man and God through love were being felt and assessed. As noted, Preston's position differs measurably from that of the earlier generation of Cambridge Calvinists dominated by William Perkins, for whom man's love of God was not a primary concern. Preston's real quarrel is not with the Calvinist thrust of *sola fides* in the direct communion between man and God, but with its some-times singleminded exclusion of direct love of God. He simply points out for his reader the path of interpretation that de-emphasizes without ignoring the social thrust of Paul's text. For him, Paul is talking first about the love of God that follows directly from the commitment in faith and precedes charity to others. That is, centre stage of the argument had shifted, and Preston assumes a broader Christian context than a stricter Calvinist would allow.

Thus, Preston stands against that stricter Calvinism to obey the first half of the Great Commandment more warmly, accepting the need to love God. But he must struggle with a problem inherent in the

New Testament response to God's love. That is, the love revealed to man in Christ calls forth faith, even though psychological realism might suggest that the answering response would be warmer love of God by man. This love would then, in turn, be the impetus for faith. Such psychological realism can be seen emerging in unexpected places. Even Luther, for whom the priority of faith is paramount, would seem to admit at least an admixture of love in the initial response: '*if we rightly consider it,* love comes first, or at the same moment as faith. For I could not trust God if I did not think He desired to be favorable and gracious towards me.'[33] Yet Luther's psychological realism is left in embryo form, neglected in favour of his emphasis on *sola fides*.[34] The priority of faith to love in New Testament thought strongly supports such emphasis in Paul, as noted, and in John's 'knowledge' that is faith.[35] For his part Preston recognizes both the danger of excluding affection in the initial response to God's love, hence encouraging a compartmentalization of faith and love, and also the dangerous tendency toward an unemotional, overly intellectual cast to Calvinist articulations[36] of the 'knowledge' that is faith. But like Donne[37] he assumes that the believer comes to faith, first, through the understanding supported by the will: '*Fides est actus intellectus,* It is an act of the understanding, assenting to Truths for the Authority of the Speaker; therefore the mind and will must concurre to make up this Faith.'[38] Preston's characterization of the will's 'consent' to reason reveals a noteworthy emphasis in his thought, representing as it does his attempt to suggest a more affective response to God's love that works against a compartmentalization between faith and love. In order to 'take and receive Christ,' the will must 'embrace them [the promises] ... take them, ... lay hold upon them.'[39] We can hear some loud echoes in this terminology. To 'lay hold' or 'to take hold' is a favourite contemporary term going back to the Bible, Paul in particular,[40] popularized by Luther,[41] and used widely by British Protestants[42] to express the act of belief. In Preston it merges with the idea of sexual embrace and the attendant notion of 'marriage' between the human Spouse and the divine Bridegroom.

Preston's suggestive mixture of traditional motifs characterizing the will's participation in belief comes to rest in the love embrace of marriage. But, significantly, that action also characterizes the union in love. The believer must first take the Person, by believing in him, 'as the Wife takes the Husband.'[43] This notion of intimate, personal union carries through Preston's characterization:

> Faith is not onely the beleeving of a truth which is delivered, from the authority of him that doth deliver it; but it is a resting upon Christ, a casting of ourselves upon him ... it is of necessity required that you must bee unbottomed of your selves, you must altogether leane upon him, you must cast your selves wholly upon him.[44]

Only when that is done, and the justifying union in faith is completed, does love for God necessarily follow. After 'the match is made,' then one must love. 'It is required that you love your Husband, *Iesus Christ*, that you forsake Father and Mother, and become one Spirit with him, as you are one flesh with your Wife; for you are now bone of his bone, and flesh of his flesh.'[45] The marriage union between the Spouse and Christ is a constant in the characterization of both faith and love. Of course, Preston's critics could well argue that he wants it both ways: love both is and is not part of the act of faith. Perhaps, but his intention is to break down any rigid compartments between love and faith by suggesting closely related, but distinct, actions of the same voluntary faculty that marries the soul to God. Unlike Paul, Luther, Calvin, and Perkins, he is carefully clearing ground for man's direct love of God, while preserving the priority of justification by faith.

The presence of similar ideas in the works of the popular Richard Sibbes suggests their currency in Herbert's Cambridge. That Sibbes lent a sympathetic hand in editing Preston's works posthumously merely adds to our sense of convictions expressed harmoniously among several 'Calvinist' Cambridge voices. More to our point, Sibbes is no less eager than Preston to encourage man's love of God. His emphasis, like Preston's, sharply separates him from Calvin and many of his British followers. For Sibbes, love of God is the pivot in a spiritual psychology more complexly developed than Preston's. For him all 'inward worship of God is in the affections,' and love is the 'commanding affection of all others.'[46] Love is 'primary, the first-born affection of the soul, from which all other affections are bred';[47] and through love of God the human creature is fulfilled. Sibbes has problems in accommodating this emphasis on love in his psychology to his Reformed theology. Like Preston he regards justification by faith in Christ's person as the necessary precursor to loving God; and, similarly, for him the marriage between the human Spouse and the Husband, Christ, involves both faith and love. But while he emphasizes love as the master affection, by focusing on the importance of affection in worship he runs the risk of displacing faith as

central. Part of his problem is that he must distinguish clearly
between the experiences of faith and love. Faith begins through
'hearing,'[48] a response to preaching that is guided by reason and
illuminated by the Spirit. Man thereby can get the evidence of God's
love revealed in Christ. Such faith leads him to love God, who first
loved him, as the preaching reveals. Like Preston he desires to show
the union of faith and love, sometimes speaking of faith as simply one
more affection. But his conception of faith as established by reason
and supported by the will disturbs his characterization of the
affections as having, we would say, an emotional content.

Sibbes divides the affections, which are the varying ways in which
the soul is emotionally disposed, into two basic categories. On one
hand, there are the penal *affections of humiliation,*[49] such as shame,
sorrow, grief, and fear. On the other hand, there are the more
immediately constructive affections that fulfil the soul: love, joy,
zeal, delight, hope, trust, admiration.[50] His occasional characterization of faith as an affection[51] follows from his conception that an
affection is a disposition of the will; and the will is necessarily
involved in faith, in spite of its primary roots in the understanding.
First, the understanding must be 'persuaded' about spiritual truth,
which must then be embraced by the affections:

> This is the order of God's Spirit; first to open the eye to see, and
> by sight to persuade, and upon persuasion to stir up the heart and
> affections to embrace; for good things are brought into the soul
> through the understanding, by the spiritual sight of the understand-
> ing, and from that into the will and affections by embracing the
> things we know. This is God's course daily. Therefore he saith they
> first saw them, and then were persuaded of them, and then em-
> braced them.[52]

But this clear, formulaic sequence is clouded by the will's necessary
participation in the act of persuasion. That is, the will must, with the
Spirit's aid, choose what reason discerns and then 'cleave' to it.[53] But
the intellectual activity of faith suggests that, if it is an affection, it is
sharply distinguished from all other affections.

Still, the blurring in Sibbes' categories is consistent with his need,
like Preston's, to show the intimate coordination of both faith and
love in the Spouse's close union to the Husband. Faith through the
understanding 'apprehends,' then 'cleaves' through the will; then,
the will further through the affections 'embraces' Christ and his

promises. The modulation from apprehending, to cleaving, then to embracing carries faith from the understanding through the affections:

> When the soul is persuaded of heavenly things and of its interest
> in them, and is carried to them by the sway and weight of the affec-
> tions of love, and joy, and delight, – which is called here embrac-
> ing, – then the things embraced transform the soul to be like them,
> as they be heavenly, and glorious, and excellent.[54]

Sibbes usually reserves the notion of embrace not for faith, but for love and joy, even though like Preston he regards faith as 'the marriage of the soul to Christ.'[55] 'In marriage there must be a consent. This consent is faith.'[56] By means of this consent, one 'takes' Christ; similarly, one 'lays hold' or 'cleaves' to the person of Christ as Husband.[57] The embrace that follows – through love, delight, and joy – is faith working by love, thus revealing a happy consistency with Paul's Galatians text. [58] To 'be married' to Christ is not only 'to take him for an husband,'[59] but also to unite with him in mutual love, in a mutual embrace between Spouse and Husband, conforming man's affections to Christ through union and communion.[60] Sibbes' mutual 'embrace' in love takes the sexual metaphor one step further than does Preston without disturbing the basic likeness in their thought. Both are making a concerted attempt to define man's love for God as a fulfilment of his faith.

A theological reason for this attempt may lie in the 'experimental predestinarianism' of English Calvinism described by R.T. Kendall.[61] In Calvin's own doctrine the Elect have 'a firm and certain knowledge of God's benevolence' to them.[62] They are 'fully persuaded'[63] of their election without needing later assurance from evidence of a sanctified life. However, many of Calvin's followers sought further 'experimental'[64] evidence of election following the initial faithful conviction of salvation. According to Kendall, this search was begun early on the European continent by Theodore Beza and the Heidelberg theologians; it was continued in England by William Perkins and many of those who came after him at Cambridge, such as John Preston and Richard Sibbes. For the influential William Perkins, who like Calvin emphasized the intellectual nature of justifying faith, assurance was achieved through reasoning about such effects of sanctification as the willingness to repent. Later divines like Preston and Sibbes emphasize instead the experience of the affections as assurance of election. In particular, love of God and man gives assurance that one is saved. Both Preston and Sibbes reveal such developed notions of loving God, which are absent in Calvin and Perkins.

These developed notions provide us with one clear vantage point for surveying what Herbert's *The Temple* is and is not. Together with Herbert, Preston and Sibbes reveal a concerted attempt in their contemporary Cambridge to define how faith works by direct love of God. Since Preston and Sibbes represent a widely influential and popular[65] Calvinist vein in British Christianity, Herbert's sharp difference in the matter of love embrace is significant. More generally, he experiences serious problems in defining man's love of God, as we learn immediately in 'The Church.' In 'The Sacrifice' Christ is lamenting from the Cross, his grief conveying his radical love of man. Then follows in 'The Thanksgiving' a violation of our expectations that the terms necessary to complete John's initial logic, that we love him because he first loved us, will be given:

> Nay, I will read thy book, and never move
>   Till I have found therein thy love,
> Thy art of love, which I'le turn back on thee:
>   O my deare Saviour, Victorie!
> Then for thy passion – I will do for that –
>   Alas, my God, I know not what.   ('The Thanksgiving,' 45–50)

Herbert is dramatically announcing the difficulty in finding terms to understand man's answering love of God. It is not that man does not love God, but that expressing love in traditional terms is fraught with difficulty. The terms of conformity, so clear in Preston's and Sibbes' conception of spiritual marriage, are not clear to the speaker at all. The problem lies not in defining God's love for man as we find in 'The Agonie': 'Who knows not Love, let him assay / And taste that juice, which on the crosse a pike / Did set again abroach' (13–15). Christ's sacrifice is a clear expression of his love; the problem lies in knowing how to love God in turn. At best, the terms of man's conformity are problematical.

This obtuse speaker's immediate problem in 'The Thanksgiving' – of finding a proper 'art' for loving God – is the general problem of love in *The Temple.* He tries assiduously to get around his initial sense of the difficulty of thanking Christ; he wants to 'revenge me on thy love, / And trie who shall victorious prove' (17–18). The curiously ambiguous 'revenge' expresses a desire to repay God by suffering imitative grief for his suffering; at the same time it admits the speaker's desire to get even for the invidious situation in which he finds himself. His fumbling, ambiguous response, largely the result of congenital human limitations, expresses an answering love, but no clear 'art.' His palpable humanity is the truth of him; and fairness says that we cannot blame all his limitations on his pride. Unlettered, he must learn the 'art' of loving God. And that art is training all his powers to identify and to enjoy the taste of love's strange sweetness. For Herbert developing the poet's art is necessarily included in that training.

Both Rosemond Tuve and Barbara Lewalski recognize in differing ways the problematical nature of man's love of God in *The Temple*, but not as a problem of 'art.' Tuve asserts that 'all but some twenty of the hundred and seventy odd poems raise one or more of the many traditional questions which surround the problem of the nature of Christian love'; she further claims that 'Herbert addresses himself to it with a theologian's care and profundity.'[66] Her analysis of God's love for man, however, is more informative than her sketchy analysis of man's answering love for God. Admittedly, she rightly sees man's gratitude to God and Augustinian '*fruitio Dei*' as primary components.[67] But there is more to be said about the ways in which Herbert is posing the problem of man's love for God. For her part Lewalski sees that mutual love between friends, not between heterosexual lovers, is the crucial mode in *The Temple*; but then she forces an unsubstantiated argument that a Song of Songs vocabulary articulates this love.[68] On the contrary, it is the infrequency of references to the Song of Songs and to love embrace that expresses Herbert's crucial point. Recognizing that negative point is part of learning the right terms to express the art of love. Diana Benet is quite right in saying that *The Temple* examines the search to express love to God.[69] More precisely, expression is integral to the prayerful art of obeying the Great Commandment.

At this point, a more searching look at the relationship between faith and love is necessary for understanding this 'art of love.' The real value of Strier's claim that justification by faith is at the heart of *The Temple* is that the experience of love cannot be understood separately from faith. God's power and love meet man's love and trust, making 'an every where.' Trust is the *sine qua non* of faith in the person Christ; it is the 'fiducia,' the 'confidence' undergirding Reformation spiritual psychology.[70] For Herbert, like Preston and Sibbes, this faithful trust is love's foundation. A basic contemporary vocabulary of faith is ironically invoked early on in 'The Sacrifice.' The crucifying Jews 'lay hold' on the person of Christ, 'not with the hands / Of faith, but furie' (45–6). Like all sinners they violate Christ's person rather than surrender to the power of his love and its promises. To lay hold of Christ or to hold fast to him spiritually is to trust in the promise of his love; this trust, this belief, constitutes the faith, the 'hold fast'[71] that supports believers. Herbert's poem 'The Holdfast' assumes this essential psychology of trust in the person of Christ that surrenders dependence upon the self:

> I threatned to observe the strict decree
>> Of my deare God with all my power & might.
>> But I was told by one, it could not be;
> Yet I might trust in God to be my light.
> Then will I trust, said I, in him alone.
>> Nay, ev'n to trust in him, was also his:
>> We must confesse that nothing is our own.
> Then I confesse that he my succour is:
> But to have nought is ours, not to confesse
>> That we have nought. I stood amaz'd at this,
>> Much troubled, till I heard a friend expresse,
> That all things were more ours by being his.
>> What Adam had, and forfeited for all,
>> Christ keepeth now, who cannot fail or fall.   (1–14)

The inner voice of the Spirit, the 'friend,' brings the speaker to recognize that his identity is fulfilled by trusting all to God, not to his own powers. The conviction in this trust, that is, faith itself, is the holdfast.[72]

In general, the speaker's surrender resembles the psychology of trust to be found in both Preston and Sibbes. To 'take and receive' the person of Christ, Preston tells us, is to subject the self to him as a wife does to a husband, surrendering without qualification to his powers. This 'laying hold' of Christ 'drives a man out of himselfe,'[73] thereby 'casting' himself and 'resting upon Christ.'[74] In turn, Sibbes says that the believer 'goes out of himself' and 'casts himself upon God's love and mercy.' This is to 'rely on' Christ, to 'trust' him, a vocabulary indebted to Paul, to Luther, and to Calvin.[75] This trust or confidence is a passive surrender to God's love that identifies man's power as Christ's. But the obverse is also true: to relinquish the self is not to eradicate it, but to follow Christ's direction without uncertainty so that God's power seems like one's own.

That this Pauline faith works by love pointedly informs Preston's and Sibbes' understanding of the Great Commandment, first to love God, then man. A necessary corollary is that the programmatic test of love is, concurrently, the test of faith. For Preston, we know we love God if the affections of love and joy stir within, if love is experienced as delight, that is, if there is enjoyment of the beloved and love itself, and if there is a desire to please God.[76] Sibbes is even more exacting than Preston, offering a general principle that 'The nature of love is seen in four things: 1. In admiring of some secret good in the thing beloved, which stirs up the soul to make out for it. 2. In a studiousnes of the contentation of the person beloved. 3. In a desire of union and fellowship with the person we affect. 4. In a resting and solacing of ourselves in the thing we love.'[77] He then applies these four norms programmatically as a means of ascertaining whether or not we love God. Like Preston, he assumes that the proof of love is concurrently the proof of faith; thus, love is a necessary, continuing reminder of one's trust in God. Just as faith works by love, love is evidence of faith; or, put negatively, the absence of love proves an absence of faith.

This is the dark side of the notion. God shows his love directly in his favour and in his presence; disfavour and absence seem like the withdrawal of love. And the apparent loss of God's love can weaken the whole logic of loving a God who first loved man. In turn, the loss of man's love for God erodes its foundation in trust. We see Herbert's darkness in the autobiographical 'Affliction (I),' which chronicles the growing contradiction between God's enticement and affliction. The final stanza jangles with self-contradiction:

> Yet, though thou troublest me, I must be meek;
> > In weaknesse must be stout.
> Well, I will change the service, and go seek
> > Some other master out.
> Ah my deare God! though I am clean forgot,
> Let me not love thee, if I love thee not.   (61–6)

Rebellious, he clearly recognizes that his feeling of love, now shaken, is the touchstone of his service. Self-blame for not loving God barely muffles rebellion against the affliction that erodes his love and trust. It also fractures a Reformation logic of causality by assuming perversely that a capacity to love God is a reward based on merit for already loving God. This broken logic still darkly figures forth his disturbed service. Fortunately for the believer such moments do not last; the darkness can lighten; and evidence of love can be found for man's continuing love and trust. The true logic is that God's motions cause both faith and love; and the believer must find that logic informing the welter of light and darkness in God's dealings with man. Included in the art of love is learning to detect this logic, which can sustain love and its foundation in faithful trust.

In more general terms, the art of love is a search to discern, define, and express the conformity to God that will save man. This art of love is an art of revision, for God's communications with man characteristically exceed the terms man develops to comprehend how God manifests himself. But in this revision lies an essential conformity to the divine artist, who revises his own art of love to meet changing conditions. At first, God transcribed the Law on stone tablets: 'of old the Law by heav'nly art / Was writ in stone' ('Sepulchre,' 17–20). Now, God writes on the 'fleshly tables of the human heart' (2 Corinthians 3:3), however hardened by sin: 'And though my hard heart scarce to thee can grone, / Remember that thou once didst write in stone' ('The Sinner,' 13–14). God must 'write there' in the 'heart' the New Law expressed in Christ's sacrifice ('Good Friday,' 23). Just as God revises his art of love, so must man, in likeness, learn to revise his. But such basic likeness is defined paradoxically by profound difference. Whereas God's art of love both creates and renovates his subject, man's art of love can only honour God by recognizing that everything is already done for man. In fact, God's greatest 'Master-peece,' we are told in 'Love' (Williams manuscript), is to make man realize that his efforts to show love to God are always far surpassed by God's love to man:

> Thou art too hard for me in Love:
> There is no dealing with thee in that Art:
>   That is thy Master-peece I see.
>   When I contrive & plott to prove
> Something that may be conquest on my part,
>   Thou still, O Lord, outstrippest mee.   (1–6)

The riddle of Herbert's conformity is implicit here. His poetic acknowledgment of God's 'Master-peece,' which emphasizes the contrast between their respective arts, paradoxically conforms him to the loving divine artist by expressing his own love. Just as the incarnate Word expresses God's love to man, man's love, in conformity, must be expressed in words.

The true art of love guides the heart's loving search for the right words, and in this connection we can approach Herbert's parody of secular love poetry.[78] Like God, he is writing an *Ars amatoria* and a *Remedia amoris*. In two sonnets about divine love poetry, 'Love (i) and (ii),' Herbert parodies the conventional Petrarchan lover-poet examining the necessary connection between his love and his poetry. The sonnet form itself is love's art of praise. But Herbert's speaker laments that 'heart and brain,' which are God's 'workmanship' ('Love (i),' 7–8), are devoted to loving and praising women, not God, the 'authour of this great frame' (1). God's correction is necessary. By petitioning God to 'kindle in our hearts such true desires' of love that will 'consume our lusts' ('Love (ii),' 4–5), the lover-poet seeks the flames of divine correction that are fired by God's love. Reason and will could then join to praise the loving God, who first created and now must restore the damaged soul to achieve its proper end in love. As in secular love, the right words of praise are the measure of true love.

The breadth and detail of love parody, admirably mapped in modern Herbert scholarship, rest uneasily with his rejection of love embrace to express the believer's union with God. In general, Herbert carefully walks a razor's edge, using secular love conventions to say both what his love is and is not. For example, the love-dialogue[79] in 'Love (iii)' suggests neither the shepherd's hut nor the pregnant bank, but the communion table and heavenly marriage. The 'Come away,' / Make no delay' (1–2) of the *aube*[80] in 'Dooms-day' does not invite the beloved to seize the day, but asks the powerful divine lover to save a sinful, temporal world. Also, Herbert invokes the secular origins of the broken heart, but always under the shadow of Christ's broken body as the complicated model for man's grief. Herbert readers can find the traces of sacred parody everywhere throughout *The Temple*. But Herbert pulls up short when exploiting the idea of full heterosexual union to depict divine love. In one uncharacteristic allusion to the Song of Songs ('I am sick of love,' 2:5), the love-sick soul may be 'wed' to God ('Frailtie,' 20–1), but the central bond – Lewalski is quite right – is friendship, not heterosexual union. A mark of the love between God and man is that heterosexual love, embodied in the available conventions of secular love poetry, can suggest man's union with God only in a qualified way.

Herbert would agree with Sibbes that in 'true love' to God there is a *'desire of union and communion with him.'*[81] Like Sibbes he finds more than one way to express his sense of the union and communion. In Sibbes the ruling notion of the love embrace interacts with the notion of spiritual taste and the Eucharist; the common denominator is the conception of the marriage feast between the believer and Christ. In Herbert the love communion in language between friends or between master and servant interacts with the experience of tasting love's sweetness. The three poems on love, pointedly related to each other by their titles, lead to this centre of love communion, to speaking and eating. In 'Love (ɪ)' and 'Love (ɪɪ),' the choice of the love-sonnet form cinches tightly together the experiences of love and praise. To love is to express praise. The even larger truth is the communion in the dialogue poem, 'Love (ɪɪɪ),' in the speaking and eating between Christ and the soul. Here, the relationship of 'friends' which Lewalski finds throughout *The Temple* can bear its full fruit, if seen in terms of language as well as eating. That is, the crucified Christ of 'The Sacrifice' prepares us for the host Love in 'Love (ɪɪɪ)'; and the Spirit of Christ appears as the Friend in *The Temple*.[82] Here is the Protestant sense of faithful communion with a personal God. The communion of friends, which modulates into the master/servant and father/child relationships, expresses the emphasis not only on faith in the Person of Christ but also on communion with the indwelling Person of the Holy Spirit. But it is the Eucharistic essence of 'Love (ɪɪɪ),' its centre in the communion between man and God, which suggests how the soul is 'wed' to God in Heaven. Not heterosexual embrace, but assimilation through eating and speaking, through taste and language, as we will see in some detail in chapter three, expresses the love union in Heaven. Here is the centre of man's love of God, to which all elements in union and communion must be referred.

The role of language in Herbert's art of love includes terms for identifying God. These terms denote qualities in divine Persons and essential relationships with the believer; and using these terms when calling the beloved Person acknowledges the identities of both the human and divine lovers. Identification can be mutual, merging into dialogue, as in the sweetened 'commerce' (29) of 'My Master' and 'My Servant' in 'The Odour.' In 'The Collar' the concluding exchange finally calls back to order the rebellious child, rushing headlong out of control: 'Me thoughts I heard one calling, *Child* / And I reply'd, *My Lord*' (35–6). Elsewhere, sacred love parody is obtrusive. In 'The Search' the unanswered, anguished voice seeking 'My Lord, my

Love' (2) echoes the unrequited secular lover separated from the beloved or suffering from Cupid's disfavour. By identifying the divine person and, reflexively, himself as well, the speaker thereby clarifies the nature of their relationship. The terms reveal essential truths.

The real thrust of such identifying is what it tells us about possession in the love union between man and God. Herbert's fondness for explicitly calling on God expresses possession self-consciously, although at times the possessive 'My God' can seem like the frantic whistling in the darkness of separation. At other times he speaks with full conviction. In 'The Call' he invokes God: 'Come, my Joy, my Love, my Heart' (9). This invitation to the beloved follows hard on two varyingly biblical invocations: 'Come, my Way, my Truth, my Life ... my Light, my Feast, my Strength' (1, 5). The culminating lover's invocation, intimate and heartfelt, further expresses parody of love possession that often colours Herbert's addresses to God. Herbert persists throughout *The Temple* in examining the relationship of 'mine' and 'thine' between God and man.[83] The pronouns repeatedly express the complex modulations in the mutual possession to be distinguished by the art of love. The basic terms in Herbert's psychology of love possession can be found in 'Love (I) and (II).' There, the opposition of 'true desires' and 'lusts' ('Love (II),' 4–5) assumes that desire powers all love, as it does all affections.[84] Herbert would agree with Sibbes that love is the 'commanding affection of all others, and setteth the whole man sweetly a-work to attain its desire.'[85] The object of the 'hearts desire' ('Discipline,' 5), the love parody assumes, is union with the beloved, expressed as mutual possession, 'mine' and 'thine.' At this point Tuve's claim that much in Herbert does 'closely resemble the *fruitio Dei* of Augustine' is most useful.[86] For Augustine, and Herbert after him, both desire and its fruition in the enjoyment of God are components of love.[87] Love's desire is the will's movement to enjoy the love object. For Herbert that fruition, which is the goal of his art of love, is experienced as a joyful possession of God's person.

Unfortunately, such love possession can be a knotty matter in Herbert. His distinctions can seem more tentative than conclusive. The invitation that God 'come' in 'The Call' is followed immediately in 'The Clasping of Hands' by an attempt to understand possession which the heart desires. But even the title is knotty. After all, heterosexual love desire, as the sacred parody implicitly reminds us, would not usually be satisfied with a mere clasping of hands. Herbert is playing with the idea of love embrace, suggesting mutual union, but only with clasped hands and not the arms of the soul.[88] But even though we have been forewarned about the 'true desires' of divine love ('Love (ɪɪ),' 4), the poem's failure to talk explicitly about either 'hands' or 'clasping,' while rejecting love embrace, leaves us questioning. To this end Herbert alludes ironically to mutual possession in the Song of Songs ('My beloved is mine and I am his,' 2:16) while rejecting the lavish physicality that defines it. But he and his God do possess each other:

> Lord, thou art mine, and I am thine,
> If mine I am: and thine much more,
> Then I or ought, or can be mine.
> Yet to be thine, doth me restore;
> So that again I now am mine,
> And with advantage mine the more,
> Since this being mine, brings with it thine,
> And thou with me dost thee restore.
>   If I without thee would be mine,
>   I neither should be mine nor thine.   (1–10)

Imputation of Christ's righteousness explains man's possession of God, while preserving the distinction between human and divine. The human self is restored by Christ's indwelling presence; hence his righteousness now belongs to the speaker. In turn, God now owns the believer in his new commitment to follow in God's way. So far so good – until the speaker's desire for union unsettles his understanding of their necessary relationship:

> Lord, I am thine, and thou art mine:
> So mine thou art, that something more
> I may presume thee mine, then thine.
> For thou didst suffer to restore
> Not thee, but me, and to be mine,
> And with advantage mine the more,
> Since thou in death wast none of thine,
> Yet then as mine didst me restore.
>   O be mine still! still make me thine!
>   Or rather make no Thine and Mine!   (11–20)

Seen in human terms, Christ's death for man is a self-surrender ('none of thine'), seemingly unsettling Christ's possession of man. The speaker instinctively recognizes the fault in this reasoning; after all, the surrender of Christ to man left his divine nature self-sufficient, separate from man. But love's powerful desire for union unwittingly leads the speaker dangerously close to a proud failure to keep clear essential differences between human and divine ('make no Thine and Mine'). The irony is powerful: the strength of his 'true desires' confuses the proper terms for their true satisfaction. But, then, the enigmatic title has implicitly warned us that possession is no easy matter.

Still, love's desire for mutual possession and communion can find moments of clear satisfaction when God seems close; by contrast, his seeming absence or inattention causes anguish. Among the rare moments of satisfaction is the mutual traffic in sweetness between 'My Master' and 'My servant' in 'The Odour.' Unfortunately, Herbert's God elsewhere seems as much absent as present, as much unheeding as attentive. Like the secular lover aggrieved by the beloved's distance, Herbert regards coming to terms with God's varying distance as a primary task in the art of love. Here, sacred parody is at its most telling. In 'The Search' the aggrieved speaker, distanced from God and longing for union, seeks 'My Lord, my Love':

> For as thy absence doth excell
> > All distance known:
> So doth thy nearenesse bear the bell,
> > Making two one.   (57–60)

Perceiving his aggrieved sense of separation as a great space, he envies the stars in their proximity to God ('poore I pine,' 16). Like the secular lover's, his grief is frustrated desire for union ('Making two one'). But he lacks a conviction of God's presence. In 'Longing' frustrated desire yearns for the attention of an unhearing Christ; inattention is perceived as distance ('on high,' 57). Bold love parody compares Christ to a wounding Cupid perversely cold, distant, and hard:

> > My love, my sweetnesse, heare!
> > By these thy feet, at which my heart
> > > Lies all the yeare,
> > > Pluck out thy dart,
> > And heal my troubled breast which cryes,
> > > Which dyes.   (79–84)

Ironically, the parody in expressing love's frustrated desire for union is an art for communing with God: 'Lord of my soul, love of my minde, / Bow down thine eare!' (20–1). In capturing his feelings of separation and dispossession, the parody embodies love's desire; for only love's fruition is absent, not love itself. A further irony is that his anguished love, if conformed to Christ's own grief, is the ultimate way to possess him through love's art.

At this point, the broader assumptions of that art deserve closer scrutiny. We have already seen that the basic experience of love – desire, fruition, spiritual communion, possession – cannot be separated from self-conscious literary and linguistic skills. The artifact is constructed through adaptation, revision, and parody of existing forms as a necessary expression of love. The reverse holds true, as well: without these self-conscious artifacts, love remains unformed, without the possibility of fruition. The importance of the artifact lies in the nature of created reality, which is itself the artifact of the divine artist. In conformity the poet must use his God-given gifts to love and honour him. But this conformity does not grant a special election to artists alone, since the broader application is that all believers are similarly obligated to develop their arts of serving God. This broader assumption emerges frequently in Herbert's time – in Sibbes' 'The Art of Self-Humbling' and 'The Art of Mourning,'[89] Donne's 'art of salvation,'[90] Hall's *The Art of Divine Meditation*,[91] Marvell's Cromwell, whose 'Arts of Peace' must later be replaced by the '*Arts*' that '*gain*' and later '*maintain*' power.[92] Stretched even more broadly, the assumption is that living itself is a self-conscious art of loving and honouring God.

Herbert's Protestant notion of vocation is relevant here. For, if living is an art, so too is any God-given calling, particularly those concerned with making artifacts. More specifically, his own personal 'art of love,' embodied in *The Temple* in a way that serves his readers, merges into the fulfilment of his vocation as a poet. Basic assumptions of the Protestant notion of calling come into play here. Like most Protestants of his time, Herbert is quite explicit about the 'necessity of a vocation' (*The Country Parson*, p 274) in fulfilling man's service to God. It has been suggested that performing the obligation of one's calling was an 'essential kind, of Christian worship' for Protestants.[93] In any event, the calling was an essential relationship whereby God could be served by serving other humans. Further, the Lutheran roots of this notion are that actions in a calling must be guided by love.[94] We have already seen the theological basis of this notion: that is, faith works by love and service to other humans, which express love and service indirectly to God as well. Thus, the work of one's calling expresses love directly to other humans and indirectly to God, thereby obeying the Great Commandment. A corollary is that a believer cannot love either God or man truly without working in his vocation.

Essential motions in *The Temple* embody Herbert's desire to satisfy the demands of the Great Commandment. Although love of God occupies the centre of Herbert's spirituality in the work, his charitable concern for others is necessarily implicated in his sense of his poetic calling. Rosemond Tuve once took George Herbert Palmer to task for accusing Herbert of self-enclosure, a 'self-centered piety' he called it. Her refutation is unequivocal:

> Herbert's wellnigh perfect understanding of what it means to *love*
> our neighbor is assuredly visible in his poems, and is firm, just,
> clear, subtle, bearing fruit inescapably in constant actions of high
> generosity and a humility so based as to rehabilitate the very word
> *charity*.[95]

Diana Benet provides a detailed defence of this claim, showing how Herbert's clear sense of charity to his readers informs *The Temple*.[96] Herbert himself encapsulates it: *'Love God, and love your neighbour.'* But these are 'dark instructions,' he also tells us ('Divinitie,' 17, 19). His dramatization of his 'many spiritual Conflicts that have passed betwixt God and my Soul,'[97] revealing at best a frustrated art of love, is offered to his reader as a paradoxical 'taste' of 'The churches mysticall repast' ('Superliminare,' 4) that illustrates the 'dark' ways the commandment can be obeyed. But these dark instructions, centring as they do on directly loving God, inspire motions of spirituality that make *The Temple* what it is.

This chapter has been less explicit about spirituality than about love, but the bond in love between man and God necessarily shapes the spiritual communion between them. The prayerful Christian life, like the love that quickens it, is for Herbert an art. For the devotional poet writing in a prayerful mode, that truth is more obvious and compelling, but no more ultimately true than for any other Christian believer. That shared truth is a primary bond not only between Herbert and his artist God, but also between him and his reader.

Herbert's own experience of these bonds takes on the special coloration of his own spiritual temperament. The following chapters on Herbert's spirituality suggest in detail why the essential qualities of sweetness, fitness, delight, and quickness distinguish Herbert's prayerful communion with God and man.

3 *Tasting and Telling Sweetness*

'Love (III)' has a special place in *The Temple*. This final lyric in the long, devotional middle section, 'The Church,' configures the heavenly result of the earthly devotional life. The host Christ, who is Love, after 'sweetly questioning' (5) the reluctant believer, invites him to sit down and 'taste my meat.' The believer's direct response concludes the dialogue: 'So I did sit and eat' (17–18). The clear lines of this drama emphasize some essentials of Herbert's spirituality: the sweetness of love, the taste and consumption of God, and fulfilment through language. The relationships between these essentials determine many of the distinctive qualities of his devotional poetry. A few illustrations at the outset will suggest the importance of the relationships between these elements.

In 'Jordan (II)' the 'friend' admonishes the speaker to '*Copie out onely*' the '*sweetnesse readie penn'd*' (17–18) in the experience of God's love. There is much to be heard in this whispered admonition. Self-serving poetic decoration, we are told, is just that, the indulgence of self that denies the true subject of devotional poetry. And not merely love is the true subject, but love experienced as 'sweetnesse.' For Herbert, there is a necessary relationship between language and the sweetness of love. Significantly, Herbert defines one kind of sweetness by another. The harmonies of poetic language are denied here; but even when allowed elsewhere, 'sweet phrases, lovely metaphors' ('The Forerunners,' 13) are not essential. Although enticing, such harmonies do not always serve the spiritual sweetness that may inform language differently.

Such poetry, in treating sweetness, expresses the natures of both God and man. In interrupting the posturing self, the whispered admonition of the loving, divine 'friend' in 'Jordan (II)' is itself sweetness ready penned; the soul that can hear even whispered divine motions is a soul already sweetened by divine love; and the divine voice that informs the soul, swiftly, simply, intimately, reveals God's loving nature in the informing action itself. Thus, in its seemingly homely simplicity in 'Jordan (II),' the idea of sweetness leads paradoxically to many sides of a complex truth which Herbert takes as a primary subject of devotional poetry.

But the expression of sweetness assumes the 'taste' and consumption of God's love. In 'Love (III)' Christ's invitation to 'taste my meat' is a necessary ingredient in the communion between man and God that also includes the spoken dialogue. And the experience of tasting God's sweetness characterizes Herbert's spirituality. In 'The Agonie,' for example, to 'taste' the 'liquour sweet' (16–17) of Christ's blood is to know what love is. So, too, in 'Love (III)' the speaker will taste the sweetness of Christ's sacrifice while eating his meat. Here Herbert points more explicitly to the role of taste as one part of a whole: tasting occurs while consuming and assimilating God's love. That is, the soul tastes or experiences the effects of God's indwelling presence as it conforms the believer to God himself. That conformity in love, which is pervaded by the sense of sweetness, is the centre of Herbert's poetry.

By beginning with necessary inferences drawn from 'Love (III),' we can comprehend Herbert's centre more fully. This is particularly true of the sense of sweetness pervading Herbert's spirituality. The primary Christian truth here is the sweetness of the Godhead, a notion which, in its biblical origins and its enrichment through later variations, reveals a deeply sensed spiritual reality. In its broadest reaches God's sweetness suggests his goodness and benevolence in regard to his creatures.[1] What is 'sweet' in Latin translations of the Bible is 'good' in others.[2] More specific biblical identifications of sweetness assume the broader meaning, such as the sweetness of God's words (Psalm 119:103) or his judgments (Psalm 19:10) or the effects of the Spirit's presence (Isaiah 61:1). Later allegorical interpretations of the perfumed Bridegroom in the Song of Songs pointedly identify sweetness as divine love. Modulations between the respective sweetness of love and goodness occur easily, given the Christian linkage of these qualities in the divine nature.

The frequency of such modulations in St Francis de Sales, Herbert's French contemporary, bears witness to the Christian spirituality of sweetness and its vitality in Herbert's time. Francis argues that man was created to love goodness, in particular to love God's goodness, which is 'better and sweeter than all things.'[3] By nature of his goodness, God continuously aids the soul in this love, revealing the 'sweetness of his love' to man,[4] an enticement to man's own appropriately sweet love of God. The sweetness of both God's goodness and love can be seen in the benefits of his providential care that Francis celebrates in joy: 'Ah! is there a sweetness like unto this sweetness?'[5] It should be noted, however, that the sweetness of love is subordinated to that of goodness.

For Richard Sibbes, Herbert's influential contemporary, the language of sweetness refers primarily to divine love. The commonplace Reformed coordination of the Son with the Holy Spirit, whose activities apply Christ, is experienced as a pervasive sweetness. The Spirit's 'sweet motions'[6] transform the believer's soul in a loving marriage to the Bridegroom; and Sibbes' prose is perfumed by the language of the Song of Songs to characterize that union with Christ. The sweetness of Grace, through the Spirit's motions, whether in the 'sweet voice' of the ministry[7] or in the Church's sweet ordinances, especially the Sacrament,[8] or in the private motions in the virtuous, sweetened soul, has its foundation in Christ's sacrifice as the fullest expression of the sweetness of divine love.

The traditional character of Herbert's sensitivity to divine sweetness is coloured by his own spiritual temperament. For him, like Sibbes, divine sweetness is first a matter of love. Accordingly, in 'Providence,' his hymn to the harmonious, providential coordination of the created world, he praises the Spirit's divine 'power and love' that 'so strongly and so sweetly' moves (29–31) the world and its coordinated parts. Herbert's emphasis on providential care as evidence of the sweetness of divine love stands a revealing half turn away from Francis' consideration of providential care as first illustrating goodness. Similarly telling is that Herbert's temperament does not find in the union of Bridegroom and Spouse, the perfumed centre of the Song of Songs, a congenial expression of love between the believer and God.[9] Yet Christ's sweetness is the spiritual centre as much for Herbert as for Francis and for Sibbes.

When expressing the soul's experience of divine presence, Herbert does not naturally turn to the marriage of Spouse and Bridegroom. To see that is to see the importance of a different traditional strain in his spirituality, the spiritual senses. Not lovers' union, but the taste, smell, and sound of sweetness distinguish achieved spiritual life as Herbert knows it. Again St Francis de Sales and Richard Sibbes give us measuring sticks. The sweet 'sense' of God's presence, especially in the Sacrament of Holy Communion, is a Christian commonplace; both men sympathetically respond to this live commonplace, just as both respond spiritually to the commonplace notion of the marriage between Spouse and Bridegroom. However, Herbert excludes the marriage idea, revealing a different sensibility with both poetic and spiritual consequences.

Of the spiritual senses, taste plays the most important role in Herbert's spirituality of sweetness. This is only a matter of emphasis since 'The Odour. 2. Cor. 2.15,' one of Herbert's most important poems of sweetness, concentrates upon spiritual smell. And we have already 'heard' the whispered admonition of the divine voice in 'Jordan (II).' Nonetheless, the notion of taste, in contrast to the other senses, has crucial spiritual implications in Herbert's thought. Unlike the other senses, taste is possible only when the objects perceived are actually consumed by the body. The tree seen, the rock touched, the music heard, or the flower smelled – all remain outside the perceiver.[10] By contrast, the honey or bread eaten and the wine drunk are all taken within the body to be broken down and tasted. Tasting, consuming, and assimilating represent much more closely the intimate relationship with the loving God, who enters, inhabits, nourishes, and conforms the believer to himself. Through love the soul tastes the sweetness of the indwelling God. In that taste of God's sweetness, which in turn sweetens the believer himself, lie the pleasure and joy that are one goal of Herbert's spirituality.

His emphasis upon tasting is quite congenial with Christian belief. With the Communion table standing at the centre of Christian religious life, its bread and wine conveying Christ's sacrifice in love, a theology of spiritual feeding and tasting follows as if by necessity. Sibbes repeats the commonplace to Herbert's contemporaries: 'There is a wondrous beauty in the sacrament; for therein we taste the love of God, and the love of Christ.'[11] Herbert, in turn, observes that the 'taste' of the Saviour's blood at 'his board' cleanses the believer ('Conscience,' 14–15); and to 'taste that juice ... that liquour sweet' of Christ's blood is to taste divine love ('The Agonie,' 14–17). Similarly, the soul tastes the 'sweetnesse in the bread' ('The Banquet,' 13) that perfumes the heart. Herbert's poetic modulation, from consuming the truth in the bread and wine to consuming truths revealed in other media generally, assumes the taste of God's love manifest in the Sacrament as one referent for all Christian truths. For example, the 'infinite sweetnesse' of Scripture is the truth of Christ, the 'hony' gained by the heart that sucks 'ev'ry letter' ('The H. Scriptures (I),' 1–2) and tastes as it consumes.

As a bee collecting honey, act by act, the heart both sharpens and extends this discussion of sweetness in Herbert as it relates to God and also to the soul. The honey, its sweetness permeating each letter of Scripture, blends the Psalmist's sense of divine 'words sweeter than honey' (Psalm 119:22) and the received notion of Christ as honey,[12] which for Herbert expresses the sweetness of God's love, into a widely shared Protestant conception of Scripture. In this conception all Scripture, first prophetically and typologically, expresses the later truth of Christ, the eternal Word.[13] For Herbert divine love is most fully manifest in the Sacrifice as the 'hony' that is 'gall' to Christ's persecutors ('The Sacrifice,' 111); the sweetness in all Scripture is fulfilled in that earthly Sacrifice. However, it is not just Christ's sweetness sucked in every letter of Scripture that bears consideration here, but also the nature of the heart itself. Behind Herbert's claim that the heart sucks the sweetness of Scripture lie precise assumptions about how specific human faculties appreciate God's sweetness. A further look at 'The H. Scriptures (I),' this time in its necessary relationship to 'The H. Scriptures (II),' reveals how these faculties are engaged.

The adhesive holding these two companion sonnets together is the assumption that God's love and truth, his sweetness and light, which are the two basic ingredients of Scripture, are perceived respectively by the will and reason, by the heart and brain.[14] Just as there is sweetness of God's love in 'ev'ry letter' ('The H. Scriptures (I),' 2), the light of truth 'shines' not only in each verse but in 'all the constellations of the storie,' making a 'book of starres' that 'lights to eternall blisse' ('The H. Scriptures (II),' 4–14). Truth as light, again in regard to Scripture, is flatly stated in 'Divinitie':

> But all the doctrine, which he taught and gave,
>> Was cleare as heav'n, from whence it came.
> At least those beams of truth, which onely save,
>> Surpasse in brightnesse any flame.   (13–16)

A similar economy in 'Heaven,' that gives light to the 'minde' or reason and joy to the will,[15] distils a standard Reformed conception of the bipartite soul.[16] The work of reason is to judge, argue, know, and understand; the work of the will is to fear, love, grieve, and enjoy. Herbert's corollary, that the 'taste' of God's sweetness is an affective experience, agrees with the conception of 'taste' in Western spirituality, specifically with those who relate it to the will.[17] By loving, the will tastes God's love.

This concept of taste provides a foundation for examining Herbert's sense of sweetness as a condition of the soul itself. Tasting God's love sweetens the soul; it becomes like what it tastes, perceiving in its own sweetness its spiritual fruition. Moreover, the good 'sent' ('Life,' 17) of the 'sweet and vertuous' soul ('Vertue,' 13) preserves the soul against sin's ruin. Virtue is the daily business of the will disciplined to goodness, and the sweetness of virtue is the healthy moral and spiritual condition motivated by love of God. The very lyricism of the poem 'Vertue' is related to this condition. That lyricism plays a keen nostalgia for lost earthly beauties against a reassurance of salvation for the 'season'd timber' (14) of the virtuous soul. In the spring of the year, the 'box' of 'sweets compacted' of sweet days and roses (10), lie the ephemeral enticements of natural pleasures. The pun on 'season'd' timber invokes the cycle of seasons and the repeated moral and spiritual testing, through losses in time, which develops the fragrance of virtue. And the nostalgia for lost earthly beauties tests the believer's willingness to abandon the things of the world. Such willingness characterizes the sweetness of the good soul.

A brief aside is helpful here, for the poem's nostalgia admits a subtle ambivalence toward earthly beauties. Herbert is shifting around his emphases in a basic truth. In general, he justifies his love of nature, most feelingly expressed in a love of botanical elements, as a loving creature's proper response to this 'great frame' created by 'Immortal Love' according to 'beautie which can never fade' ('Love (I),' 1–2). The beauty and coherence of this world, its several parts coordinated in praise of God, serve man's pleasure and his 'use' ('Providence,' 149). In 'Vertue' the shift to nostalgia confesses not an ultimate contradiction, but the fuller truth that death's and time's corruption serves God's end. In 'Life' we embrace the fuller truth:

> Farewell deare flowers, sweetly your time ye spent,
> Fit, while ye liv'd, for smell or ornament,
> > And after death for cures.
> I follow straight without complaints or grief,
> Since if my sent be good, I care not if
> > It be as short as yours.   (13–18)

The very justification of earthly sweetness here puts in perspective the nostalgia expressed in 'Vertue.' Even opposition of nature's sweetness to the soul's requires the material reality to define the spiritual. Although unlikeness between the two realms warns against the limitations of earthly life, the poem's subtler truth is that natural sweetness fulfils one proper 'use' when it serves this definition of the soul's sweetness. The title not only refers to the gamut of natural and theological virtues that discipline the soul to regain and preserve its natural goodness; it also refers to the more general sense of the power and efficacy of any creature, including the soul, to fulfil its function as in the 'vertues both of herbs and stones' ('Providence,' 74). The title 'Vertue' can be seen as embracing both kinds of sweetness in the poem.

Thus, in the soul's sweetness of virtue, we find created goodness brought to fruition after having been soured by sin. And we also find Herbert assuming that all virtue is established in a loving will moved by a loving God. Again, in Herbert we must refer sweetness to love and, again, we can see Herbert's intentions more clearly in a traditional light. Since both Francis de Sales[18] and Richard Sibbes[19] look to Bernard of Clairvaux as a spiritual master, we can find in his spirituality a useful perspective on Herbert. In Bernard there is in sweetness an essential conformity, through mutual love, between human and divine wills. Goodness, mercy,[20] and love comprise the sweetness in God's nature; but love especially dominates his spirituality. Taking his scriptural cue (1 John 4:8) that God is love, Bernard stresses that the incarnate Word *is* love and that his full pattern of virtues, to which the rectified human soul conforms, carries the sweetness of his divine substance. Christ's four perfumes – wisdom, righteousness, sanctification, redemption[21] – draw the believer, who is motivated basically by love of Christ, as a pattern for the human virtues of prudence, forgiveness, temperance, and pa-tience. There is in Christ, as Bernard has it, a 'fulness of of virtues,'[22] the fragrant lilies 'among' which he 'feedeth';[23] in other words, 'every part of his character is a lily, that is, a virtue.'[24] Thus, in his virtues can be tasted his essential sweetness and to follow his pattern of virtue is to become sweet. In Bernard's broadest terms, the sweetness of the virtuous human soul reveals a believer's basic conformity to Christ in love. Similar assumptions explain the pun on 'vertue' in Herbert's 'Peace.' The 'sweetnesse' of the dead Prince, typologically Christ, can be tasted in the grain growing from his grave; the 'secret vertue' of that grain brings 'peace and mirth' (35) to those who eat of the bread made from it. The same assumptions lie behind the sweetness of virtue in 'Vertue.'

But even a virtuous soul, its 'season'd timber' conformed to the Cross, experiences sourness or bitterness. Predictably, for one like

Herbert, minutely attentive to the variations of spiritual events, there is more to sweetness than just identifying one attribute of the Godhead or the nature of virtue. Herbert's God is tasted as much by his absence as by his presence. And the congenitally sinful soul, however virtuous, can only wait, helplessly, though observantly, for God's return. The taste of bitterness is frequent. God's unpredictable comings and goings plus the soul's varying hopefulness and discouragement enact the drama of Herbert's 'poetry of Grace.'[25] But for Herbert the varying savour of sweetness and bitterness distinguishes the relationship between man and God. Thus, the nature of bitterness and the way that God enters and departs from the soul are both at stake.

We can begin most usefully with the opposition to sweetness that defines bitterness (interchangeably sourness). Herbert works on this opposition in 'The Sacrifice,' pitting Christ's 'sweet sacrifice' (19) and 'hony' (111) against the bitterness of his tormentors, who maliciously give him 'vineger mingled with gall' (237). Christ's love opposes man's hate; his sweetness opposes their bitterness. Herbert forces the ironies by superimposing God's perspective on sinful man's. Christ's honey tastes like gall to his tormentors (111). To those who hate goodness or, more generally, to those who are sinful by loving things possessively and selfishly, love tastes bitter. The same truth is stated more wryly in one of Herbert's *Outlandish Proverbs* (no 422, p 335): 'Who hath bitter in his mouth, spits not all sweet.' This homely wryness of practical Christianity reminds the believer to guard against the bitter taste of his own sin. Herbert's belief in the sweetness of each creature's function, in man's case the created sweetness of a will loving God, is the foundation for viewing sin as a bitter perversion. Thus, even the virtuous believer tastes a mixture of sweetness and bitterness because of sin inherited through Adam's fall.[26]

But bitterness itself is a compound taste. Violating a God-created function deserves punishment; the bitterness of sin deserves the bitterness of punishment. The poem 'Bitter-sweet' complains to the 'deare angrie Lord' (1) about 'sowre-sweet dayes' (7) given for the speaker's correction. An orthodox pattern emerges here in the pain of God's corrective affliction which, joined with the mortification of repentance, remedies the sinful will within the lengthened shadows of Christ's 'bitter crosse' ('The Sacrifice,' 195). Christ's humble and patient suffering, the payment to divine justice for man's sin ('charg'd with a world of sinne,' 205), sets the terms for human penitential practices. The 'bitter' cross reflects both crime and remedy, and the believer participates in both. However, the bitterness has sweetness. From the traditional paradox that suffering is both punishment and remedy for sin springs the 'sowre-sweet dayes' of Christian life. In the bitterness of remedy can be found the sweetness of God's love, which reclaims his sinful creatures. To participate in the bitter cross is to find love's sweet sacrifice; it is to find the sweet rose that purges, the love expressed in the pattern of suffering that purges man's sin ('The Rose,' 28).

This mingling of sweetness and bitterness lies in God's hands. The unpredictable departures and returns of Herbert's God, who determines all spiritual events, keep man at his mercy, even the repentant believer who confesses his sins and accepts the 'Bitternesse' that 'fills our bowels' ('Repentance,' 27). God sets all terms of punishment, its length and its severity. The worst punishments may stretch tightly man's willingness to endure, pushing him close to despair. God's afflictions cause the longing for release from the 'bitter grief' ('Longing,' 59) of fatigue and discouragement:

> My love, my sweetnesse, heare!
> By these thy feet, at which my heart
> Lies all the yeare,
> Pluck out thy dart,
> And heal my troubled breast which cryes,
> Which dyes.   ('Longing,' 79–84)

God's apparent deafness to man's pleas to come and end the bitter punishment is experienced as a desertion that increases the bitterness. This sense of God's absence is embittered all the more by memory of his presence earlier as in the whispered admonition of 'Jordan (II).' The punishment ends at God's return; renewed taste of his sweetness stands in sharp contrast:

> How fresh, O Lord, how sweet and clean
> Are thy returns! ev'n as the flowers in spring;
> To which, besides their own demean,
> The late-past frosts tributes of pleasure bring.
> Grief melts away
> Like snow in May,
> As if there were no such cold thing.   ('The Flower,' 1–7)

The taste of bitter grief yields to the taste of God's love that invigorates the believer's taste for being. For the poet specifically, it revives the 'relish' for 'versing' ('The Flower,' 39).

Thus the varying experience of sweetness and bitterness is one essential way that Herbert expresses the struggle to achieve fruition in God. And that struggle sums up much of the discussion so far. While tracing out some broader lines in Herbert's spirituality of sweetness, we have seen the basis of what Herbert calls a 'traffick' in sweetness ('The Odour,' 27) between God and man. On one side is God's love, the cause of all sweetness; on the other side are the answering effects in the sweetened human soul. Although God's sweetness is expressed in the harmonies of the created world and in his providential care, it is most fully expressed in the influence of Christ's Sacrifice in the individual human soul. As we will now see in greater detail, the believer's conformity to Christ's love inspires sweetness in the soul; the business of the soul is to sense – in particular, to taste – its own sweetened condition as well as God's sweet presence within. In the very refinement of its sense of sweetness and bitterness, the soul reveals its greater conformity to Christ and hence approaches its fruition.

The broad lines of the preceding discussion give us the necessary boundaries for examining 'The Odour' and 'The Banquet,' which, in their preoccupation with sweetness as a spiritual fruition, have a special importance in *The Temple*. In both poems Herbert pursues further the link between sweetness and language expressed in 'Jordan (II)' and in the 'relish' for 'versing' in 'The Flower.' In that linkage Herbert finds a primary figure for perceiving ultimate reality. Both poems engage the task of investing language with the experience of divine sweetness – that is, the task of speaking sweetly. This is an earthly equivalent to the heavenly dialogue shared with a loving God 'sweetly questioning' in 'Love (III).' And in 'The Banquet,' in the sweetness of the Eucharist, we come to the related matter of consuming God, which is so conclusive in 'Love (III)' and essential to Herbert's spirituality.

In 'The Odour' Herbert looks most searchingly at the relationship between language and love's sweetness. The poem turns on Paul's claim that the believer in Christ partakes of his nature, becoming a 'sweet savour of Christ.' Herbert defines that relationship in 'The Odour' by a master-servant relationship: to be able to call on God, 'My Master,' and be called 'My servant' in return is to participate in his sweetness. It is to *be* Christ's sweet savour expressed as a believer.

The expression of that sweetness in language, both by man and God, creates a 'commerce' (29)[27] in the act of speaking sweetly. The poem thus assumes the necessity of words in being, both for God and man. What they 'call' each other defines their love respectively as master and servant. Such a love seeks its expression in sweet speaking.

For man such speech coordinates both rational and voluntary motions. The experience of sweetness is specifically the domain of love, and the will does not preclude the actions of the 'minde' or reason:

> With these all day I do perfume my minde,
>> My minde ev'n thrust into them both:
>>> That I might finde
>> What cordials make this curious broth,
> This broth of smells, that feeds and fats my minde.   (6–10)

To contemplate the principles in the epithet 'My Master' is to 'thrust' the mind into them, as a nose thrust in flowers. To understand these principles is to 'perfume' the mind while feeding it and fatting it with a broth of sweet smells. The mind must understand both the 'My,' which denotes his personal relationship to Christ, and the 'Master,' which defines the principle of that love relationship. By contemplating love's expression in language, his reason increases the love itself. Mind, will, and language work toward fruition in sweetness.

Herbert trains Paul's ideas to this end. The poem's devotional emphasis ignores the social dimension of Paul's conviction that believers are the 'sweet savour' of Christ to others.[28] Instead, Herbert has in mind the Pauline root, that believers participate 'in' Christ, who in turn lives 'in' them. In 'Aaron,' the poem immediately preceding 'The Odour,' Herbert points directly to that Pauline root. The speaker is 'in' Christ 'new drest' (20), while Christ lives 'in' him (24).[29] 'The Odour' follows as a development from that state. Those 'in' Christ participate in his sweetness. The continuing ability to speak 'My Master' maintains that sweet savour; for it is to *be* the sweet savour of Christ. But here only Christ himself, not other men, is intended to taste the believer's sweetness. The master will smell and taste the sweetness inspired in the servant by his love.

The pomander image applied to the epithet 'My Master' reveals the fuller meaning of the sweetness between God and man. Consideration of that repeated epithet leads to the anticipation of God's return call, 'My servant.' That is, the pomander ball gives off its scent when warmed. That answering call, a further sweet scent, would convey God's 'pardon of my imperfection' (19), thus defining the nature of the Master's sweetness. Herbert's variation on the pomander image in 'The Banquet,' there referring to Christ's sacrifice in love, reveals the full meaning assumed in that definition:

> But as Pomanders and wood
> > Still are good,
> Yet being bruis'd are better sented:
> God, to show how farre his love
> > Could improve,
> Here, as broken, is presented.   ('The Banquet,' 25–30)

The Christ 'broken' on the Cross thereby expresses his love; the bruised pomander gives off its sweet scent; Christ's humility and suffering for sinners reveals his sweet love. This is the sweetness that inspires the pomander: 'My Master' in 'The Odour,' and it is anticipation of the Master's pardon of the speaker's sins that 'warms' the pomander anew. The poem excites anticipation of a 'traffick' (27) in sweetness between man and God, to be completed when Christ calls 'My servant.'

That 'traffick' is a fuller conformity of believer to Christ in love. Awaiting God's call requires humility and a sense of possession that is proper for that conformity. Accordingly, the mind thrust into the two words must examine both 'My' and 'Master.' A selfish possessiveness would lead to the bitterness of sin. God's possession of man differs in kind from man's possession of God: God owns the servant, not vice versa. Something else is meant by the speaker's 'My.' Another glance backward to 'Aaron' reveals the same issue: 'Christ is my onely head, / My alone onely heart and breast' (16–17). To say that Christ is his 'onely head' has a straightforward Pauline meaning: the surrender of self in humble faith in Christ, the Head of the Body and its Members.[30] However, the 'alone' is more complicated: in its two possible meanings, Herbert alludes to the Christian problem of self. To say that Christ is his 'alone' could either mean a proud possessiveness excluding other believers, or it could signify that special individuality of every believer's relationship with Christ. The self subordinated in the priestly responsibility denies sinful pride; but even that special function does not efface the humble believer's conviction that God 'lives in me' individually ('Aaron,' 24). That sense of individuality requires the humble acknowledgment of man's

unworthiness. In 'The Odour' kindred claims of individual possession express the humility necessary for conformity with Christ, the
humbled, broken Sacrifice, who speaks in love. There is such
humility in the human statement of 'My Master.'

This conformity can achieve a yet fuller sweetness when God calls
'My servant' in return. The speaker desires the full commerce in
sweetness, a business: literally a busy-ness through words, the
activity proper to his created human nature. Elsewhere Herbert
laments the absence of business:

> All things are busie; onely I
> Neither bring hony with the bees,
> Nor flowres to make that, nor the husbandrie
>   To water these.
>
> ('Employment (i),' 17–20)

In 'The Odour' the speaker yearns for the 'new commerce and sweet'
that would 'employ and busie' him all his life (29–30). For man
'business' involves a servant's words sweetened by a loving con-
course with the indwelling Master. The poem itself is part of this
business, working toward the perception of sweetness, itself busily
becoming a 'speaking sweet.' Throughout, an insistent language of
sweetness defines the repeated 'My Master' and 'My servant.' We are
first prepared for this definition by Herbert's virtuoso blurring of the
dimensions of the respective human senses, thereby suggesting a
sweetness that pervades a full experience:

> How sweetly doth *My Master* sound! *My Master*!
>   As Amber-greese leaves a rich sent
>   Unto the taster:
>   So do these words a sweet content,
> An orientall fragrancie, *My Master*.   (1–5)

We are to understand the sweetness of sound by reference to the rich
scent that is not smelled, but tasted. Sound, smell, and taste are
commingled; paradoxically, what is perceived defies set categories
while requiring these categories for definition. Herbert's virtuosity
serves his intentions further: the mind itself is perfumed, fed, and
fattened with a 'broth of smells' (10). The senses, the body's digestive
function, the respiratory function (the 'breathing of the sweet,' 25)
suggest poetically a fullness of response to a pervasive sweetness. Just

as the body can enjoy physical sweetness, so too does the full soul perceive spiritual sweetness. That full perception is necessary for the business that the speaker desires.

Reference to physiological experience to express the sweetness of conformity to Christ carries us into the deepest sources in Herbert's thought. The ideas of eating, drinking, and tasting sweetness have a special potency that reveals an important aspect of his spiritual temperament and heightens the importance of Holy Communion. In 'The Banquet,' Herbert's most explicit treatment of its sweetness, he looks directly at the assumption only implied in the 'curious broth' of smells that 'feeds and fats my minde' in 'The Odour.' That sweetness flows from the Master's love manifest in the Sacrifice and its ceremonial embodiment in Holy Communion. Here we have an application of C.A. Patrides' observation that 'The Eucharist is the marrow of Herbert's sensibility.'[31] The even larger truth is that in eating and drinking Herbert finds his primary figures for achieving conformity to a loving God. Significantly, 'The Banquet' concludes with the speaker's desire that the wondrous experience of Holy Communion will 'take up my lines and life' (51). The poem joins eating and drinking with sweetness and language as the measure of fulfilled being.

To examine eating and drinking we must begin with 'The Invitation,' the companion poem to 'The Banquet,' for these two interrelated poems present Herbert's most detailed treatment of this subject. The poem's title refers to the first step in the Anglican Order of Holy Communion (Invitation, Confession, Absolution, and Comfortable Words), and those addressed by the speaker in his priestly function are all sinners. In its call to repentance preparatory to Communion, 'The Invitation' opposes the eating and drinking of those whose 'taste' is their 'waste' against those who would eat God 'prepar'd and drest' (1–5). All Christian believers eat and drink in both ways. That is, all sin; but repentant believers can be renewed by conforming to Christ through Communion.

A basic tenet of Herbert's thought provides the context here. The created world is to be used, to be consumed according to God's intention for man. And the divine truths represented in the physical world are likewise to be consumed – desired, understood, followed – according to their divine intention. Humans 'whom wine / Doth define' (7–8) drink not to sustain the body as a servant of the soul and to find in the exhilaration of wine a figure for rising to God. And for a dehumanized believer to 'graze without your bounds' (21) is to use the physical world, specifically food, as a material end in itself. Such grazing inverts the feeding in Herbert's 'The 23rd Psalme': those led by God eat the 'tender grasse' (5); they use the created world according to divine truths. To consume properly, to use and enjoy both the material and spiritual in light of their Creator, is to follow values divinely established according to the pattern of God himself. To eat and drink of God, to have him 'in' the believer, is to conform to that pattern.

In 'The Banquet' the focus shifts to consuming the Eucharistic bread and wine as a physical medium of God's love. The speaker desires that the reality of that medium will accompany, enliven, and inhabit him:

> Welcome sweet and sacred cheer,
>   Welcome deare;
> With me, in me, live and dwell:
> For thy neatnesse passeth sight,
>   Thy delight
> Passeth tongue to taste or tell.   (1–6)

His pressing desire for satisfaction underscores the limitations of his physical senses and of his earthly habits of comprehension. Yet the experience of sweetness pushes him to explain its presence in a physical medium. He makes two false starts. The first is a fanciful consideration that a star was melted in the wine; the second is an equally mistaken conjecture that the bread's sweet ingredients subdue sin. His adaptation of commonplace Renaissance culinary techniques – of sugar added to wine and of 'Flowers, and gummes, and powders' (16) to breads – merely accents his human readiness to explain mysteries with handy, earthly notions.

These false starts bring the soul to a true perspective, that the sweetness lies in conformity with Christ. The call to repentance in 'The Invitation' prepares the humbled believer to conform in love to the humbled God; and the Eucharistic wine and bread renew awareness of the sweetness of that conformity. The same God who 'gives perfumes' humbly assumed flesh and lived a pattern of suffering love that 'perfumes my heart' ('The Banquet,' 22–4). In the speaker's sharpened awareness of that sweetness now 'presented' in the Eucharist, Christ's 'broken' love (30) gives its sweetness again; the bruised pomander of Christ's suffering again gives its perfume;

and so does the 'wood' (25) of the Cross. Thus, Christ's sweetness is 'in' the Eucharist by being 'in' the believer; God is consumed and his sweetness tasted in that sharpened self-recognition. The poem's movement of thought toward that recognition expresses the sweetness of conformity on which it is based.

The poet manipulates our spatial sense to characterize this self-recognition in the Eucharist. Having drunk the wine, the speaker can fly to the 'skie' (44) on its 'wing' (42). His spiritual ascent fulfils a spatial relationship first introduced in 'The Invitation' in the sinful 'lower grounds' (24), which must be flooded by spiritual joy and transcended by love, the 'dove' that exalts you to the 'skie' (26–7). Herbert carries the same metaphorical mixture of space and liquid into 'The Banquet.' Christ 'Spilt' his blood with man when finding him again 'on the ground' (35–6) flooded with sensual delights. Although man was 'low and short' (40), the wine of Christ's blood met the 'taste' (39) of man on the 'wing' of the wine (42). The sense of radical elevation through love expresses the spiritual experience of consuming that sweet and sacred cheer.

This spiritual elevation solves the speaker's problems of seeing, tasting, and telling. Earlier the 'neatnesse' (4) of the Eucharist defied physical sight; now he can 'see.' His experience has subdued him to understand more fully his conformity with Christ.

> Where I wipe mine eyes, and see
> What I seek, for what I sue;
>   Him I view,
> Who hath done so much for me.   (45–8)

Similarly, his physical taste was unequal to the delight in the Eucharist. But now, his spiritual taste having been met in the cup, he experiences Christ's wondrous sacrifice. He can taste its sweetness more fully. The poem's concluding request is that his spiritual elevation in the Eucharist may be translated into the earthly efforts of living and writing poetry. He would then be able to 'tell':

> Let the wonder of his pitie
>   Be my dittie,
> And take up my lines and life:
> Hearken under pain of death
>   Hands and breath;
> Strive in this, and love the strife.   (49–54)

Since the spiritual elevation requires humility, the spatial perspective implicitly receives a paradoxical grounding through the necessary earthly commitment. Yet to love that earthly strife, inspired by one's own loving 'pitie' of the exemplary earthly suffering of Christ, is to become 'sweet and sacred' like the Eucharistic experience itself. The result is that he would be able to see, taste, and tell accordingly.

The thrust of Herbert's poem, that the sweetness of the Eucharist must inform the essence of the human being in action and words, has the full force of Christian tradition behind it. However, it is not enough to say that Herbert reveals a deep sympathy for the Eucharist as a medium of man's union with God. Nor is it enough to say that for Herbert it was an especially powerful reminder of love's sweetness as the fruition of earthly spiritual life. Both statements are of course true. Yet as an act of eating, drinking, and tasting, the Eucharist made special claims on Herbert's spiritual temperament. Given the importance of that temperament in his spirituality of sweetness, I would like to return to some implications of the notion of eating and drinking introduced earlier.

We have noted Herbert's conviction that although divine truth is revealed in the Eucharist, it is also manifest throughout Scripture and in the created world as well. To understand the 'virtue' of a given creature, to use and enjoy it according to God's design, is to abide by the truth that it embodies. It is to consume that expression of God's truth. We have also seen that Herbert shares the Protestant assumption that all Scripture expresses the truth fulfilled in the Word himself, but manifest partially before in prophecy and typology. That is, the divine Word can be consumed wherever manifest in Scripture. We recall Herbert's claim that the Holy Scripture, a book of 'infinite sweetnesse,' has honey in every letter; each relates to God's love, most manifest in Christ. This is also the principle of his typology, and we find him frequently alluding to those types that point to the eating and drinking of Christ. He is the Eucharistic bread of life prefigured in manna;[32] and his blood is the sweet 'juice' ('The Agonie,' 14) prefigured in the cluster of grapes that must be 'pressed' for man's sake.[33] The physiological activities of eating, drinking, and tasting are always at the surface or just below the surface of Herbert's consciousness. Why this is true indicates further why the Eucharist, which is so conclusive in 'Love (III),' emerges as it does in *The Temple*.

The importance of these physiological activities in Herbert's thought expresses the body's own truth as a creature. The tongue's taste of sweetness gives to the soul a figure for its experience of God. In turn, eating and drinking furnish a figure for the soul's communion with God. For Herbert, the simple realities of eating, drinking, and sensing are necessary for the proper physical 'use' of the human creature in fulfilling man's duty to love and honour God; in providing profound figures for communion with God, these simple realities also have their spiritual 'uses.' We may infer that the body's 'virtue' lies in fulfilling these physical and spiritual uses. Thus, Herbert's belief in the spiritual truth of these physiological functions reveals an important element in his temperament. Even the most fleeting contrast with the importance of sexual embrace in Donne's poetry underlines the difference.

Very much to the point here is Herbert's attention to dietary practices and the virtue of temperance. A strong kinship binds together his poem 'Lent,' his translation of Luigi Cornaro's 'A Treatise of Temperance and Sobrietie,' and those parts of *The Country Parson* concerned with dietary matters. In 'Lent' he opposes the Lenten fast against dietary excess:

> Besides the cleannesse of sweet abstinence,
> Quick thoughts and motions at a small expense,
> A face not fearing light:
> Whereas in fulnesse there are sluttish fumes,
> Sowre exhalations, and dishonest rheumes,
> Revenging the delight.   (19–24)

The sweetness of an attuned physiology during abstinence opposes the 'sowre' digestive unpleasantness of excess or 'fulnesse.' Self-denial is necessary for conformity with Christ's humiliation, but it also becomes a figure for the sweetness of that conformity. Similarly, digestive sourness is both evidence of intemperance and sinful excess and also a figure for a spiritual condition. The connection between diet and spiritual existence accounts for Herbert's interest in Cornaro's treatise. Confessing his own earlier intemperance, Cornaro recommends the sober order of dietary temperance. Excess food and drink had undermined his health; and he recommends his reformed dietary habits, even at his advanced age, for his life 'is not a dead, dumpish, and sowre life; but cheerfull, lively, and pleasant' (p 303). In *The Country Parson* Herbert states most fully the need for dietary temperance. Dietary concerns are a necessary part of Christian life, to be taught by the parson's own example. Herbert's dietary advice is often tellingly minute, ranging from fasting to medical problems. Such practical considerations are inspired by a strong conviction that diet has related physical and spiritual dimensions.

The feeding metaphor that is Herbert's keynote for *The Country Parson* points to the broader dimensions of his purpose:

> Being desirous (thorow the Mercy of God) to please Him, for whom I am, and live, and who giveth mee my Desires and Performances; and considering with my self, That the way to please him, is to feed my Flocke diligently and faithfully, since our Saviour hath made that the argument of a Pastour's love, I have resolved to set down the Form and Character of a true Pastour, that I may have a Mark to aim at: which also I will set as high as I can, since hee shoots higher that threatens the Moon, then hee that aims at a Tree.   (p 224)

The type is Christ, the Good Shepherd, who feeds his flock. Herbert, in turn, must feed his pastor-readers; then, they must feed their parishioners. The notion of feeding relates to the Christian life in which the believer 'feeds' within physical, moral, and spiritual dimensions. All principles, whether dietary, moral, or spiritual, are to be 'digested'; all work toward the same larger truth. The prose work continuously introduces analogies between physical and spiritual dimensions to achieve that truth. The pastor himself must feed and digest in all these dimensions if he is to feed his parishioners:

> Now if a shepherd know not which grass will bane, or which not, how is he fit to be a shepherd? Wherefore the Parson hath throughly canvassed al the particulars of humane actions, at least all those which he observeth are most incident to his Parish.   (p 230)

The good pastor imitates the Good Shepherd Christ by teaching his flock, by word and deed, how to feed both their bodies and souls. It is not beside the point to recall here that in Herbert's hands the twenty-third Psalm becomes a poem about eating and drinking.

Herbert's emphasis upon eating, drinking, and the concomitant experience of tasting expresses a temperament that avoids deliberate intellectual complexity to seek profound truths in simple realities. He looks to the body as man's most immediate physical reality, and to eating and drinking as its most immediate need. For him the power of the Eucharist is that it offers this simple human need as a figure for the soul's highest communion in love with God. And for Herbert the

truth of the body and its physiology required the dietary and
penitential disciplines that he recommends so firmly. The actual
eating and drinking of daily life must be tempered, disciplined, to
maintain the 'virtue,' both physical and figurative, of the body as a
creature of God. As to taste, which Herbert regards as the most
important spiritual sense, the body likewise provides a simple figure
for a spiritual reality. Just as the tongue's taste perceives the nature of
the body's fare and its own digestive state, taste also provides a figure
for the soul's perception of the sweetness or bitterness of spiritual
fare and its effects on the soul's own condition. Fully conceived, taste
is inseparable from consumption and assimilation because it measures their results. In short, the full physiological reality of tasting
configures profound spiritual truths.

Significantly, the depth of this physiological reality is most
compellingly expressed in the Eucharistic conclusion of 'Love (iii)':
'You must sit down, sayes Love, and taste my meat: / So I did sit and
eat' (17–18). The taste of Love completes the words sweetly spoken
between man and his loving Creator. That simple communion of
speaking and tasting expresses the essential conformity with God
that fulfils man's created nature. Man's pattern for this conformity
lies in the nature of the Creator himself, who expresses his love
sweetly in words and who assimilates to man's physical nature so
that man, in turn, can assimilate to his sweet love. We began this
chapter by noting the special importance of 'Love (iii)' in capturing the
essential relationships in Herbert's spirituality between language,
sweetness, tasting, and consuming. We can conclude by considering
that the simplicity with which the poem captures these relationships
is a fulfilment of his art. That simplicity reveals how Herbert would
taste and tell the sweetness of spiritual fulfilment.

4 Fit Framing

The ideas of architecture and space play important roles in Herbert's prayerful art. The 'Architect, whose art / Could build so strong in a weak heart' ('The Church-floore,' 19–20), also built 'this great frame' ('Love, (i),' 1), the physical world. Herbert's reader knew himself to be a temple built by God's loving hand and placed in an earthly space specially framed and fitted for him. In *The Temple* references to architectural forms like the church porch, windows, and floor apply further to the human temple in terms of framed spaces. So do extended, three-dimensional forms like the altar and church monuments. In particular, the shaped poem 'The Altar' speaks doubly to the eye, for its words, which we must see in order to read, are also framed and fitted together to imitate the shape of an altar. And hieroglyphic form – here as a complete poem, elsewhere in stanzas or the arrangement of poetic lines – demands that we 'see' truth framed spatially as well as linguistically. Herbert leads the reader to see that building the human temple spiritually requires our sense of physical space in which objects are made to fit. This rudimentary spatial sense, in turn, establishes the necessary grounds for a complex notion of spiritual and vocational fitness in Herbert's art of love.

Our primary business is this notion of fitness, but first we need to see briefly how Herbert works on our spatial sense as its basis. The poem 'Good Friday' offers a pointed and useful example. In asking how to measure Christ's love and suffering, the speaker is also asking how to measure spiritual realities in artistic form:

> O my chief good,
> How shall I measure out thy bloud?

How shall I count what thee befell,
   And each grief tell?   (1–4)

Measuring, counting, and telling are simultaneously both a poetic and a spiritual problem. But God's suffering love is a 'vast, spatious' thing ('The Agonie,' 4) making both rational comprehension and poetic expression different. Nonetheless, to solve the problem of measurement is to imitate Christ's suffering:

Since bloud is fittest, Lord, to write
Thy sorrows in, and bloudie fight;
My heart hath store, write there, where in
One box doth lie both ink and sinne: (21–4)

The heart's 'bloud,' its affections, must be rightly ordered in penitential suffering; they must be conformed, fitted to Christ's suffering. And this solution is expressed formally: the poetic stanza or fit becomes box-like, fitted hieroglyphically to form the heart. Then, Herbert plays further on the fitness of the rectangular stanzaic pattern:

That when sinne spies so many foes,
Thy whips, thy nails, thy wounds, thy woes,
All come to lodge there, sinne may say,
No room for me, and flie away.

Sinne being gone, oh fill the place,
And keep possession with thy grace;
Lest sinne take courage and return,
And all the writings blot or burn.   (25–32)

The heart is the 'room'; but so, too, is the equivocal Italian *stanza*, to be fitted with the suffering Christ, thereby excluding sin. We see the stanzaic box (or rectangular fit), a visual reality fitted in space; at the same glance we also 'see' the underlying spiritual issue.

Here is the necessary link between two kinds of fitness distinguishing Herbert's art. When the speaker answers his own opening question, he reveals a spiritual fitness empowering him to construct the spatially 'fit' stanza or 'room,' thus conforming man's faculties to God; that fitness, in turn, strengthens his power to find poetic form. The two kinds of fitness interact in the sequence running from the

one pattern poem, 'The Altar,' to the other, 'Easter-wings.' For
Herbert the 'fit heart' ('Sepulchre,' 19), appropriately 'broken' by
contrition ('The Altar,' 1–2), is not a sepulchre for Christ but a
properly framed altar; it has 'room' ('Sepulchre,' 5) for the crucified
Christ so vividly present in 'The Sacrifice' and recalled again in 'Good
Friday.' That fit heart can rise on Easter wings to praise the crucified
Christ. This sequence of poems consistently investigates the link
between the fit heart and fit verse forms. Words work on both the
understanding and the physical eye. The pattern poem merely
displays the interplay between spiritual and spatial fitness most
obviously. More broadly, the individual poems can be said to fill
space, not only in individual pages, but also in relation to each other
over several pages as parts of an encompassing poetic and architectural frame, *The Temple.*

The interplay of spatial and spiritual fitness is intimately related to
the importance of framed spaces in Herbert's spirituality. He thinks
in terms of frames: the heart is a box; the Trinity and Incarnation are
'two rare cabinets' ('Ungratefulnesse,' 7); the world is a stately
'house' ('The World,' 1); and the whole poem and its parts are
conceived as a temple. As an artifact, any framed space embodies the
values, either human or divine, informing it. As in 'The Altar,' the
spatial fitness of the poetic frame tells us much about the necessary
fitness of the heart that 'thy hand did frame' (3); it also tells us much
about the divine architect and builder. Even more important is what
it tells us about the likeness between God and the poet who builds a
poetic 'frame' (11) to praise God.

This likeness between God and the divine love poet, as makers of
fit frames, carries into the likeness binding the poet to his readers.
The poet's fit use of words is at the heart of this likeness, although we
need to step beyond the basic likeness between the divine Word and
the poet, and the poet with other men. The poet's gift of linguistic
fitness parodoxically separates him from non-poetic readers. Instead,
we need to look to the contemporary Protestant notion of the 'fit'
vocation, which binds the poet to God and to other men. In chapter
one[1] we have already discussed in passing the importance of the
Protestant calling in Herbert's spirituality. Each believer takes his
'fit' place in the community, in the church, the family, and the
commonwealth. More specifically, each believer has a particular
professional calling to serve God by serving the community. Thus,
answering God's call to the 'fit' vocation in a given space is a primary
tie to both God and other men. All men must use their gifts, whatever

they may be, to serve God and man. This is a shared problem, creating a basic likeness binding Herbert to his readers. For all, the 'fit vocation' assumes the 'fit' heart, framed in conformity to the God whose love is the source of all fitness. And – a point we will return to later – it assumes that the believer frame the space in which he is called.

But the necessary tie between spiritual and vocational fitness requires detailed attention. Herbert confronts the problem of fitness in a calling when he bares his own raw nerves about being a priest. 'I am both foul and brittle; much unfit / To deal in holy Writ' ('The Priesthood,' 11–12). Yet he recognizes that, just as 'earth is fitted by the fire and trade / Of skilfull artists' (16–17), so too the artist God can fit congenitally sinful men for the priesthood. To dress the 'true Aarons' ('Aaron,' 5) is to make the poor, sinful priest spiritually fit for his priestly role. That is done by conforming the believer to Christ: 'That to the old man I may rest, / And be in him new drest' (19–20). The priestly dress, the requirement of the office, involves the same spiritual problems for all 'true Aarons'; similarly the formulaic stanza in the poem focuses on the same spiritual issues at the same points in each stanza. The individual priest achieves spiritual fitness through conforming to Christ, whose type is Aaron, and the poet implicitly expresses this same spiritual fitness necessary for divine poetry by fitting his stanza to his subject.

The foundation for understanding the connections between vocational and spiritual fitness is commonplace in Protestant commentary on calling. Basically, the Protestant notion is a coin with two sides: one, a general calling, and the other, a particular calling. As Robert Sanderson puts it, the general calling to salvation 'is that wherewith God Calleth us ... to the faith and obedience of the *Gospel*, and to the embracing of the *Covenant* of grace and of mercy and salvation of Jesus Christ.'[2] To deny this calling, William Perkins says, is to 'make our selves unfit for the kingdome of heaven.'[3] Further, to obey this calling by performing its duties, to serve God and man, is 'to be a child of God, a member of Christ, and heire of the kingdom of heaven.'[4] For a time Herbert's speaker in 'The Collar' rejects the discipline inherent in these responsibilities, with their 'cold dispute / Of what is fit' (20–1). He would no longer be 'in suit' (6) for God's help to obey his law, spiritually dressed, suited, fitted like the new Aaron for his duties. Rather, he would 'serve his need' (31), not his God's pleasure. In response, God's call is simple, assuring his adoption; his renewed obedience, in imitation, is appropriately swift and simple:

> But as I rav'd and grew more fierce and wilde
>   At every word,
> Me thoughts I heard one calling, *Child!*
>   And I reply'd, *My Lord.*   (33–6)

This child of God can once again answer the general calling of the elect.

On the other side of the coin, the particular calling is the individual's specific office or responsibility in the community. Not separable from the general calling, this particular role, consciously played in the church, the family, or the commonwealth, gives proof of obedient faith in God. Perkins says:

> Every man must ioyne the practise of his personall calling, with
> the practise of the generall calling of Christianity, before described.
> More plainly: Every particular calling must be practised in, &
> with the generall calling of a Christian. It is not sufficient for a man
> in the congregation, & in common conversation, to be a Christian,
> but in his very personal calling, he must shew himselfe to be so.
> As for example. A Magistrate must not onely in generall be a
> Christian, as every man is, but he must be a Christian Magistrate, in
> executing the office of a Magistrate in bearing the sword.[5]

The believer must seek that calling for which he has been fitted with special gifts. Sanderson advises choosing a calling 'not only for which we are *competently* fit, but for which we are *absolutely* fittest.'[6] In step, Herbert says, 'Wherefore all are either presently to enter into a Calling, if they be fit for it, and it for them; or else to examine with care, and advice, what they are fittest for, and to prepare for that with all diligence' (*The Country Parson*, p 275).

For some particular callings physical gifts are most fit; for others, intellectual gifts. Some intellectual gifts are necessary for edifying the church: Sanderson includes the 'natural dispositions' like 'promptness of wit ... quickness of conceit ... fastness of memory ... clearness of understanding ... soundness of Judgement ... readiness of Speech.'[7] In 'Dulnesse' the speaker complains that just such mental and linguistic gifts are dulled: 'Where are my lines then? my approaches? views?' He laments, 'Sure thou didst put a minde there, if I could / Finde where it lies.' He concludes with a petition:

> Lord, cleare thy gift, that with a constant wit
>   I may but look towards thee:

> *Look* onely; for to *love* thee, who can be,
>> What angel fit?   (17–28)

The speaker needs God's help to 'cleare' his mind and his poetic expression. He knows enough to blame his dullness not on the 'gift' itself, but on his spiritual condition; and he now feels even less 'fit' spiritually to praise God than a weak creature could do normally. Here is the recurrent plight of the devotional poet called to offer his own experience to those 'who shall make a gain' ('The Dedication,' 5). Using the intellectual and linguistic gifts in his calling depends on spiritual fitness.

As noted earlier, the basis of fitness is conformity with Christ, who is also the model for both the general and the particular callings. Perkins explains both the theology and the spiritual psychology:

> The sonne of God takes not to himselfe the office of Mediatour, but he is called and sent forth of the father: whereby two things are signified; one, that the office of a Mediatour was appointed of the father: the other, that the Sonne was designed to this office in the eternall counsell of the blessed Trinities. And so, that we may please God in our callings and places, we must have a double assurance in our consciences; one, that the offices and callings which we performe, are good, pleasing unto God: the second, that we are designed and called of God to the said offices and callings. ...
>
> The sonne is *sent forth*, that is, he comes from his father, laies aside his maiestie, and takes on him the condition of a servant. The same minde must be in us, to humble and abase ourselves before God, to thinke better of others than our selves.[8]

Christ is the model for the faith, obedience, humility, and charity necessary in a particular calling. The general and the particular callings here merge; for in conformity to Christ also lies the spiritual fitness for answering the general call to be a Christian. For Richard Sibbes such conformity is a disposition of 'chaste affections' for spiritual things,[9] leaving the Christian, like Christ, 'full of goodness' and 'fitted to do good to all.'[10] Work in a particular calling embodies that goodness.

Thus, likeness between man and God defines work itself. Whatever else it is, the Protestant calling is a doctrine assuming that work is natural for God and man alike. There is a familiar Protestant ring to Herbert's claim that Adam had a particular calling in Paradise (*The*

Country Parson, p 274). Biblical claims about the sanctity of work readily support Protestant claims that work is not naturally penal, only by sin's debasement. Rather, work can be a joyful expression of human nature. The Creation pattern of work and rest established not only the sanctity of work, but also the likeness between human and divine actions. This likeness is inherent in the biblical notion of God's 'works,' either his deeds or things made.[11] In short, work by both man and God is productive action expressing their natures. Accordingly, Perkins says that God's 'workes' are done 'out of himselfe, that is, out of his divine essence'; such works are either his 'decree, or the execution of his decree.'[12] And Herbert notes that 'Gods works are wide, and let in future times' ('The Bunch of Grapes,' 13). To the divine 'workman' ('Mattens,' 19) belong the 'works of thy creation' ('The Thanksgiving,' 35) and the 'work' of grace in a human soul ('Grace,' 15). In sum, man's likeness to the divine workman is the most compelling reason for the works in his calling.

That work or 'business' is natural applies more broadly to all creatures; to be is to work, and to be busy. Just as bees 'work for man' ('Providence,' 65), winds 'work ... Be the season cold, or hot' ('Businesse,' 10). And 'flames do work and winde, when they ascend' ('Jordan (ɪɪ),' 13). The more limited notion that work is toilsome modulates into the sense of work as an action natural to a given being. Like men, other creatures resemble God, whose words and deeds are all 'works.' Also, the language of 'business' inherent in Protestant commentary on the particular calling similarly modulates between the specific commercial sense and the broader conception of action natural to a given species. Herbert could agree easily with Thomas Adams' depiction of man's created nature: 'But he [God] that gave him a heart to meditate, gave him also busines to doe; hands fit to worke, and worke fit for his hands.'[13] Such 'busines' suggests commercial activity and, more generally, actions necessary in one's calling. Also, it expresses the democratic tolerance for all callings characteristic of Protestantism, while alluding more broadly to action as man's natural responsibility as a creature. As Herbert puts it: 'Life is a businesse' ('Employment (ɪɪ),' 16). So, too, life is work.

The vocabularies of work, of commercial business, and of fitness – all coalesce in the profound truth of calling in Herbert's thought. Finding and maintaining a vocation requires conformity to God leading to fit activity, physical and spiritual. In 'Employment (ɪ)' the speaker laments that 'All things are busie' (17), but not he.[14] In 'Employment (ɪɪ)' his desire to be that 'busie plant,' the 'Orenge-tree'

(21–2), its blossom and fruit concurrent, expresses a similar lament. In *The Country Parson* his strictures against those who are not busy are unequivocal: 'Idleness is twofold, the one in having no calling, the other in walking carelessly in our calling.' After all, '*fit* imployment is never wanting to those that seek it' (pp 274–5). Yet behind the firmness of these strictures lies Herbert's own vocational reluctance and uncertainty. Self-stricture against spiritual idleness in *The Temple* alludes to the necessary 'business' of working in one's vocation. For Herbert spiritual idleness leads personally to the poetic failure to praise God ('Employment (I),' 14), thus compromising the work, the business of his fit poetic calling.

A 'busy' calling has much to do with the question of Herbert's relationship to his readers. On the one hand, Herbert's own voice asks questions about the priestly and poetic roles. On the other hand, allusions to commercial and manual labour look to callings quite different in kind. For example, the heart is a spinning wheel, its work disturbed by 'grief and sinne' ('The Glimpse,' 28); but with God's help the 'busie' heart can 'spin' praise of God 'all my dayes' ('Praise (III),' 3). Similarly, reference to believers who 'graze without your bounds' and surrender to their 'lower grounds' ('The Invitation,' 21, 24) calls to mind more homely agricultural occupations. Likewise, the language of commerce, trade, and law, although it is tied to Christ's ransom,[15] recalls those professions. Such allusions are most illuminating in reference to Herbert's Protestant conception that calling is a primary tie with God and with other members of the church and the commonwealth. These bodies *are* their members. In both bodies any particular calling 'belongs' to other members through mystical participation in them. Accordingly, the experience of the shepherd, the farmer, the weaver, the tradesman, the judge, the priest, and the poet all belong to other members; nonetheless the problems of Herbert's own calling are no less personal for having value for other members of the Body.

The common bond is the legacy of Adam: 'So that even in Paradise man had a calling, and how much more out of Paradise' (*The Country Parson*, p 274). Like Adam every man is a husbandman, whatever his calling. Perkins plays a common note when he says that Adam 'was ... called and appointed to dresse the garden of Eden.'[16] To live is to tend the garden – pruning, dressing, watering – working our way to heavenly paradise in a given calling. The father's calling is 'to labour Christian soules, and raise them to their height, even to heaven; to dresse and prune them, and take as much joy in a straight-growing childe, or servant, as a Gardiner doth in a choice tree' (*The Country Parson*, p 275). The first Adam in a paradisal garden is one model to follow; the second Adam, Christ, is another. Just as Christ 'dressed me' to produce fruit ('Employment (II),' 25), believers must work in their gardens to dress and prune, to produce proper fruit. Conformity to the second Adam is the life of every particular calling; in such life there is business – and fitness, and fruition.

The equivocal 'dressing' brings us back to the relationship between the particular calling and, as its necessary condition, fitness. Richard Sibbes plays another familiar note in depicting Christ's work in the 'garden,' the church; he says that Christ 'dresseth and fits it to bear spices and herbs.'[17] The plants are dressed, made to fit their places in the church; dressing is a proper mixture of feeding, training, and pruning[18] to encourage growth. The poet Herbert similarly dresses, trains and prunes in the poem 'Paradise,' to encourage spiritual fruitfulness:

> When thou dost greater judgements S P A R E,
> And with thy knife but prune and   P A R E,
> Ev'n fruitfull trees more fruitfull   A R E.
>
> Such sharpnes shows the sweetest F R E N D:
> Such cuttings rather heal then   R E N D:
> And such beginnings touch their   E N D.
>
> ('Paradise,' 10–15)

In one proverb Herbert goes a step further in exploiting the equivocal 'dressing': 'A garden must be lookt into and drest as the body' (*Outlandish Proverbs*, no 129, p 325). Not only the body, but the full being is a plant to be made fit for paradise, just as Aaron must be dressed, fitted for his calling. And the poet Herbert, if the soul is fitted to its proper dress in the right size, can dress the poetic plants in the garden of his calling. A poet with a fit soul will find fit language.

Inevitably, we have come around once again to the matter of language in *The Temple*. Herbert saw himself as a poet called to build a fit temple in language; but there is more to be said about *calling* here in a very rudimentary way that underlies his conception of the fit temple. Embodied in *The Temple* is the simple linguistic reality of persons calling to each other; Herbert's God calls his creatures and, in turn, his human creature invokes him or replies. In 'The Collar' God calls the unruly speaker, rebellious in both 'lines and life' (4), his blasted metrical and stanzaic forms flouting his spiritual unfitness. He replies, calling to God by name and thus solving the problem of both lines and life, both poetic and spiritual fitness. But his reply is specifically that − a reply to a God who calls in language. We can detect recognizable Protestant markings here, the 'effectual call,' that is, the Spirit's actual call within the specific believer.[19] But formal theology merely expresses here a very rudimentary human conception of a personal God who calls to his creatures as one of his primary works − and expects a call in return.

Herbert's biblical God, who calls to Jacob and Israel, is the same God whose voice called the world into existence:

> Hearken unto me, O Jacob and Israel, my called; I am he; I am the first, I also am the last. Mine hand also hath laid the foundation of the earth, and my right hand hath spanned the heavens: when I call unto them, they stand up together.   (Isaiah 48:12−13)

This creator God calls to man through his likeness, imprinted in his creatures and comprehensible to man. More important, he calls directly to man by speaking to him, first to Adam, then to others like Jacob after him. Most obviously, he calls to man through his incarnate Son: 'he calleth his own sheep by name' (John 10:3). And it is the Son 'that hath called us to glory and virtue' (2 Peter 1:3). Paul's design for salvation assumes this God calls to his creatures: 'Moreover whom he did predestinate, them he also called: and whom he called, them he also justified: and whom he justified, them he also glorified' (Romans 8:30). This parent design generated its offspring (election, calling, justification, adoption, sanctification, glorification), which Lewalski rightly finds everywhere in British Protestant thought.[20] The calling to salvation here is merely a specific stage in an itinerary of salvation planned by a God ever calling to his human creatures in diverse ways.

By its nature, *calling* blurs the distinction between words and deeds, for both God and man − and the simple reality of persons calling each other becomes less simple. Heather Asals rightly stresses Herbert's words as the natural linguistic response to a God who is the Word. But the ambiguity of *calling* does suggest a more complicated likeness involving the notion of work as well. In 'The Collar' God's calling '*Child*' is a summons, a call to order, and an identification; to reply '*My Lord*' is to obey the summons, to end the rebellion and to accept the identification by God. On both sides words are also deeds.

More broadly, all God's deeds and creations – his 'works' – speak to man as if they were words; and, similarly, all man's fit 'works' express love and honour to God. The boundary between words and actions, between words and works blurs equivocally before us. For man to answer fully God's calling, both the general and the particular, lies in a fitness of both word and deed, or word and work. The boundary line between words and works stays blurred, and our understanding of what it means to answer the calling to build a fit temple, both human and literary, is stretched.

We stand on uncertain ground here, but there is a linguistic fitness that applies especially to the poet. To begin with, actions are and are not words. Fit actions are and are not distinct from fit words. And poets and other humans are and are not the same; for the poet's calling has much more to do with fit language, with literary 'work.' Although he resembles the gardener, who trains and fits plants to grow fruit, or the tailor, who fits the body with proper clothes, the poet is called instead to dress language. Just as good discipline or affliction prunes the human plant, even so the poet must prune his language to make it fit his poetic forms and subjects. Just as the priest must be fitted spiritually to fill Aaron's priestly office, the poet must fit his language to his spiritual purpose. He is called specifically to linguistic fitness.

The emphasis upon fitness as a poetic norm is a familiar contemporary strain. Herbert could agree with Ben Jonson that the poet expresses 'the life of man in fit measure, numbers, and harmony.'[21] And Jonson's translation of Horace, in confirming the norm, identifies a secular heritage assimilated in Herbert's conception of the devotional poet. The proper relationship between language and subject is fitness. For example, 'Sad language fits sad lookes.'[22] In portraying humans the poet must 'give fitting dues to every man.'[23] The ability to determine this fitness must come from within, from knowledge and wisdom gained through experience. The Horatian lineaments implicit in Herbert's notion of poetic fitness would not have gone unnoticed by those Herbert readers who shared his classical preparation and recognized his allusions to other classical criticism in The Temple.[24] For these readers Herbert's extension of the Horatian line in devotional terms, that is, by emphasizing inner, spiritual fitness as the foundation for poetic fitness and the basis for fulfilling his poetic calling, would have left a deep imprint.

The devotional poet Herbert answers his calling by building a poetic temple with words properly dressed or fitted. In the necessary connection between God's calling to man and His building human temples, we find a fundamental notion in *The Temple*. But here we step back onto equivocal ground. The title refers most obviously to Paul's temple of the Holy Spirit to be built in every believer's heart, including the poet and his readers. Also, it is the larger temple, the church of Christ, comprised of its many members and housed in a physical building. And the poem itself is conceived as a temple, as the bold structural frame makes clear: 'The Church-porch,' 'The Church,' 'The Church Militant.' Similarly, the individual poems make the natural Pauline subject matter likewise inescapable. In 'The Church-porch' the poet tells his readers that 'Christ purg'd his temple; so must thou thy heart' (423). In 'The Windows' the 'holy Preachers' (8) are windows through whom God's truth shines on others in his communal 'temple' (3). Herbert also reminds his audience in 'The Sacrifice' that the model for both the individual and the communal temples is the suffering Christ, 'the Temple to the floore / In three dayes raz'd, and raised as before' (65–6). That there are many hands in Herbert's equivocal title is not in itself problematical, but the relationships between them are.

The more vexing problems are rooted in two closely related issues. One is inherent in Paul's notion of the human temple, a building paradoxically still being built. Stanley Fish rightly underscores the importance of Paul's notion of spiritual 'building,' both as a noun and as a verb.[25] Chosen as God's temple, the believer is, nonetheless, made incomplete by sin. The building is still being built. For Fish poetic movement in *The Temple* catechizes the reader, leading him to spiritual insight that builds the temple of the heart. Fish's tightly circumscribed argument reduces all movement to 'catechism' of the reader, thereby slighting the role of Herbert's own spiritual experience embodied in the work. Nonetheless, Fish's attention to Herbert's method of reformulation has left an enduring imprint on Herbert criticism. Motion and not rest, building and not completion – these are Herbert's mode. But Fish's argument pays too little attention to the self-conscious 'dressing' or 'building' of these motions in language. This brings us to the second issue: the self-reflexiveness of Herbert's title and the poem as a temple of language. Here again is Herbert's emphasis on man as essentially a linguistic creature; the temple to be built in his heart must be expressed in words. The poem, *The Temple*, embodies the movement of thought in spiritual building and the search to express that movement in prayer and praise.

A glance in passing at 'Sion,' which works from a commonplace opposition between physical and spiritual temples, illustrates these matters. In the speaker's change – from his wonder at the splendour of Solomon's temple to his understanding that contrition is proper worship – we see the spiritual temple, the 'frame and fabrick' now 'within' (12), being built:

> And truly brasse and stones are heavie things,
> Tombes for the dead, not temples fit for thee:
>   But grones are quick, and full of wings,
>   And all their motions upward be;
> And ever as they mount, like larks they sing;
> The note is sad, yet musick for a King.   (19–24)

Brass and stones stand for the physical temple; and contritional sorrow, for the spiritual temple. In the heart conformed, fitted to Christ's suffering, lies the power to sorrow for one's own sin. The synecdoche assumes that contritional prayer, a 'good grone' (18), measures the heart's fitness. Both the heart and its expression are fit temples. In that neither exists without the other, they share the same architecture.

The devotional poet who builds a fit temple in language edifies his readers by leading them to examine their own experience as spiritual and linguistic creatures. Thus, Herbert's own experience embodied in the long devotional centre, 'The Church,' can contribute to building in others. Further, the poet's calling contributes to that communal 'building fitly framed together' in Christ that 'groweth into an holy temple' (Ephesians 2:21). All Christians, Paul argues, have a responsibility to edify other members of that temple through encouraging, correcting, and promoting them.[26] Herbert's 'holy preachers,' the 'windows' of the temple, are like the devotional poet in fulfilling Paul's claim that preachers and those in other vocations are necessary for that building.[27] Moreover, the poet's calling carries out Paul's emphasis that fit language strengthens the bonds of the temple.[28] The full weight of the poet's responsibility is implicit in Herbert's inclusion of 'The Church Militant,' which assumes that the building of that temple is incomplete and stretches out through historical time. Thus, Herbert's equivocal title reflects his sense of his own responsibility to edify other believers, both as individual temples and also as living stones in a communal temple fitly framed and extending through time.

But edification requires the indwelling God, who begins all motions of building and who has been largely ignored in the foregoing discussion of spatial frames, spiritual fitness, calling, and temples, both spiritual and linguistic. The church and its individual members can be 'fitly framed' only when God inhabits them and gives them life. Paul tells his readers, 'Ye are a temple of God, and the Spirit of God dwelleth in you' (1 Corinthians 3:16). Herbert's attraction to Paul's conception is clear:

> My God, I heard this day,
> That none doth build a stately habitation,
>   But he that means to dwell therein.
>   What house more stately hath there been,
> Or can be, then is Man? ...   ('Man,' 1–5)

Herbert's adaptation of Paul embraces other biblical characterization of God's presence in man and man's participation in God. Accordingly, the implications of God's 'indwelling' require some attention in assessing Herbert's concept of the temple. The primary ways of conceiving divine indwelling come from immediate human experience. The artist in his work, the father in his children, the inspiration of one person in another, a person inhabiting a dwelling – each conception helps to characterize God's presence in man, although none pretends to comprehend it. Most conceptions go beyond the more materialistic sense of one object contained by another, although Herbert shares the affection of biblical writers for concrete notions to express indwelling. John's similes for God's indwelling presence come readily to Herbert's mind, such as 'light' that illuminates and the 'bread of life' to be eaten. Also, Herbert's botanical notions are strengthened by John's notion of the 'true vine' and its 'branches.' The crucial point is that Herbert passes freely from one biblical figure to another in characterizing God's dwelling in man and man's participation in God, but all must be referred to Paul's notion that God inhabits the temple.

Paul laid the foundation for the Protestant experience of the indwelling Spirit[29] shared by Herbert:

> But ye are not in the flesh, but in the Spirit, if so be that the Spirit of God dwell in you. Now if any man have not the Spirit of Christ, he is none of his. And if Christ be in you, the body is dead because of sin; but the Spirit is life because of righteousness. But if the Spirit of

> him that raised up Jesus from the dead dwell in you, he that raised
> up Christ from the dead shall also quicken your mortal bodies by his
> Spirit that dwelleth in you.   (Romans 8:9–11)

Herbert, in turn, calls to the Spirit to 'spread thy golden wings in me'
('Whitsunday,' 2). But the Spirit does not come alone. Paul easily
interchanges the indwelling Spirit for the indwelling Christ (for
example, 'Christ liveth in me,' Galatians 2:20), expressing the truth
of Pentecost that the Spirit is Christ's. Wherever the Spirit, there is
Christ. The assumption in 'Whitsunday,' which closes by shifting the
address from the Spirit to the 'Lord,' that 'same sweet God of love and
light' (25–6), is that Christ dwells in the Spirit's presence. Thus, to
find the Spirit in the heart is to experience conformity with Christ. It
is to have Christ's 'sorrows ... and bloudie fight' written in the heart
('Good Friday,' 22). God's indwelling thus involves a likeness to
Christ moved by the Spirit.

For Herbert, questions about God's indwelling involve both spiritual and literary considerations. A brief comparison with Donne serves
to point out such complications. For example, in 'Jordan (ɪɪ)' a divine
'friend' actually speaks, but nowhere in Donne's devotional works
do we 'hear' the Spirit's voice. God dwells in the believer more
directly in Herbert's poems than does Christ, for example, in Donne's
'Good Friday, 1613; Riding Westward.' There Christ is merely
remembered as an unmoving member of a set tableau, however
vividly portrayed. By contrast, in Herbert's 'The Collar,' in which
God calls 'Child,' and in 'Love Unknown,' in which the inner friend
advises the speaker, we hear God speaking. For Herbert, the Spirit is
'in' the believer in a way quite different from Christ's merely
remembered image in Donne's poem. From these spiritual differences follow literary differences as well. In 'Jordan (ɪɪ)' is an experience of God 'readie penn'd' and the speaker must 'Copie out onely
that, and save expense' (17–18). Ultimately, we must split the hair
and note that the poem is actually *recalling* the Spirit's words, which
cannot be present 'in' the poem just as they were 'in' the speaker. But
the real difference from Donne remains in either case. In Herbert
there is more than just indwelling through behaviour conformed to
Christ and aided by memory, although such conformity, the spiritual
fitness through likeness, is a necessary precondition. Rather, the
most fit words for the poet's use are God's own words spoken directly
to his poet to be recaptured in verse. In both Herbert poems God's
voice is 'in' the believer and also 'in' the poem; God dwells much

more immediately in both the human temple and in the poetic temple than he does in Donne.

In 'The Collar' is a subtle variation. Again, we hear God's voice dwelling 'in' the poem, calling 'Child.' Few Protestant explications of 'adoption' are more immediate. Through conformity to the Son, Christ, the believer participates in the filial bond with God. Paradoxically, the speaker is already God's Son as his created image and likeness. God, the Father, is thereby already dwelling in him through likeness. Also, he is a member of God's Elect whose effectual calling is dramatized before us. God's voice calling effectively 'in' him assures him intimately of being 'in' God and enjoying his filial favour.

Not only God's voice is dramatized as dwelling 'in' the poems directly. Heather Asals points out how God's hand guides the poet's in the act of transcribing the poem.[30] For Herbert God's presence seems almost automatic, at least involuntary: 'Though didst at once thy self indite, / And hold my hand, while I did write' ('Assurance,' 29–30). Also, God seems almost to dress himself in man's own words:

> My heart did heave, and there came forth, *O God!*
> By that I knew that thou wast in the grief,
> To guide and govern it to my relief,
>   Making a scepter of the rod:
>   Hadst thou not had thy part,
> Sure the unruly sigh had broke my heart.
>
> ('Affliction (iii),' 1–6)

The speaker's heaving '*O God!*' reveals more than just a creature so conformed to Christ's suffering that he becomes a likeness of God himself. As well, it reveals God actively moving the speaker's contritional response to God's affliction. This poem differs from 'Jordan (ii)' and 'The Collar,' since God though present is once removed; these fit words are not God's, but the speaker's. Here, we have a 'good grone,' a temple fit for the God actively building, hence dwelling within it.

Paradoxically, the sense of God's absence is as much a part of his indwelling as a sense of his presence. In 'The Glimpse' and 'The Glance' lost delight expresses that sense of absence. In 'Longing' the recognition that, as God's child, he still participates in God seems to exacerbate, not ease the speaker's anguish:

> Thou tarriest, while I die
> And fall to nothing: thou dost reigne,
> And rule on high,
> While I remain
> In bitter grief: yet am I stil'd
> Thy childe.   (55–60)

He fears that God's apparent absence will devastate his words: 'Let not the winde / Scatter my words, and in the same / Thy name!' (22–4). But God dwells 'in' the speaker's very desire to possess him; for God moves that desire which, in conformity with God, expresses a love for what is good. Also, for the elect child of God, who is also God's chosen temple, the indwelling God is never really absent, just not manifest; and cries that God 'come' or 'show' himself are really petitions that he turn and manifest himself. The God who anticipates all events dwells 'in' the absence that moves the speaker's love suffering; and the same God who creates even 'poysons' to 'praise' him ('Providence,' 85) inspires suffering as a mode to save man. The request that Christ 'Furnish & deck' the human soul so that it be a better 'lodging' ('Christmas,' 13–14) for Christ allows that suffering in God's absence can actively contribute to building and furnishing that lodging. Thus, God dwells both 'in' his absence and 'in' his lodging, but with varying directness.

God's presence in Scripture likewise poses questions about his indwelling in *The Temple*, which itself assimilates Scripture in varying ways. We have already heard the Spirit speaking directly in 'Jordan (II),' fit words 'readie penn'd.' But Christ's Spirit speaks differently, less directly to man in Holy Scripture, which is the 'pasture ... thy word,' where man feeds ('Christmas,' 19). God's written words work accumulatively and progressively, as they are consumed, assimilated in heart and mind and expressed in man's words, thoughts, and deeds:

> Such are thy secrets, which my life makes good,
> And comments on thee: for in ev'ry thing
> Thy words do finde me out, & parallels bring,
> And in another make me understood.
>
> ('The H. Scriptures (II),' 9–12)

And the words of Scripture find out Herbert in *The Temple*, directly,

allusively, pervasively. In 'The Thanksgiving' the crucified Christ
speaks to us directly out of Matthew 27:46: '*My God, my God, why
dost thou part from me*' (9). In 'The Forerunners' Herbert repeats
Psalm 3:14: '*Thou art still my God*' (5) and in 'Divinitie' the Great
Commandment emerges without serious modification (17–18). Direct quotations, verbal echoes, allusions – the Bible is everywhere in
The Temple. Protestant assumptions about Scripture, that 'ev'ry
letter' ('The H. Scriptures (I),' 2) expresses Christ's love and that the
Holy Ghost, the author of Scripture, also moves the reader,[31] suggest
that God dwells variously in the faithful reader who can 'Suck ev'ry
letter, and a hony gain' (2). Enlightened and sweetened by Scripture,
assimilated to its truths by the Spirit, and hence conformed to Christ
– the believer finds God dwelling in the scriptural verses fitted to his
actions, thoughts, and words.

That God dwells variously in man, nature, artifacts, and Scripture
demonstrates the varying manifestations of his mystery. Herbert
would not be disturbed to be reminded that God dwells much
differently in the human heart than in his poetic representations of
that indwelling in *The Temple*. These representations are only
artifacts, however 'fit' they may be. Nor would Herbert be disturbed
to be reminded that the Spirit would dwell much differently in
different members of the church that read *The Temple*. After all,
Christ's own earthly dwelling in his creatures was various and
mysterious. Incarnate, his own body a temple, Christ was first
housed in Mary's womb, then in the world at large, then in the
Eucharist and the believer's heart. Similarly, God is not fully or
simply or comprehensibly contained in any one of his earthly
temples, but only in a partial condition of building. The greatest
anguish expressed in *The Temple* is a loving God's mysterious
absence from the human temple; and the request that God, who built
so 'brave a Palace,' should 'dwell in it' ('Man,' 50) can be satisfied only
occasionally with his close presence. Variously, God may call
'Childe' or speak of 'sweetness readie penn'd' or even talk at length
with man ('The Dialogue') – but only infrequently and unpredictably.
Unfortunately, the heart's unsatisfied but saving desire not only to
speak but also to dwell with God, as in 'Love (III),' creates hope that
leads as much to pain at God's mysterious absence as to delight in
momentary consummation. Nonetheless, the soul's self-consciousness of God's various and mysterious indwelling and its role in the
soul's fitness contributes to building the inner temple.

Such effects of indwelling make us confront more specifically the paradoxical fitness of the temple still being built. In that paradox that denies stasis – but not established forms – we find the full truth of fitness. To understand that truth, we must return to the notion of framed space discussed earlier, for this notion lies behind Herbert's notion of the physical temple also intended by the equivocal title. There is a 'spatial' dimension in *The Temple*, a sense of living space which assumes that the physical temple is a primary referent for all experience, hence for the mystery of existence itself. And it provides the primary figure for true fitness. Thus, to conclude this discussion of fitness in Herbert's spirituality, we need to look more searchingly at how Herbert conceives space. For him it is in that architectural space, the physical temple building, that the individual perceives his mysterious edification in a communal temple extended through time.

Herbert's commitment to the physical church and its furnishings is striking. For example, his experience in rebuilding, in 're-edifying'[32] the church at Leighton Bromswold should not be taken too lightly. Walton underlines Herbert's refusal to swerve from his intention to rebuild Leighton Ecclesia, in spite of Magdalene Herbert's great concern about his health.[33] Nicholas Ferrar conveys Herbert's sense of this architectural mission, saying that God 'ordained him his instrument for reedifying of the Church.'[34] This passion, shared by the Ferrars at Little Gidding, led to Herbert's influential modification of the reading-pew that made it equal in height and size to the pulpit. Here is a very 'Anglican'[35] emphasis on necessary ties between the physical church, its fittings, and the public liturgy:

> The seventeenth-century liturgists loved to build churches and
> re-plan the interior of old ones, with special reference to the celebra-
> tion of the liturgy as the act of the whole body of the faithful. The
> reading-pew for the officiant at the offices was usually at the east
> end of the nave, opposite the pulpit. At Leighton Bromswold George
> Herbert had the reading-pew and pulpit of equal height, so that
> prayer and preaching might enjoy an equal honour and estimation.[36]

This same will that guided Herbert to re-edify Leighton Ecclesia and redesign the reading-pew guides his scrupulous advice to country parsons to take a 'speciall care of his [God's] Church, that all things there be decent, and befitting his Name by which it is called' (*The Country Parson*, p 246). The minuteness of Herbert's attention to the fitness of the church and its liturgy assumes that he will not separate the inner temple of the soul from the physical temple containing the body and housing the communal temple.

Pauline principles of decency and edification strengthen the backbone of this conviction, both in Herbert and in like-minded contemporaries. Herbert's advice to country parsons about caring for the physical church assumes a necessary interplay between these two principles:

> And all this he [the country parson] doth, not as out of necessity, or as putting a holiness in the things, but as desiring to keep the middle way between superstition, and slovenlinesse, and as following the Apostles two great and admirable Rules in things of this nature: The first whereof is, *Let all things be done decently, and in order*: The second, *Let all things be done to edification*, 1 Cor. 14. For these two rules comprize and include the double object of our duty, God, and our neighbour; the first being for the honour of God; the second for the benefit of our neighbor.
>
> (*The Country Parson*, p 246)

Like those contemporaries who objected to stripping the physical church, Herbert believed that the edification and re-edification of the church building itself contributed to bond together and edify the vaious members of the mystical Body. Necessary was the decency, the fitness of everything within. Herbert's similar argument from Paul undergirded the rigorous, at times virulent Anglican reactions against both Catholic and Puritan practices.[37] Though not combative like some, Herbert was on the same side as Hooker, Andrewes, and Laud on this issue. For him, like them, the church as a consciously formed, edified public space is necessary for building up the church community of individual souls. Pauline decency and edification are unquestioned norms.

But Herbert's innovation in the reading-pew is most revealing. Simultaneously it embodies Paul's principle of edification while demonstrating further that we must maintain a clear sense of the physical temple when reading *The Temple*. The new equality of the reading-pew and the pulpit gave 'neither ... precedency or priority of the other,'[38] thereby recommending visually the importance of prayer. John Booty's crucial observations on the organic role of the *Book of Common Prayer* in *The Temple* are to be taken together with his reminder that Herbert, the child of Magdalene Herbert, then Andrewes' charge at Westminster School, later a canon at Lincoln

Cathedral, and, finally, the attentive shepherd of his Bemerton flock, would never make a strict separation between public and private prayer.[39] From the reading-pew modified for public view is read the communal prayer that publicly edifies the members of that temple; the prayerful communion with God in *The Temple* dramatizes the private side of this edification. Physical temple, mystical communal temple, individual human temple – the edifying centre is prayer.

Herbert and other seventeenth-century liturgists assumed both that edification was the purpose of reading the prayer book in its public setting and that the full person, physical body and spiritual soul, is involved. The liturgy edified man's whole life:

> The principle of edification means that the liturgy, if it is to be
> the prayer of the Church, must be something which will help the
> average man to worship as a member of the Church, and inspire
> him to lead a life, which is true to the ideals of the liturgy, so that he
> may attain his destiny as a child of God.[40]

The emergence of prayer-book language and the lineaments of its spirituality in the more private, devotional *The Temple* suggests the strength of that visibly public edification in the church. Moreover, Herbert's instructions that country parsons integrate physical gestures into the full truth of the public readings affirm the truth of a visible, physical reality in edifying souls: 'The Countrey Parson, when he is to read divine services, composeth himselfe to all possible reverence; lifting up his heart and hands, and eyes, and using all other gestures which may expresse a hearty, and unfeyned devotion' (*The Country Parson*, p 231). This respect for physical gestures in a devoutly contrived architectural setting reflects a characteristic Anglican emphasis on the body's role in liturgy. Similarly, Andrewes speaks to that role: 'But if He hath framed that body of yours, and every member of it, let Him have the honour both of head and knee, and every member else.'[41] The liturgy is to build up souls in Christ, engaging the whole person, body and soul, in a fit space.

Here is a strong 'Anglican' sense of extended forms in framed spaces. For Herbert the even profounder truth is that in the formal arrangement of space, which itself is a creature of God, lies an essential figure for understanding God's nature as the informing Giver. We noted much earlier that Herbert conceived of all existence in terms of framed space: the world is alternately a 'cupboard of food' or a 'cabinet of pleasure' ('Man,' 29–30); man is a 'stately habitation'

(2); the body is a frame; the heart, a box or an altar. The divine models include the 'two rare cabinets,' the Trinity and Incarnation ('Ungratefulnesse,' 7); the 'palace,' heaven ('Sunday,' 23); the temple of Christ's body; and the cross itself. In particular, Herbert's temperament seized on the temple, a framed space, as a primary expression of God's informing influence in the created world. This informing influence is the origin in Herbert's poetry of all proper measure, size, fitness; and it is the origin of the spatial sense of fitness distinguishing his spirituality.

The paradoxical 'building' that is both a completed frame and a continuing process explains the contradiction between Herbert's sense of spatial fitness and its striking distortions. The 'crumme of dust' stretched 'from heav'n to hell' ('The Temper (I),' 14) or the 'wonder tortur'd in the space / Betwixt this world and that of grace' ('Affliction (IV),' 5–6), stretch painfully, intolerably our sense of spatial limitations. We are confronted with images akin to radical distortions in the visual arts. Only the realization that no earthly form is absolute can ease our discomfort; the distortion denies spatial rigidity, thus breaking through proud desire to fix idolatrously on earthly realities as absolutes. Paradoxically, however, spatial distortion or the plasticizing of set form can be 'measured' only by our firm sense of spatial fitness. The instinctive shock at distortion yields to the realization that earthly fixations must be broken as part of building the temple in the human heart. Yet that temple, that building, already exists as formed by God, however unfulfilled, just as existing spatial frames can have a God-ordained fitness, whatever the limitations in their truths. Such paradoxical competition between set form and its distorting motions conveys Herbert's sense of live space, which accommodates both form and its distortion. The distortion that plasticizes forms in space suggests a human reality fulfilled in motion, and a created space alive in time. The motions of stretching, extending, contracting, breaking apart, and scattering in vast spaces – all express the suffering that conforms the believer to Christ, whose 'stretched sinews' ('Easter,' 11) and broken body are the pattern for all suffering. Just as Christ's suffering body redefines both bodily and spiritual realities, so too the distortion of established spatial forms expresses that new reality. Paradoxically, both set forms and their distortions can be 'fit.'

A useful concluding reminder is that in Herbert the spatial sense is distinguished by linguistic realities. Since the spatial forms we see in the poetry are made with words, their fitness is perceived by the eye as well as the ear and, more important, the heart and the mind. We recall how Herbert adapts the emblem poem, building the visual emblem out of the words themselves, breaking the compartments, respectively, for the eye and the ear. Herbert would not separate experience from a linguistic conception of it. And the fitness necessary in all experience, built up throughout the believer's life in conformity with Christ, must be achieved in language. In general, all believers are called to this fitness in accordance with their gifts. In particular, the poet is gifted to speak, not only for low creatures as a 'Secretarie of thy praise' ('Providence,' 8), but also for humans. The devotional poet is called to express prayerfully how the human being, an essentially linguistic creature, becomes built as a fit and living temple of God.

5 *The Baits of Delight and Grief*

The gradual discovery when reading *The Temple* that Herbert is a poet of delight comes unexpectedly. Admittedly, in 'The Church-porch' he promises to make poetry a 'bait of pleasure' that 'may finde him, who a sermon flies, / And turn delight into a sacrifice' (4–6). But this claim, by suggesting enticement, allows questions about the ultimate value of delight, while the poem's repeated warnings against earthly pleasures put us further on our guard. Moreover, early emphasis in 'The Church' on Christ's grief and agony, then on man's frustrated attempts to conform to Christ's experience, may leave some readers wondering whether or not there is any bait at all. However, *The Temple* increasingly shows how delight draws man upward to God. As Herbert puts it, God uses a 'double line' of 'joy and grief' and 'sev'rall baits in either kinde' ('Affliction (v),' 13–17). In *The Temple* there is bait on both lines that raise the soul to God. The paradoxical ways that Herbert works the two lines cause our surprise when we discover that delight, no less than grief, conforms man to God.

How delight can be turned into a sacrifice is a good place to start in understanding the relationship between the two lines and their baits. The assumption is that to enjoy *The Temple* is to be like the suffering Christ; this apparently entangling paradox ties man's delight to his likeness to Christ's sacrificial pain. Within this paradox is Herbert's firm sense that man was created for delight and not grief, for pleasure and not pain. Man's delight likens him to God, who naturally enjoys himself and his creatures. In turn, the devotional poet appeals to man's delight in God's truth and in the literary invention embodying its various elements. As for Christ's sacrifice, it provides a painful model for repairing man's loss through humility, obedience, and love.

Delight, like any other Christian sacrifice that honours God, such as prayer and praise, must conform to these virtues. In ultimate terms grief and delight only seem to jar against each other; in fact, the two lines work to return man to his original condition of enjoying God and his creatures.

In practical terms delight is a much more problematical matter in *The Temple*. To begin with there is the problem of Herbert's vocabulary. Sometimes he uses 'pleasure,' 'delight,' and 'joy' synonymously; other times he makes important distinctions between them. There is no mystery in this usage, for which there is sound biblical precedent, supported by Christian tradition. The basic distinction is that, strictly speaking, pleasure refers to the glow accompanying the satisfaction of a physical desire; in contrast, joy refers to the equivalent spiritual experience. At the end of 'The Church-porch,' we seen this distinction operating clearly:

> In brief, acquit thee bravely; play the man.
> Look not on pleasures as they come, but go.
> Deferre not the least vertue: lifes poore span
> Make not an ell, by trifling in thy wo.
>> If thou do ill; the joy fades, not the pains:
>> If well; the pain doth fade, the joy remains.   (457–62)

This strict distinction between pleasure and joy also explains a basic meaning of delight, which is simply an intensification of pleasure, of physical satisfaction. Such delight, if corrupted, opposes joy:

> He that doth love, and love amisse,
> This worlds delights before true Christian joy,
>> Hath made a Jewish choice: ('Self-condemnation,' 7–9)

The objects of desire differ: on the one hand, the objects are fleshly; on the other, they are spiritual.

But Herbert, consistent with Christian precedent, also breaks down these clear distinctions, interchanging the terms as he wishes. In 'The Rose' the 'pleasure / In this world of sugred lies' (1–2) translates into the 'scourge' of 'Worldly joyes' (26). The interchange also works in the opposite direction. The heart and lute are invoked to make a song 'Pleasant and long' ('Easter,' 14) to celebrate Christ's resurrection. Clearly, pleasure and joy are both ambivalent. So, too, is 'delight,' as we have already seen in the pejorative 'worlds delights'

('Self-condemnation,' 8) versus the sacrifical 'delight,' the knowledge of Christ crucified ('The Church-porch,' 6).

The status of earthly 'pleasure' is especially troublesome. As Herbert and his contemporaries knew well, it could never work free from its tainted reputation as debased hedonism, even though legitimate physical and spiritual pleasures were often taken for granted in Western thought. To say that Herbert manipulates the ambivalence of 'pleasure' is not only to point to an important fact in *The Temple*; it is also to see him self-consciously working within a long tradition familiar to his audience. Herbert's knowledge of the Platonic dialogues,[1] his direct attack on Epicureanism, his close association with Augustine's works,[2] his daily experience of the Psalms[3] – all suggest his experience of the various elements contributing to the uneasy history of 'pleasure' or 'delight.' Many of his contemporary readers would recall Plato's truce with physical pleasure; Plato's early attack on it was mollified later by his claims that man's instinct for pleasure, which could be satisfied intellectually and spiritually, did not necessarily exclude all physical satisfaction.[4] Epicurean pleasure was likewise a vexed matter. Herbert's more perceptive readers might suspect that his frontal attack upon the debased '*Epicure,*' for whom 'Lust and wine plead a pleasure' ('The Church-porch,' 57, 60), deliberately caricatures Epicureanism to score an easy moral point. Here he chooses conveniently to ignore the Renaissance rehabilitation of the true Epicurus and his emphasis on intellectual pleasures.[5] Herbert is clearly willing to exploit the troublesome nature of physical 'pleasure' for local purposes.

At the same time, Herbert knows that his Christian audience, however wary about bodily pleasure, shares a long Augustinian tradition that allowed legitimate pleasures in sensory experience. For Augustine, bodily sensation was a necessary occasion for the soul's perception. More important, Augustine emphasized delight as the will's movement in love to embrace the images of physical stimuli perceived, judged, and stored by the soul. Augustine calls delight the 'weight' of the will's desire in movement toward its objects, however low or high they are.[6] Not delight, which occurs in any event, but its object determines the virtue of the soul. Even 'unlawful and unclean things afford pleasure, and it may also exist in that carnal pleasure which is permitted.'[7] But lawful pleasure in sensory experiences contributes to the spiritual pleasures that lead man to God.

Such spiritual delight so essential in Herbert's Augustinian tradition is strongly biblical. When Paul says, 'I delight in the Law of God after the inward man' (Romans 7:22), he expresses his Old Testament rearing. A similar delight in God runs like a refrain through Psalm 119. For the Psalmist, like Paul and like Augustine, man's experience of God is leavened by delight in his being, righteousness, justice, strength, mercy, and love. And it is brightened by knowledge that God, in turn, delights in those who obey his commandments. Delight in God's nature does not preclude delight in his physical creatures, like 'every tree' in Eden 'that is pleasant to the sight' (Genesis 2:9). Rather, delight in the creator God establishes the ground on which man can delight in God's creatures. This is the same ground for rejecting earthly delights for their own sakes. Otherwise, the spiritual consequences are severe: 'He that loveth pleasure shall be a poor man' (Proverbs 21:17). Such biblical usage establishes the ambivalence of delight, in its physical and spiritual dimensions, as a commonplace in the Christian tradition.

It is significant how this ambivalence emerges as a central element in Herbert's thought. His strong emphasis upon physical pleasures at times seems unexpected. For example, 'The Odour' turns on the distinction between physical and spiritual sweetness, making physical pleasure a necessary figure for spiritual pleasure:

> For when *My Master*, which alone is sweet,
>   And ev'n in my unworthinesse pleasing,
>   Shall call and meet,
>   *My servant*, as thee not displeasing,
> That call is but the breathing of the sweet.   ('The Odour,' 21–5)

The necessity of remembered physical pleasures confirms that they are indispensable as a bond in man's spiritual relationship to God. One inference is that to use and to enjoy the things of the created world is essential in man's well-being. There are related orthodox assumptions here about the microcosm, man, who corresponds to the physical world while it serves and delights him:

> For us the windes do blow,
> The earth doth rest, heav'n move, and fountains flow.
>   Nothing we see, but means our good,
>   As our delight, or as our treasure:
> The whole is, either our cupboard of food,
>   Or cabinet of pleasure.   ('Man,' 25–30)

In man's 'good' there are distinct categories: 'food' and 'treasure' are in one, and 'delight' and 'pleasure' in another. The Augustinian distinction between *uti* and *frui*, which Heather Asals rightly finds in Herbert's poetry, is helpful here.[8] Some earthly things are to be used now in preparation for enjoying God in eternity. Other things are to be both used and enjoyed now.[9] Whenever man uses and enjoys earthly creatures, he must do so with God's purpose in mind. Since man was created both to use and enjoy the physical world, his fulfilment, as well as the world's through him, its 'high Priest' ('Providence,' 13), requires both experiences. Objects seen, heard, tasted, smelled, and touched are 'full of dutie' ('Man,' 37) to serve man, who will serve God now in time, later in eternity. Man's proper use and delight in the goodness of these objects in the macrocosm confirm the natural goodness of his own human faculties, whatever their damage through sin.

Abuses do occur when delight in earthly creatures leads man to forget the Creator. But such abuses do not nullify the value of delight, even though Herbert repeatedly reminds his readers of difficulties with the senses. Herbert pulls firmly on the reins of temperance, endorses spare and demanding Lenten discipline, and reminds readers of their physical limits. But such self-conscious controls merely qualify and guide the need for sensory delight. Man's physical nature responds to the beauty of 'Sweet day, so cool, so calm, so bright' ('Vertue,' 1) or to the 'cabinet of pleasure' ('Man,' 30), even though awareness of mortality complicates his response. Whatever the limitations, delight fulfils a nature created to enjoy the God who made both man and the sensory world.

Yet light arising from the senses can be a far cry from the spiritual 'delights on high' ('Heaven,' 1) for the reason and the will:

> Then tell me, what is that supreme delight?
>   *Echo.*   Light.
> Light to the minde: what shall the will enjoy?
>   *Echo.*   Joy.
> But are there cares and businesse with the pleasure?
>   *Echo.*   Leisure.
> Light, joy, and leisure; but shall they persever?
>   *Echo.*   Ever.   (13–20)

Here the spiritual nature of 'delight' is to be understood psychologically. The supreme delight for the 'minde,' the reason, is 'light'; for the 'will' it is joy (15). Here 'joy' and 'delight' are interchangeable words, both capturing the heavenly goal of the earthly life.

The notion that reason can experience delight requires clarification, given the Augustinian-Calvinistic cast to Herbert's psychology and the practice of regarding joy as the domain of the will. A quick look backward to love as, first, the cause of joy and, second, the handmaiden of understanding solves the apparent problem. The will loves and enjoys: love is its natural activity, and joy is the satisfying possession of its objects. That is, the will enjoys possessing what it loves. The notion is Augustinian, adapted and supported by Calvin, then by others like Donne and Herbert who live in the lengthened shadow of both earlier writers. In Augustinian-Calvinistic psychology the will also empowers the understanding, since the will through love guides the direction of reason's gaze and embraces what reason comprehends as true. The will lovingly embraces these truths as good, hence delight through the will is necessarily implicated in reason's grasp of truth. The soul's faculties are distinct, but never separate, and in their fulfilment mutually dependent. Reason recognizes its own supreme good in its comprehension of divine 'light,' and the will enjoys that supreme good most.

There is much in the will's own supreme delight. To say that the will 'shall ... enjoy ... Joy' (15–16) involves two factors. One is that is enjoys something within the soul itself, its own joy. The other is that it can enjoy powers existing independently, such as God's own joyful nature and that of the heavenly community. Similarly, the light enjoyed by reason includes the mind's perception of its own enlightened grasp as well as the light of God existing independently from it. On the will's enjoyment of joy, Helen Vendler says: 'To feel feeling, to enjoy joy, to love love – these are all ways of establishing semantically and syntactically that perfect completion of the self in which subject and object are one.'[10] To enjoy supreme delight is to experience fulfilled motion in the faculties, when the subjective experience becomes the object of desire. But Vendler's insight requires theological coaching since this 'psychological' explanation brushes aside the theological point that the true objective source is God himself, from whom the human subject remains essentially separate. Man and God are 'one' only in that man can return to his likeness to God through the fulfilled motions of his reason and will, not in the sense that God and man cease to be objectively different beings. But man can learn to enjoy as God enjoys, that is, in the full capacity of his given being. Like God he would enjoy his own enjoyment of goodness. This self-reflexiveness is only a likeness, since only God can fully understand and enjoy himself as the giver of joy to his human creatures. But man can enjoy unfettered delight in both God, the source of his joy, and in the fully satisfying experience of supreme delight.

What we have been calling the ambivalence of pleasure, delight, and joy respectively is really an accommodation of extremes: at one extreme is pleasure in physical creation, and at the other is the joyful heavenly union with God. This notion of ambivalence becomes less workable when applied more broadly to the full spiritual experience of *The Temple*. But the notion does provide the basic frame for observing Herbert's shifting use of pleasure, delight, and joy when examining an essential relationship between God and his human creature, a composite of body and soul. Strictly speaking, except for the spiritual 'supreme delight' anticipated in heaven, no experience excludes either the physical or the spiritual. Even rudimentary pleasures of sight, smell, sound, touch, and taste – except for a rough, clumsy hedonism – should lead to acknowledging the Creator's goodness in giving man pleasure, and to what end.

The 'line' of joy variously draws man throughout his life. Many techniques are simple. There is man's 'stock of naturall delights,' including the beauty of the natural world, 'thy furniture so fine.' There is God's favour translated into 'milk and sweetnesses' for the young ('Affliction (I),' 5–7, 19). Such simple evidence of God's favour pales by contrast before the 'sugred strange delight' of God's presence; such delight can remain to 'work within my soul,' controlling later grief ('The Glance,' 5, 14). And there is the Eucharistic spiritual delight that 'Passeth tongue to taste or tell' ('The Banquet,' 6). For Herbert few of the delights that draw man through this earthly existence are separated from love of language. In Herbert's own case, joy in man's completion as a linguistic creature is expanded by his delight, his 'relish' for 'versing' ('The Flower,' 39) in his poetic calling. That same love of language finds in the Holy Scripture a 'masse / Of strange delights' ('The H. Scriptures (I),' 6–7), for in the words of Scripture are expressed the essential truths of the Word. For Herbert the search to conform to the incarnate Word, who is 'All my delight' ('Affliction (II),' 13), is a search through language. The God who uses various baits on his line of joy knows his creature's delight in words.

At the same time that God draws man with one hand by the line of joy, he draws him on the line of grief with the other. We must now look at the complicated relationship between the two lines with particular attention to Herbert's very mixed response to God's methods. Both lines are used to bridge the great distance between the believer and God, who draws man upward on a pulley, as Herbert also puts it,[11] and on a fishing line. Man is lured, drawn, raised by a powerful God. But the notion of 'baits' ('Affliction (v),' 17) negatively suggests enticement and jostles disturbingly against the accompanying Eucharistic overtones ('board,' 'taste,' 11–12). Moreover, the reader's mind struggles with the paradox that affliction is a 'bait,' and that we are attracted by what repels us. Herbert is not like Paul or Donne after him in finding joy in suffering.[12] The matter is more subtle, more complicated, and less easily comprehended. Herbert never ceases to weary of the grief that saves him, to regret that the line of joy cannot in itself be sufficient without the line of grief; nor can he muffle his creature's annoyance that struggling man must take the baits as they are offered, not as he would have them.

Herbert's own experience of the two 'lines' strengthens its importance in *The Temple*. The frankly autobiographical 'Affliction (i)' traces the lines of Herbert's life, the increasing pain after initial pleasure. Barely veiled rebellion against God's method ends in abrupt capitulation, postponing without resolving the very human vexation:

> Yet, though thou troublest me, I must be meek;
>> In weaknesse must be stout.
> Well, I will change the service, and go seek
>> Some other master out.
> Ah my deare God! though I am clean forgot,
> Let me not love thee, if I love thee not.   (61–6)

No real accommodation occurs between chagrin and resignation. The reasons lie in a lifetime of increasing frustration with a God who apparently plays on man's natural desire for pleasure, while causing him increasing pain. The carrot seems to get smaller as the stick gets bigger.

The poem's ultimate irony, that God's method alienates and does not win the speaker, appears to work against God. The characterization seems damaging. First, he entices (1) the speaker, flooding him with earthly pleasures that seemed to be evidence of favour but are then belied by sorrows of all kinds – illness, loss of friends, an academic occupation antagonistic to his upbringing. Just as God has earlier enticed him with youthful pleasures, he now palliates him with the pleasure of 'Academick praise' (45). But the rod of sickness again falls and the given academic calling teaches no resignation: 'Now I am here, what thou wilt do with me / None of my books will show' (55–6). God has backed him into a corner.

Even when we locate the source of the poem's ironies in the speaker's narrow and immature comprehension of God's method of keeping the tension on both 'lines' simultaneously, the accusation of enticement is unsettling. God has turned the natural desire for pleasure against the speaker, using it as a 'bait' to draw man more strenuously into God's service. But Herbert's ironies force us to recall the dangers of earthly delights. The language of 'delight' and 'entice' share the same discoloured etymology: *delectatio* (delight) never works free from its source *delicto* (allurement or enticement from the right path), which in turn recalls *delicere* and *lacere* (to allure from the right way).[13] The undertones of enticement accuse God of using delight to allure man to his disadvantage, of tricking him into believing that he will reach an immediate, pleasurable end. Yet the irony can entrap us here. The speaker unwittingly reveals a subtle hedonism that cannot allow pain. That God 'entices' is the speaker's immature perspective on how God should draw with just one line and not two. The strongly autobiographical flavour admits a self-censure, a strong self-awareness of his desire to avoid grief. The reader's uneasiness about God's 'enticement' admits a similar human chord that cannot accept that both 'lines' must draw man.

In 'Affliction (I)' the speaker cannot accept that earthly delight will not be continual. He does not yet know how to interpret his various delights in terms of less comforting events. More important, he does not see the full implication of God's 'gracious benefits' (6), the spiritual evidence of less tangible favour. Having a continued life even when seemingly extinguished by grief, pleasure can be known in more ways than one. The speaker does not understand that delight viewed as evidence of God's favour can continue in memory even in the face of grief. The spiritual advance occurring between 'Affliction (I)' and 'The Glance' indicates a dimension in delight that the speaker in the earlier poem cannot understand. He does not see how previous experience of delight can continue to live.

Delight refined by competing griefs can be translated into a new form continuing in later experience. Herbert investigates this spiritual truth in 'The Glance.' Here is an autobiographical focus on a single event, the intitial, joyous experience of God's presence:

> When first thy sweet and gracious eye
> Vouchsaf'd ev'n in the midst of youth and night
> To look upon me, who before did lie
>   Weltring in sinne;
> I felt a sugred strange delight,
> Passing all cordials made by any art,
> Bedew, embalme, and overrunne my heart,
>   And take it in.   ('The Glance,' 1–8)

Later, in spite of 'many a bitter storm' of grief (9), this 'sweet originall joy' (13) both sustained his defences against punitive griefs and also served to characterize, hence predict, heavenly delight later. Thus, the poem enters three different dimensions of the same 'sweet originall joy,' past, present, eternal future. In contrast, the speaker in 'Affliction (I)' lacks the spiritual maturity to see the continuing life of previous joy, of God's 'gracious benefits.' In the latter poem joy teaches the necessary perspective on much grief.

Herbert struggles to be precise about this incomprehensible joy, which continues to work in the soul. It is 'sugred' and 'strange,' but not fully conveivable by any human standard ('Passing all cordials made by any art'). The sweetness is God's love felt in the soul, its varied effects to be apprehended, though not fully comprehended. It is felt to 'Bedew, embalme, and overrunne my heart, / And take it in.' The poet struggles for precision. What is comprehensible is that delight is the effect of perceiving God's loving presence and its permanent effect in the soul. That presence is progressive: first, a pervasive moistening that mollifies sinful hardness, then, a sweet embalming tincture that establishes the soul's goodness before, finally, overrunning it in enveloping liquefaction that takes the moistened, tinctured soul into a divine experience greater than itself. These effects constitute a 'mirth,' a joyous identification with God's powerful goodness that continues to 'work within' (14) the soul after first being 'open'd' and then 'seal'd up' again (18). Such continuing 'work' strengthens the soul in combat against harmful, destructive grief at the same time that it creates expectations about the strength of delight later in 'heav'n above' (24).

These expectations of fullness, necessarily involving God's 'sweet and gracious eye,' extend the notion of delight. Man's enjoyment of God's watchful love manifest in his initial glance creates the expectation of wondrous comprehension:

> If thy first glance so powerfull be,
> A mirth but open'd and seal'd up again;
> What wonders shall we feel, when we shall see
>   Thy full-ey'd love!
> When thou shalt look us out of pain,
> And one aspect of thine spend in delight
> More then a thousand sunnes disburse in light,
>   In heav'n above.   (17–24)

The concluding sun image points to the conception of light included in the sweet love expressed by God's eye. That man will 'see' God's light suggests reason's perception of truth, of God's love, which the speaker has 'felt' since God's first glance. Thus, feeling and understanding will be joined in heavenly joy. Herbert may also be suggesting that reason has already played a role in the 'originall,' inchoate experience of delight, which has left such powerful, lasting effects, affirmed in 'The Glance.'

The contradiction between 'Affliction (I)' and 'The Glance' is problematical, especially for those who would argue that the two poems have autobiographical roots. The first complains that God-given delight does not defend against grief; the second runs in the face of that claim. One explanation of this contradiction is that the two poems, instead of embodying the experience of just one consciousness, represent instead two concurrent, but mutually exclusive, possibilities. Another explanation is Louis Martz' notion that there is a spiritual progression toward a 'plateau of assurance' in *The Temple*.[14] According to that principle, the two poems can be seen as sequential, with the second expressing a later, more true realization. Yet another explanation is that Herbert's spiritual realism allows sharp contradiction. The rebellion of 'The Collar' contradicts the satisfied 'commerce' (29) between God and man in 'The Odour,' just as 'Affliction (I)' contradicts 'The Glance.' Such contradictions can be taken to express the ups and downs of spiritual life.

Herbert's larger point is that delight in relation to grief must be understood within a broad field of dramatic possibilities. The companion relationship between 'The Glance' and 'The Glimpse' helps to make this point. Both poems examine man's perception of delight, turning on the notion of the momentary look and its effects. In 'The Glimpse' the focus narrows on man's glimpse of divinely given delight, not on God's glance at man. In both cases the effects of man's perception continue, but in markedly different ways. In 'The Glance,' the 'sweet originall joy' is an irreversible first experience. Its powerful sweetness contrasts sharply to life 'Weltring in sinne' (4), creating a desire that can be satisfied only by full delight. In 'The Glimpse,' the bewildered complaint – 'Whither away delight?' (1) – speaks not to a unique, but to a recurring event expected from a God who comes and goes. Desire makes preparations that will encourage the return of delight.

In working on man's desire, God pulls both lines together. Love's unfulfilled desire is the subject of poems like 'The Glimpse,' 'The Longing,' and 'The Search.' But this desire, which is the will's movement in love toward fruition in joy, causes grief when unsatisfied: 'Thy short abode and stay / Feeds not, but addes to the desire of meat' ('The Glimpse,' 11–12). The speaker, beleaguered for 'many weeks of lingring pain and smart' (4), then comforted for 'one half houre' (5), is now even more powerfully conscious of his incomplete state. Yet in his realization that delight will always be rationed and that he must work to tie God to him, we see one way that God works the two 'lines' together. The speaker's heart 'Pickt here and there a crumme' of pleasure (17), realizing that only momentary delights, a few 'droppings of the stock' and not the whole 'heap' of pleasures, will be given (23–4). Single delights whet desire amid 'many weeks of lingring pain and smart,' and these must be enough to 'tie' a 'gentle guest' to God (20). Throughout The Temple we find God coordinating one line with the other in tying man to him.

But Herbert never really makes his peace with the line of grief. Unlike Paul or Donne he cannot rejoice in suffering. Too often we find his speakers at the end of the tether, anguished by God's absence: 'I sent a sigh to seek thee out, / Deep drawn in pain' ('The Search,' 17–18). This speaker complains that grief is as 'large' (45) as his absent God's distance from him. Frustrated complaints express a sense of abused helplessness:

> With sick and famisht eyes,
> With doubling knees and weary bones,
>   To thee my cries,
>   To thee my grones,
> To thee my sighs, my tears ascend:
>   No end?

> My throat, my soul is hoarse;
> My heart is wither'd like a ground
>   Which thou dost curse.

> My thoughts turn round,
> And make me giddie; Lord, I fall,
>   Yet call.   ('Longing,' 1–12)

Here is the bared nerve of spiritual desire, aggrieved and frustrated in its attempt to have God, its most desired object. Mere resignation is not enough, for the will naturally desires and enjoys possessing its object. Grief impedes enjoyment, the soul's fruition.

Grief exacerbates a congenital restlessness that too often seems like another form of grief. Fruition necessarily includes rest, an escape from searching and straining desire. But the same God who draws man on the lines of joy and grief also denies him rest, as a 'pulley' to attract him. In fact, no delight on earth can give complete rest to the striving soul. Admittedly, man may 'runne, rise, rest with thee' ('Trinitie Sunday,' 9) in moments of spiritual delight, but God strictly rations the number and duration of these moments. And most earthly rest is not the self-conscious enjoyment when the will's desire is satisfied by possession. Rather, most rest is mere cessation of grief. Herbert sees such rest, like 'relief' and 'comfort,' as short-lived therapy for the constant griefs that thwart a natural desire for unbroken delight. This therapy is often little more than a respite from grief and 'repining restlesnesse' ('The Pulley,' 17) of human life.

A deep ambivalence accompanies Herbert's complaint that much life is lived at the end of the tether. On the one hand, rejection of life's affliction by refusing to 'sigh and pine' ('The Collar,' 3) is regarded as proud rebellion. The believer knows what is expected of him. He accepts the need for continual grief, even complaining that his verse lacks 'both measure, tune, and time' to express it ('Grief,' 18). On the other hand, he must always wrestle with his desire to avoid the affliction, even when conformity with Christ clearly requires it:

> Ah my deare Father, ease my smart!
> These contrarieties crush me: these crosse actions
> Doe winde a rope about, and cut my heart:
>   And yet since these thy contradictions
> Are properly a crosse felt by thy Sonne,
> With but foure words, my words, *Thy will be done.*
>   ('The Crosse,' 31–6)

Herbert's fear of the dangers of excessive affliction joins a desire to experience delight without impediment. There is little in Herbert that resembles joy in affliction as a mark of God's favour or of martyrdom for the Body. Instead, Herbert's ambivalence releases cross-currents at times barely contained in *The Temple.*

Herbert's deep resistance to suffering does not mean that he rejects the essential orthodoxy of grief and affliction. Quite the contrary. He sets out the two basic tenets unequivocally in *The Country Parson:* first, that only Christ's 'sorrow' can perfect human redemption and, second, that 'affliction ... softens, and works the stubborn heart of man' (p 249). The sorrowing Christ not only pays the debt to divine justice through his grief and affliction; at the same time he establishes the model for penitential practices and man's necessary response to affliction. To conform to that model, to accept grief and affliction, is to find Christ's earthly experience continuing 'in me' ('Affliction (III),' 15). This conformity often involves punishing affliction that mortifies sin by breaking the hardest soul as a means of 'building' it ('Affliction (IV),' 29). Men are 'trees,' whom 'shaking fastens more' ('Affliction (V),' 20); their natures, though sinful, are strengthened by this orthodox punishment.

Herbert's resistance to grief and affliction could bend more easily if conformity to Christ's suffering were more readily comprehensible. But the human creature must strain painfully in attempting to understand that relationship. The article of faith, that the God-man suffered human pain, vies with knowledge that his experience was vastly different. How can man 'measure out thy bloud ... count what thee befell ... each grief tell'? ('Good Friday,' 2–4). This logic of incalculability continues to vex Herbert. He pleads that God 'Kill me not ev'ry day' ('Affliction (II),' 1). No matter how many times God mortifies him with affliction, he can never conform to Christ's death, 'since thy one death for me / Is more then all my deaths be' (2–3). Nor can his tears of contrition conform to Christ's tears; for all men's tears together 'Into one common sewer, sea, and brine' (7) are nothing in comparison to Christ's. As the primary earthly expressions of God's love, 'vast, spacious things' ('The Agonie,' 4), Christ's grief and painful death seem to lose their human comprehensibility.

The other 'vast spacious' thing, sin, poses related problems that defy practical limits. Every sinner in killing Christ daily commits an incalculably heinous crime which no human act can requite. He simply cannot cry enough tears of contrition:

> O who will give me tears? Come all ye springs,
> Dwell in my head & eyes: come clouds, & rain:

> My grief hath need of all the watry things,
> That nature hath produc'd.   ('Grief,' 1–4)

Poetic 'measure, tune, and time' (18) aid little in expressing his
inadequate, 'rough sorrows' (14). A despairing practicality can ask
what value lies in expressing such paltry grief anyway. An even more
practical objection reveals a rudimentary sense of human limits; the
amount of grief conceivable, however inadequate that estimate may
be, simply exceeds our human powers:

> Lord, I adjudge my self to tears and grief,
> > Ev'n endlesse tears
> > Without relief.
> If a cleare spring for me no time forbears,
> > But runnes, although I be not drie;
> > I am no Crystall, what shall I?   ('Ephes. 4.30,' 25–30)

Practicality pulls back from excessive grief, knowing that too much
suffering threatens the human spirit. That sense of human limits
questions the possibility of conformity, even though Christ 'makes
good / My want of tears with store of bloud' (35–6). Conformity
remains mysterious to basic humanity.

We should not, of course, overstate this uncomprehending humanity in Herbert, even though it resists his faithful conviction that one
can conform in some measure to Christ's suffering. This resistance is
less dissipated than outweighed by a deepending sense of how the
individual participates in Christ's suffering. The seemingly incalcu-
lable distance between the individual and Christ seems much less as
the believer experiences how Christ's earthly life is extended further
in the suffering members of his Body. The speaker in 'Affliction (III)'
discovers Christ's presence 'in' (2) his own aggrieved sigh, 'O God,'
thereby experiencing his conformity to Christ in a most immediate way:

> Thy life on earth was grief, and thou art still
> Constant unto it, making it to be
> A point of honour, now to grieve in me,
> > And in thy members suffer ill.
> > They who lament one crosse,
> Thou dying dayly, praise thee to thy losse.   ('Affliction (III),' 13–18)

Recognizing how the experience of the Cross remains incarnate in the individual members forces another perspective on the Christ whose tears seem to outnumber the collective tears of all men. Christ through the Spirit conforms to the speaker, breathing in his breath, speaking in his words, and moving him to understand his conformity to Christ. At bottom is the faithful trust that identifies Christ's power with the believer who imps his wing on Christ's. So empowered, the collective grief of individual members becomes far less paltry than a strict 'practical' sense can allow. The speaker's understanding of Christ's presence 'in' his grief helps explicate an earlier claim that 'Thou art my grief alone' ('Affliction (II),' 11). The ambiguous 'alone' connects man's punitive suffering to his crime against Christ, while it also makes claims of individual conformity enjoyed by each individual member. That sense of Christ's specific attention to the individual can convince the speaker that his own suffering is less paltry than it first seems.

This assured conformity with Christ does not disentangle completely Herbert's mixed feelings about affliction, nor does it dismiss the problem of conformity posed by Christ's divine incomprehensibility. But it does explain affliction and grief as a 'bait' that draws man to God. God's presence in grief to 'guide and govern it to my relief' ('Affliction (III),' 3) demonstrates one of two necessary paths to salvation, grief and joy. The sense of immediate conformity, that is, God 'in' the grief, assures the believer of God's favour and demonstrates his intentions with compelling directness. To say 'Oh God,' clearly identifying the God within who draws man, is to take one bait that saves.

The two baits of grief and joy come together in the Eucharist. In this ceremony of love, the emblems of affliction, the wine and the bread, are offered as delightful objects to be eaten both literally and spiritually:

> Welcome sweet and sacred cheer,
> > Welcome deare;
> With me, in me, live and dwell:
> For thy neatnesse passeth sight,
> > Thy delight
> Passeth tongue to taste or tell.   ('The Banquet,' 1–6)

This is a supreme earthly bait, offered regularly to believers having already received the 'sev'rall baits in either kind' less formally. The bruised 'pomander,' the broken Christ through whose suffering man can atone for his sins, is offered in love. Man's own continuing conformity to that suffering makes the love understandable; but the emphasis here is on enjoying more what the bloodshed and broken body reveal than on how they were suffered. The Passion is experienced as a manifestation of God's love that man enjoys. This Eucharistic delight in the ceremony of love gives an earnest of heavenly delight that raises man on the wing (42).

'The Banquet' concludes with the relationship between poetry and the Eucharist implicit throughout *The Temple*. The Eucharistic experience of love and delight elevates the speaker to a comprehension of God that, he prays, will inform his 'lines and life' (51). Appropriately, it will require his 'strife' (54), a struggle that will further conform him to Christ's struggle of love. Making devotional poetry is the struggle to incorporate the truth of the Eucharist and its delight into earthly life and the poetic vocation. All poems in *The Temple* can be related to that struggle.

This delight adds further to what Herbert told his reader at the outset in 'The Church-porch' about delight and its essential role in devotional poetry. Verse is offered as a 'bait of pleasure' that in the reader will 'turn delight into a sacrifice.' The delightful nature of the lines themselves will create delight in the reader. And, as we have just seen in 'The Banquet,' delight must guide the life of the poet who writes them. There are three kinds of delight involved here: in the poet, in the poem, and in the reader. All are sacrifices to God, which like prayer, praise, and Christian life itself must honour and celebrate God; as sacrifices they remind us that conformity to Christ's suffering, through humble repentance and obedient service, is the selfless ground on which true delight becomes possible.

That being said, we need to ask more specifically how delight is turned into a sacrifice, first, for the reader of *The Temple* and, then, for the poet. For the reader it occurs when one finds in *The Temple* those Christian experiences that quicken grief, love, and joy, thus bringing one into conformity with Christ. God's love is inherently delightful, but souls impaired by sin cannot taste its sweetness. The poet's art serves God by working on those damaged faculties for whom love's delight is shrouded. It is not just the 'sweet youth ... who a sermon flies' ('The Church-porch,' 1, 4), but all readers whom devotional verse entices by appealing to man's natural impulse to delight. The reader's experience of delight can become obedient, worshipful service to God, a sacrifice.

The poetic artifact is also the poet's sacrifice of delight. Not all

English Renaissance poets are as self-conscious about their poetic art as Herbert. The reasons for his attention lie in his notions of man's linguistic nature and of his own vocation as a builder of word structures, prayerful temples for the worship of God. Such imaginative structure of language please both the reader and the poet. The 'sparkling notions,' 'sweet phrases, lovely metaphors' ('The Forerunners,' 4, 13), the harmonies of metrical arrangement, the surprises of form and subject — these delights attract both the reader and the devotional poet in sacrificial service to God. The devotional poet's delight is sacrificial if it answers the needs of his devotions and his vocation. Thus, his baits of pleasure involve both the poet and his human reader.

Even more important, the poet's sacrifice of delight involves his divine audience. Even without Herbert's alleged account of *The Temple* as a 'picture of the many spiritual conflicts ... betwixt God and my Soul,' there can be no doubt, given the many poems addressed to God, about that divine audience. What man's 'sacrifice of delight' means from God's perspective must be considered. Herbert's incessant concern about proper devotional language demonstrates his desire to please God. The deliberately clumsy admission that 'if I please him, I write fine and wittie' ('The Forerunners,' 12) humourously denigrates human powers while emphasizing God's pleasure as an end of devotional poetry. More often Herbert does not denigrate his poetic sacrifice to God, however self-conscious he may be:

> My God, if writings may
> Convey a Lordship any way
> Whither the buyer and the seller please;
> Let it not thee displease,
> If this poore paper do as much as they.   ('Obedience,' 1–5)

For Herbert, God's pleasure in his creature's poetry is part of their basic relationship. He petitions God: 'O let thy sacred will / All thy delight in me fulfill!' (16–17). With divine help he can please God by making his life and lines a sacrifice of obedient and fruitful service.

Just as the nature of man and of his devotional poetry are involved, so too is God's nature. The God who loves and enjoys himself likewise loves and enjoys the creatures made in his likeness. A primary element in the conformity between the human creature and God is man's delight in both God and his creatures. For man's part, to love and enjoy goodness is to be like God. Therefore, man delights both in his own linguistic nature and also in his given calling among God's other earthly creatures. In particular, Herbert knows the devotional poet's delight in building his experience into temples that encourage a sacrifice of delight in others. Lower earthly creatures become involved in his delight also. He knows that 'All creatures have their joy' ('Mans medley,' 3), whatever their limitations; and he accepts that to use and to delight in that 'cabinet of pleasure' ('Man,' 30) and its creatures serving man is to accept the responsibility as the 'worlds high Priest' to present the linguistic 'sacrifice for all' ('Providence,' 13–14). His praise and his joy are part of his created nature just as God's delight in his creatures and his providential care are part of his nature. In sum, Herbert's delight in his calling expresses conformity to the primary member of his audience, to God. In the desire to please God in his calling, he becomes increasingly like God, who requires man's sacrifice of delight in order to save him.

That the delight is a *sacrifice*, however, is the continuing reminder that earthly comprehension of God hinges on the truth of suffering. The line of grief ever draws Herbert. The God whom he desires to please in *The Temple* is the biblical God whose justice requires his suffering. The Bible leaves no doubt that this God delights. He delivers those in whom he 'delighted' (2 Samuel 22:20); and he 'taketh pleasure in them that fear him' (Psalm 147:11). And in acknowledging the 'beloved Son, in whom I am well pleased' (Matthew 3:17), he proclaims delight in his own being. Yet it can never be forgotten, in spite of Herbert's resistance to grief, that this God of delight translates his being to man through grief. The suffering Son is a pattern of love, in grief and affliction; and, as Herbert puts it, he '*Left all joyes*' ('Dialogue,' 31) to share our line of grief. Though God's grief is primarily channelled through Christ, as payment for man's sins, it can also be expressed by the Spirit: 'Grieve not the Holy Spirit of God, in whom you were sealed for the day of redemption' (Ephesians 4:30). Paul's verse works the line of grief between God and man, but in a different way.

Herbert's poem ('Ephes. 4.30, *Grieve not the Holy Spirit, & c.*') on this popular but troublesome text of Paul alerts his contemporary readers to the continuing problem of God's grief. Important sermons on the text by prominent Protestants agree that the divine Spirit cannot actually be said to grieve. That would, as Sibbes clearly tells us, admit deficiency in God:

The Holy Ghost cannot properly be grieved in his own person, because grief implies a defect of happiness in suffering that we wish removed. It implies a defect in foresight, to prevent that which may grieve. It implies passion, which is soon raised up and soon laid down. God is not subject to change. It implies some want of power to remove that which we feel to be a grievance. And therefore it is not beseeming the majesty of the Spirit thus to be grieved.[15]

Like Calvin before them,[16] Lancelot Andrewes and Joseph Hall stress that the scriptures merely speak in an understandable human idiom, throwing over the Spirit a recognizable human cloak.[17] In contrast, Herbert's poem ignores the problem. His simple, unstated point is that grief is how man conceives much of his relationship with God, especially if he believes that Christ continues to grieve 'in' his living members ('Affliction (III),' 16) through his Spirit. The spiritual truth, simply put, is that the believer knows God by knowing what it means to grieve.

This knowledge is a continuing process involving the whole Trinity. In 'Ephes. 4.30' the speaker first addresses the Spirit (1), then the Father (25), while discussing the suffering Christ. Since 'the God of love,' the Spirit, 'doth grieve' (7), so too should man grieve for his sins. But contritional 'tears and grief' (25) inadequately serve his purpose; and, when his penitential energies give out, they must be supplemented by Christ's blood:

> Yet if I wail not still, since still to wail
>   Nature denies;
>   And flesh would fail,
> If my deserts were masters of mine eyes:
>   Lord, pardon, for thy Sonne makes good
>   My want of tears with store of bloud.   (31–6)

At this point the poem implicitly circles back on itself. The title's injunction not to grieve the Spirit through sin assumes that the Spirit does grieve, especially since penitential grief cannot eliminate sin. Only Christ's sacrifice, applied to man by the Spirit through affliction and renewed rounds of repentance, can do so. The circle must begin anew. Thus, God does seem to grieve, for he is felt 'in' man's own grief. That this grief is merely God offered through a human perspective, as Calvin, Andrewes, Sibbes, and Hall tell us, is not the point for Herbert. Man comes to know God through that very human experience.

That same God continually grieving 'in' man is the God whom Herbert must please through both grief and joy. And Herbert's own struggle to establish that conformity in himself is the same attempt to embody it in *The Temple*. We find Herbert's self-consciousness about this conformity even at the end of his life, as Walton's account suggests. Herbert asked that Nicholas Ferrar be told about the 'decaying condition of my body' and also about his assurance that he had 'become now so like him [God], as to be pleas'd with what pleaseth him. ...' Herbert's message to Ferrar continued:

> and tell him, that I do not repine but am pleas'd with my want of health; and tell him, my heart is fixed on that place where true joy is only to be found; and that I long to be there, and do wait for my appointed change with *hope* and *patience*.[18]

As we have seen, such self-conscious conformity to a God known through grief as well as joy is a wellspring of spiritual energy throughout *The Temple*. Herbert's pleasure at the end of his own life is still defined by affliction, though now his exasperation appears to be gone. Among the 'many spiritual conflicts' between his God and his soul was his resistance to God's methods, including the therapy of affliction. On his deathbed this resistance is gone. He now can anticipate the supreme pleasure, the 'true joy' of heaven gained by learning to take the baits of both grief and delight. The dying man now looks to a life when the problem of grief will be sloughed off and he will be able to enjoy unbroken delight in God.

6 *Life and Its Quickness*

The New Testament promises new life to the believer. For Herbert's contemporaries, a 'true and lively faith' quickened by a 'living God' could fulfil that promise. This renewal involves both human and divine life in ways intimately affecting the tenor of Christian spirituality in Herbert's art. Not only is God alive 'in' the believer but also that indwelling is experienced in the variations of the soul's own spiritual liveliness or quickness. The special emphasis which Herbert and his contemporaries placed on the Christian ideas of 'life' and 'quickness' in the soul distinguishes their spirituality. In turn, that emphasis distinguishes the spirituality of *The Temple.*

First, we need to ask in a general way what was meant by 'life' in its close relationship to 'quickness.' Herbert gives the bare essence in 'Coloss. 3.3' when he says that '*Life* hath with the sun a double motion' (2). Human life involves motion, whether the animal body's or the rational soul's. And such movement assumes vigour, a combination of energy, force, and strength, as in Richard Sibbes' claim that 'life is the vigour proceeding from soul and body.'[1] To Sibbes' emphasis on vigour, John Preston's definition adds quickness: 'life consists in quicknesse, and motion.'[2] This 'quicknesse' suggests readiness, promptness, liveliness; and its biblical family includes the opposed 'the quick and the dead' and the verb 'quicken,' meaning to give or restore liveliness and life.[3] In sum, full 'life' is vigorous, quick, purposive motion.

Such motion can be fully understood only in relation to its source, the living God. For example, Herbert's human flower, now green following the tempest of God's anger, has been watered by a 'spring-showre' of his Grace; it has experienced God's 'Killing and quickning' ('The Flower,' 16–28). The cycle of spiritual life is moved by the purposive motions of God's will. This cycle is created and sustained by the God whose 'sacred Providence ... from end to end / Strongly and sweetly movest' ('Providence,' 1–2). Thus, Herbert's 'ever-living Lord God' (*The Country Parson*, p 288) is related to his creatures through quickening motions. These motions also describe both the divine nature and the heavenly state. Herbert fancifully invokes a star propelled by its 'trinitie of light, / Motion, and heat' ('The Starre,' 17–18) to fly him to the heavenly place, where his own motions can assimilate to Christ's:

> Get me a standing there, and place
>   Among the beams, which crown the face
>   Of him, who dy'd to part
>   Sinne and my heart:
>
> That so among the rest I may
>   Glitter, and curle, and winde as they:
>   That winding is their fashion
>   Of adoration.   (21–8)

Such an 'ever-living' God is William Perkins' biblical God, whose life assumes motion:

> Hitherto we have spoken of the perfection of Gods nature: Now followeth the life of GOD, by which the Divine Nature is in perpetuall action, living and mooving in it selfe. Psal. 42.2. *My soule thirsteth for God, even for the living God, when shall I come and appeare before the presence of God?* Heb. 3.12. *See there be not at any time in any of you an evill heart to depart from the living God.*

The motions of 'perpetuall operation'[4] lie in the nature of the living God, and the believer comes to understand the motions of his own life only in relation to God's motions.

Life experienced as a relationship between man and God raises two questions. The first is what the believer perceives as the motions of a living God; the second is what are the human soul's own corresponding motions. The answer to the first lies in the nature of the biblical 'living God'[5] of the Protestants. The immediacy of this God is striking. He appears as a person, whether as a speaking voice, a human form, or a spiritual presence. The same God who speaks directly to Adam, Moses, the prophets, and Job also comes in love as the incarnate Christ, raises Christ from the dead, and visits man as the Holy Spirit. Protestant attention to the indwelling Spirit's presence or absence in the soul is the natural extension of this living God and his motions, both direct and indirect. In 'The Collar' the God who calls '*Child!*' is a living God whose presence directly moves, quickens the adopted believer to reply '*My Lord*' (35–6). At other times the living God is less obviously present, and his motions less immediate and direct. We have already looked at some instances when examining Herbert's minute attention to the indwelling God and the believer's anguished sense of his absence. For Herbert and his contemporaries, the varyingly explicit and implicit motions of this God prevene all motions in the living soul of the believer.

The answer to the second question, about the nature of the soul's own responding motions, is in many cases self-evident. The child enabled to reply '*My Lord*' is alive to God's presence; his own answer reveals the life within. In general, any thought, feeling, expression, or action that conforms to Christian truth reveals the motions of life. In 'Affliction (III)' the speaker's heart 'did heave, and there came forth, *O God!*' He recognizes that God 'wast in the grief' and that his 'unruly sigh' (1–6) conforms to Christ's suffering:

> Thy life on earth was grief, and thou art still
> Constant unto it, making it to be
> A point of honour, now to grieve in me,
> And in thy members suffer ill.
> They who lament one crosse,
> Thou dying dayly, praise thee to thy losse.   (13–18)

Grief quickened by his conformity to Christ's suffering and moved by the Spirit expresses the soul's own life. More to the point, recognizing his conformity most fully expresses that life. The motions of his faculties have been quickened by the Spirit of Christ's presence informing the soul's own lively perception.

Erected life in the soul's faculties fulfils its created nature. In 'Dulnesse' the speaker, in requesting 'quicknesse' (3) to praise God, asks that God 'cleare thy gift,' his 'minde.' Then the quickened soul 'with a constant wit' can 'look towards thee' (23–6). John Preston reveals a similar conception that the soul's life lies in the motions of the intellect:

> The cause of life is the understanding inlightened to see the truth;

> when the affections are right, and the understanding straight, then
> we live; when it is darkened, all goes out of order. Ioh. 1.4 speak-
> ing of Christ, it is said, that *in him there was life, and the life was*
> *the light of men*: he was life because he was light, he did inliven
> men, because he did inlighten them.[6]

To understand Christ's truth, his light, is to live; the understanding
perceives the truth it was created to perceive. And the life of the
understanding necessarily hangs on the affections of an erected will.
As Preston puts it, 'right' affections must accompany the enlightened
understanding. He cites Paul: *'Put off the old man which is corupt,*
according to the deceitfull lusts thereof; and put on the new man,
which after God is created in holinesse, and perfect righteousnesse.'
The habit of such lust or 'affection misplaced'[7] turns the will from
holiness and the love and delight in truth. Thus, the affections can
also divert the understanding from truth. Both faculties, the will and
the reason, would experience death and not the motions of erected
life.

The experience of life, known in relationship to the living God, is
further defined by its competition with death. The soul's deadly
sinfulness competes against its lively motions, impeding the faculties. Preston's analysis of the competition between death and life in
An Elegant and Lively Description of Spiritual Life and Death,
written in 1623 and published in 1633, offers a singularly useful
perspective on this same antagonism in *The Temple*, which Herbert
was writing during the same decade before his death in 1633. Preston
distinguishes three aspects of spiritual death. The first is purely legal,
the 'guiltinesse'[8] incurred for violating the Law and deserving death.
The second encompasses moral behaviour, the death through sin that
opposes the life of sanctification. The third is experiential; it is the
joyless separation from God. And it is this death that relates to our
discussion of the soul's immediate experience of life.

For Preston this death, a separation from the source of life, is to be
understood by analogy to physical death. 'This death consists in the
separating of God from the soule; when God is separated from the
soule; then man dies this death of sorrow.'[9] Like physical death one
'symptome' or 'signe' of this spiritual death is the darkened understanding, which cannot 'relish' God's ways. This symptom contributes to another, a 'want of motion'; for the failure of man's essential
rationality weakens faith, the living tie to God, which gives 'necessary motion' to the judgment and actions of religious existence. But

faith as a vital disposition to commit all one's power to serve God assumes humility. Instead, pride destroys faith, causing the symptom of 'senselessness,' the habitual hardening of the soul's capacities. No longer 'affected' with God's judgments, the faculties of understanding and feeling no longer serve God, but self.[10] The final symptom, the soul's loss of vigour and beauty, most clearly develops Preston's working analogy between the body's death and the soul's. The soul's lively beauty is its holiness, its freedom from sin, which allows proper operation of the several faculties. In sum, the dead soul, like the dead body, lacks understanding, motion, sensitivity, beauty, and vigour. When present, these qualities contribute to a life in which the soul self-consciously enjoys its fruition in God. In their absence the sorrowing soul is separated from God, the source that quickens it.

But no earthly soul is completely dead, for life and death in its faculties are relative states inseparably in competition. Herbert's request for quickness of mind admits dullness, its opposite. So does the desire of his 'heart' to receive the star's quickness:

> So disengag'd from sinne and sicknesse,
>   Touch it with they celestiall quicknesse,
>   That it may hang and move
>   After thy love.   ('The Starre,' 13–16)

The heart is double. It desires to move upward in love, ending man's separation from God; but it is also engaged in 'sinne and sicknesse' and needs quickening. Life and death compete.

But this doubleness in the soul's faculties becomes absorbed by the standard Christian paradox that death is the way to life. The paradox centres on Christ's passion and resurrection, on death turned back upon itself and becoming life:

> But since our Saviours death did put some bloud
>   Into thy face;
>   Thou art grown fair and full of grace,
> Much in request, much sought for as a good.   ('Death,' 13–16)

The mortification and vivification in repentance[11] conform the soul to Christ by turning pain and punishment, which are forms of death, into a mode of quickening. Similarly, all affliction, although a form of death, can conform the members of Christ's church to its suffering Head:

> Thy life on earth was grief, and thou art still
> Constant unto it, making it to be
> A point of honour, now to grieve in me,
>   And in thy members suffer ill.
>   They who lament one crosse,
> Thou dying dayly, praise thee to thy losse.   ('Affliction (III),' 13–18)

Christ's painful death, the pattern for the repentance that kills sin, quickens the believer. Pain and grief reach the 'quick,' that diseased, tender, and most sensitive part of the soul.[12] Conformity to the similarly afflicted and aggrieved Christ quickens the diseased believer.

Understanding how the faculties are quickened by this conformity is necessary for understanding the spiritual experience dramatized in Herbert's poetry. We have already seen in general terms the nature of this conformity. When the enlightened understanding sees the truth manifest in Christ, the soul can live; for to comprehend is to conform to that truth, while embracing it with the affections of faith, love, and joy. Conformity straightens the soul, returning it through likeness to its original righteousness. Still, these general terms do not capture the daily reality. The soul's motions, both rational and voluntary, reflect the competition between life and death inherent even in the soul conformed to Christ. For example, in 'Sinnes round' the contrite soul confesses the endless round of its sin:

> Yet ill deeds loyter not: for they supplie
> New thoughts of sinning: wherefore, to my shame,
> Sorrie I am, my God, sorrie I am.   (16–18)

But the expression of contrite sorrow counterbalances the death through habitual sin. Life works paradoxically in the rehearsal of grief for sin. These motions of life are implicit in the contrite suffering that depends on conformity to Christ.

The paradoxical identification of life with suffering suggests an even more complicated reality than we have yet allowed. For one thing, some degree of life can be expressed in any motion, even in an inanimate object, when it is moved by an animate mover. God's motions precede all motions, whatever their later perversions; and life is present wherever God moves his creatures according to his will. Put simply, any reference to constructive motions implies life. Even death's seemingly destructive 'incessant motion,' which 'Fed with the exhalation of our crimes, / Drives all at last' ('Church-monuments,' 4–6), serves God's purpose. However compromised by the sinful varieties of death, all motions can serve an all-powerful and loving God. The speaker prays: 'Yet, Lord instruct us so to die, / That all these dyings may be life in death' ('Mortification,' 35–6). For the Elect all motion, however mixed paradoxically with death, can express life.

The basic truth is that all motion comprehended by the Elect translates life to the believer. In the fanciful spiritual combat of 'Artillerie,' motions are exchanged between God and man. The star acts twice, first, landing in the speaker's lap, then, when shaken from the lap and rejected, speaking in admonition:

> Do as thou usest, disobey,
> Expell good motions from thy breast,
> Which have the face of fire, but end in rest.   (6–8)

A star has both light and fire, enlivening respectively the reason and the will. In 'The Method' the speaker has already ignored earlier 'motions' (19) but, now, again hears a conscientious voice:

> But stay! what's there?
> Late when I would have something done,
> I had a motion to forbear,
>   Yet I went on.   (21–4)

A final recognition finds God in these lively motions of conscience that first censure careless prayer, then prompt against a sinful act.

In both poems the attempt to move God expresses the desire for his enlivening presence. Both speakers struggle with the recognition that life is given on God's terms, not man's:

> Thy Father could
> Quickly effect, what thou dost move;
> For he is *Power*: and sure he would;
>   For he is *Love*.   ('The Method,' 5–8)

The request for God's presence, as live motion, is life seeking further comprehensible motions from its infinite source. Tears and prayers are man's weapons in this search:

> But I have also starres and shooters too,
> Born where thy servants both artilleries use.
> My tears and prayers night and day do wooe,
> And work up to thee; yet thou dost refuse.   ('Artillerie,' 17–20)

Such weapons of contritional sorrow and prayer involve live motions returning to their source in a living God.

Lamentably, God will not always be moved, and then the frustrated soul lives in anguish. The ironies of its unfulfilled longing show the methods of an ever-present God, who does not always reveal himself. God encourages the delusion that prayer will move him directly to return, for that very delusion quickens desire. Fleeting glimpses of God only entice, not satisfy, in order to increase desire: 'Thy short abode and stay / Feeds not, but addes to the desire of meat' ('The Glimpse,' 11–12). The dissatisfied believer is always moved, quickened by desire; his 'searches' are his 'daily bread' ('The Search,' 3). Even the conviction of regeneration, 'now ... sinne is dead' and the 'promises' that 'live and bide' ('Longing,' 66–7) cannot satisfy the quickened desire for God's presence. The irony is full. For, when the reader progresses from 'The Method,' which explicitly acknowledges God's method of using anguished desire to draw man, to 'Longing,' in which that understanding surrenders to the anguish, we see the irony of God's method in man's decreasing satisfaction. By its increased anguish the soul is quickened more than it knows. In a word, there are increasing motions of life in its desire.

But the soul's sense of its own destitution, of its lost life, is no less a measure of its condition than the contradictory life of its desires. The sense of lost motion, however contradicted by living desire, can pervade the soul, hence the 'dullness' that Herbert deplores. This torpor can be a lethal enemy to life. Herbert's exasperated complaints are heartfelt: 'Must dulnesse turn me to a clod?' ('The Forerunners,' 5). Only Grace can dissipate the sense of 'dull husbandrie' ('Grace,' 2), of violated calling. Only Grace can quicken the heart grown dull. The methods vary: in 'The Forerunners' through a sense of renewed gift; in 'Love unknown' through a therapeutic affliction, the besetting 'Thorns' of thought that 'quicken' the 'dull' heart and 'slack and sleepie state of minde' (49–66). Herbert can see only two general remedies for dullness: God must either 'move' him here on earth or 'Remove' him to heaven ('Grace,' 22–3), in which there is no dullness, only live motions.

A dull husbandry is the arch-enemy of business, the soul's

fulfilment in calling. The soul 'drooping and dull' ('Dulnesse,' 1) is the human flower deprived of its lively fruition, unlike the orange tree busily bearing fruit. For the human plant, employment assumes the motions of life: 'O give me quicknesse, that I may with mirth / Praise thee brim-full!' ('Dulnesse,' 3–4). In its inability to praise God, the dull soul breaks the cycle of live motions passing between God and man. God will not quicken the believer who will not 'move' God through praise ('Praise (II),' 4). In particular, the poet who cannot praise is a dull husbandman not tending the business of his calling. Thus, Herbert regards dullness as more than just a common spiritual malady, for it casts a special shadow over his own spirituality. His fear of dullness reflects a nagging sense of inadequacy never resolved, but revealed with touching force in the guilty hesitancy of the soul newly arrived in heaven, face to face with the 'quick-ey'd' Christ ('Love (III),' 3). The desire for quickness reflects the special needs of Herbert's temperament, which were inseparable from the business of his poetic calling. This business required the quickened faculties of thought and speech.

We need to look more closely at the notion of quickness, to see more specifically how this biblical notion of quickening, which is so important to his contemporaries, is refined by the needs of Herbert's own spirituality. The key lies in the ambiguity of Herbert's 'quicknesse,' which, in always drawing from the identification of 'quick' with 'live,' leads into the notion of vigour and rapid motion. In defining spiritual 'life' as 'motion' and quickness,' Preston occupies the same linguistic ground as Herbert. Whereas dullness results from impediment, quickness is the speed of unimpeded motion, especially thought and feeling when fulfilling their natural movement. The mind cleared can see without impediment; its intuitive grasp is naturally swift, constant. Similarly, unimpeded affections swiftly meet the object of their desires. The result is that thought and feeling naturally, quickly find words to praise God. In contrast, the 'dull husbandrie' of the poet or any intellectual believer called to make words for God reveals a soul encumbered, entangled, slowed. But the experience of quickened faculties alive in swiftness can be breathtaking, whether in witty turns, inventiveness, 'sparkling notions' ('The Forerunners,' 4), sudden realizations and – significantly – the soul's own ready pleasure in its own quickness. There is further excitement in recognizing that 'quickness' of thought, feeling, and expression are evidence of Christ living in the believer through the quickening Spirit.

The desire for this quickness becomes a ready tool of God's complex 'method.' For just as the competition between life and death defines the experience of life, so does the competition between quickness and dullness. Man is continually prodded into quickness through affliction: '*Your heart was dull, I fear*' ('Love unknown,' 56). The dull clod must be quickened by the attacking star. Like life itself the spiritual vigour and rapidity of quickness are a relative matter. The exciting, pleasurable mental agility and quickness that Herbert so desires and enjoys occur briefly, at best, then live only as a remembered ideal. We learn to recognize degrees of this quickness in the varyingly subtle motions of life embodied in the poetry. Herbert desires the unencumbered, direct motions, but finds that quickened motions of life come when entangled by experience and least expected. Ironically, the motions in the believer's '*new, tender, quick*' soul ('Love unknown,' 70) are often the surprises of God's subtle methodology: the quick insights, often through pain, that reflect back on the soul's obtuseness, its dullness, its deathly loss of motion.

As is to be expected, conformity to Christ remains the centre of God's method of quickening the believer in his ability to praise God. Christ's own paradoxical motions are the measure of all other motions in *The Temple*: 'I the Temple to the floore / In three dayes raz'd, and raised as before' ('The Sacrifice,' 65–6). The believer dies and rises with Christ; and the falling and rising motions of spiritual life must conform, therefore, to Christ's death and resurrection. The Anglican pattern of contrition and praise, of repentance and thanks-giving, which John Booty finds in *The Temple* works from this conformity. Through acts of confession and contrition, the abased Christian rises spiritually in prayer and praise of God: 'In Herbert, as in the Prayer Book, contrition yields to praise.'[13] That is, the believer rises with Christ; he humbly dies to live, conforming himself to the crucified and resurrected Christ through mortification of sin and a renewed, sanctified heart. In 'Sion' contritional sorrow distinguishes the temple being built in the believer's heart from the old, physical temple. Man now lives when God 'crosseth' him (14), conforming him through contritional suffering to Christ's own suffering: 'grones are quick, and full of wings, / And all their motions upward be; / And ever as they mount, like larks they sing' (21–3). The soul's quickened motions upward through contrition find their natural end as songs of praise in which the quickness of heart and mind are essential.

We have already seen in chapter two that the soul lifted upward in prayer and praise characterizes the spirituality of *The Temple*. These rising motions can be understood even more fully as the believer's quickening conformity to Christ that leads to songs of adoration. The two Easter poems bring together these themes which move *The Temple*. The speaker commands his heart to move upward with the resurrected Christ: 'Rise heart; thy Lord is risen. Sing his praise / Without delayes.' The poet awakens his lute, a figure for the poetic self, its strings tempered through repentance in conformity to Christ: 'His stretched sinews taught all strings, what key / Is best to celebrate this, most high day.' The rising soul, its motion aided by the 'blessed Spirit' of Christ, participates in the Resurrection it celebrates ('Easter,' 1–18). On the 'rise' in flight, the soul can 'imp' its 'wing' on Christ's, its conformity expressed in its song of praise:

> O let me rise
> As larks, harmoniously,
> And sing this day thy victories:
> Then shall the fall further the flight in me.
>
> ('Easter-wings,' 7–10)

The song would necessarily express the soul's quickened motions of ascent, in conformity with the risen Christ.

Throughout *The Temple* Herbert plays hard on the words 'rise,' 'raise,' and 'praise' to measure life quickening in the believer. The resurrected Christ, who 'riseth,' also 'raiseth thee.' Accordingly, the dejected heart is encouraged to participate, 'Arise, arise' ('The Dawning,' 12–13). Once raised, man must then, in turn, lift praise to God. But congenital human weakness stands in the way: 'To write a verse or two is all the praise, / That I can raise' ('Praise (I),' 1–2). God must help: 'O raise me then!' (17). Once lifted, the poet can sing God's praise with 'utmost art' ('Praise (II),' 9); he can 'raise' God in his heart (20) by expressing his own rising motions of life. God's raising hand is always present, though his methods may vary. For man, contrition is necessary to quicken the heart rising in praise: only 'broken bones,' the humbled faculties of the contrite heart, have life enough to raise 'together in a well-set song, / Full of his praises, / Who dead men raises' ('Repentance,' 32–5).

The lifted heart, expressing itself in song, underlines the necessary

connection between spiritual quickening and the role of music in
The Temple. Created to enjoy divine harmony, the heart too often
knows the discordant, contradictory, broken rhythms of its own
sinfulness. But its 'broken' condition is ambiguous: the communal
'consort' ('Dooms-day,' 29) broken by sin and death includes the
individual heart, broken and contrite, its humbled faculties straight-
ened by suffering, rising in praise to God. For this reason church
music is the proper form for the quickening soul that understands the
ambiguity of its condition:

> Now I in you without a bodie move,
>   Rising and falling with your wings:
> We both together sweetly live and love,
>   Yet say sometimes, *God help poore Kings.*
>
> ('Church-musick,' 5–8)

The soul's rise and fall conforms to the ascending and descending
motions of Christ and to the working motions of the dove-like Spirit.
In the music the believer finds the pattern of contrition and praise,
repentance and thanksgiving which, in conformity to Christ, quickens the heart. To be 'in' the music is to conform to the harmony,
measure, and tempo given by God to raise the quickened believer to
'heavens doore' ('Church-musick,' 12). It is to 'live and love' in the
motions of the music.

Wherever we find Herbert's self-consciousness about motion in
The Temple, we find the considerations of spiritual 'life' and
quickening that mark his spirituality. And we do well not to set our
categories too rigidly. One example is his sense of living space, the
spatial frames completed in the actions or motions occurring within
them. Such frames include buildings, natural objects, human bodies,
linguistic patterns, and poetic forms seen by the eye. Spatial frames
'live' or are 'quickened' or become translated into motion, into living
space. The hieroglyphic 'A Wreath,' which explicitly engages the
relationship between spiritual life and poetic form, becomes a living
space or frame. When the speaker comes to understand its meaning,
the connection between spiritual life and the interwoven 'garland'
form is made explicit: 'My crooked winding wayes, wherein I live, /
Wherein I die, not live' (4–5). The motions of life and poetry,
expressed hieroglyphically, are inextricable. But the motions that
quicken this frame are really the ironic countermotions that convert
the speaker's poetic gift from death into life.

The poem's ironies vary according to the speaker's incomprehension. He is not clearly aware just how his compulsively sinful nature vies with his sincere desire to praise God. His poetic form conspicuously reveals the 'crooked, winding wayes' of his proud virtuosity. Ironically, he desires the 'straight' life, yet compulsively writes a crooked and winding line; he seeks 'simplicitie' and not 'deceit' (4–9), yet he deceives himself by advertising his proud skill. Although he knows that ability to praise God is proof of life, he does not recognize that what he comes to see as a 'poor wreath' has become through his struggling humility a 'crown of praise.' The reader can see what the speaker does not – that he 'lives' through the motions of the poem's crooked, winding ways. Here is the competition between death and the motions of life working in the hearts of the Elect. Ironically, what the poem proves, though it is little comprehended by the speaker, is that the motions of life, both 'winding' and 'straight,' are relative and must be comprehended in God's terms, not man's.

Both kinds of motion can convey divine truths. In 'Coloss. 3.3' life has two kinds of motions, one, the earthly body's 'straight' (3) motion; the other, the spirit's, which 'doth obliquely bend' (4) and 'winds towards *Him*' (6).[14] The rigid categorization in 'A Wreath,' that sin is 'winding' and goodness is 'straight,' breaks down further when we recall the heavenly motions in 'The Starre':

> Get me a standing there, and place
>   Among the beams, which crown the face
>   Of him, who dy'd to part
>   Sinne and my heart:
>
> That so among the rest I may
>   Glitter, and curle, and winde as they:
>   That winding is their fashion
>   Of adoration.   (21–8)

Winding beams of light are celestial motions unimpeded by death. So, too, the winding structure of 'A Wreath,' when viewed as a means to praise God, declares its likeness to the celestial motions winding in adoration of their maker. At the same time, in that winding structure are also the perversions of pride. The irony is that the desire to praise can quicken the believer, conforming him in spite of himself to divine truth, whatever the perversion of his given nature. The motions of life can be as complex as God's methods.

Herbert's sense of this complexity quickens *The Temple* itself, as the tie between 'The Wreath' and 'Coloss. 3.3' shows. That 'The Wreath' fulfils the earlier poem demonstrates a basic conception of Herbert's poetry. It has been rightly observed that the ways in which poems interpret other poems in *The Temple* is modelled after his conception of scriptural interpretation:[15] 'This verse marks that, and both do make a motion / Unto a third, that ten leaves off doth lie' ('The H. Scriptures (II),' 5–6). Similarly, 'Coloss. 3.3' sets loose live motions fulfilled in 'The Wreath,' which in turn reflects back to the earlier poem. The two poems are fulfilled in reference to each other when their motions quicken the reader's mind and heart.

The quickening motions in the believer remain the centre of Herbert's sense of life; and that sense informs the botanical imagery which conveys spiritual life everywhere in *The Temple* and which we must now examine at length. For Herbert, like Paul and particularly like John, the idea of the plant has a special power to capture Christian experience. Paul's olive tree[16] and John's vine[17] contribute to the biblical foundation for Herbert's flower, alternately a tree, as a primary figure for spiritual life. The key is Herbert's sense of the plant as a living creature extended in space and shaped by powers outside its control. We recall from chapter four Herbert's notion of created fitness, a sense of preordained tasks and relationships that the individual must accommodate. So, too, a plant is a creature living in a given space defined by its relationships to other creatures. Examples are garden flowers, trees in a row, the communal vine and its branches. In live plants can be seen the full human reality.

The flower exerted a special claim on Herbert's imagination. In the hieroglyphic stanza in 'The Flower' – root, stem, bloom – we see human life. Man is rooted in mortality, extended in space and tested in time, to be rewarded by Heaven:

> These are thy wonders, Lord of love,
> To make us see we are but flowers that glide:
> Which when we once can finde and prove,
> Thou hast a garden for us, where to bide.
> Who would be more,
> Swelling through store,
> Forfeit their Paradise by their pride.   ('The Flower,' 43–9)

Death circumscribes and hence defines this life; but the meanings of both death and life are transformed by Christian truth. Both the physical body, its roots in the ground, and the spiritual self, when rooted in earthly pride, must also die. But virtue on earth can earn a heavenly place: blossoms once used 'while ye liv'd, for smell or ornament' can be used 'after death for cures' ('Life,' 14–15); the virtue sweetening the believer's life can be a cure against sin, thereby after death earning man the 'garden' of paradise. Answering one's calling is part of that sweet scent:

> If as a flowre doth spread and die,
> Thou wouldst extend me to some good,
> Before I were by frosts extremitie
> > Nipt in the bud;   ('Employment (I),' 1–4)

The punning 'extend' speaks of the full human, body and soul, doing his business in a given space; slantingly, it also alludes to Herbert's own poetic vocation, to writing in full.[18] The frosts of physical death cannot kill the spiritual flower that is quickened, extended, and sweetened; it earns a place 'Fast in thy Paradise, where no flower can wither!' ('The Flower,' 23).

Herbert's shifts from the flower to the tree allow related variations. In contemporary writings the works of a given calling are its 'fruits,'[19] sweet, ripe, and nourishing for other creatures. Herbert subtly, wistfully plays on this theme; his speaker would be an 'Orenge-tree, / That busie plant,' which is ever 'laden' with fruit for God ('Employment (II),' 21–3). But he bears little fruit and life goes quickly. Elsewhere, regret is more searching and the poetic figure more complicated and revealing:

> I reade, and sigh, and wish I were a tree;
> > For sure then I should grow
> To fruit or shade: at least some bird would trust
> Her houshold to me, and I should be just.
> > ('Affliction (I),' 57–60)

Herbert inverts the standard figure: the figurative tree, man, would become a literal tree. He seeks not to annihilate his life, only to exchange it for one without affliction and painful self-consciousness. He embraces responsibility and would produce that 'fruit' acceptable to God while charitably offering the 'shade' of protection and encouragement to other creatures.

But Herbert notes a spiritual trap here, one that he himself knew well in his aversion to grief. To become a tree is to turn backwards down the great chain of being in order to avoid the pain in self-consciousness. But even faithful service to God cannot exempt the believer from the punitive 'case of knives' ('Affliction (IV),' 7), the besetting thoughts that seem at times to disintegrate the very frame of consciousness. To forget that man can only be a figurative, not a real tree is to risk his own humanity. The way around the spiritual trap can be found in Herbert's bold modulation from the wounding 'case of knives' to the 'watring pots' that 'give flowers their lives' (10). Necessary afflictions quicken, go to the tender quick of the faculties that experience full human life. To say that man is figuratively a flower or a tree is not to forget that motion and quickness distinguish the essential self-consciousness of human life.

It comes as no surprise that Herbert's human tree, quickened by its suffering, is referred to the Tree of Life, just as all Christian life is referred to the crucified Christ. This Christly norm comes early in *The Temple*:

> O all ye who passe by, behold and see;
> Man stole the fruit, but I must climbe the tree;
> The tree of life to all, but onely me:
>   Was ever grief like mine?
>   ('The Sacrifice,' 201–4)

Conformity to the cross or tree, to Christ's death, gives life. The iconographic Tree of Life in *The Temple*, which contributes to the botanical truths of the poem, bears a rich, traditional load. The received link is between the Tree of Life, one fixture of Eden, and its antitype, the Cross. Whereas the Tree represents eternal life possible through obedience, but lost by Adam, the Cross restores that possibility through Christ's death. By introducing the Tree of Life, Herbert is establishing basic traditional lines in his botanical pattern.[20] Adam lost the first Tree of Life and the paradisal garden where it stood; but the loss can be restored through the Cross, the second Tree of Life, which leads to heaven, the new garden paradise. The condition is that the individual tree must conform to the Cross. The tree will revive, quicken; and in its own new motions and quickness, it will know the promise of eternal life.

For Herbert, plants play an important role in characterizing both the individual and, as we will soon see, the communal sides of spiritual life in *The Temple*. But first we need to examine further the fundamental, unifying conception of 'life' that Herbert shares with his contemporaries. This chapter began with the spiritual commonplaces, the 'true and lively faith' given by a 'living God.' This commonplace characterization of faith can be found in the obvious places in British Protestantism. Cranmer's homily on faith speaks of a 'true, lively [alternately, 'quick'] and Christian faith';[21] in the controversial Lambeth Articles it is a 'true, lively and justifying faith.'[22] The cognates are everywhere in private and public writings of Herbert's time,[23] as are the equally normative expressions of the 'living God.' Taken together these two commonplaces affirm a deeply felt spiritual reality of 'life' that distinguishes Herbert and other writers. With this faith Herbert can 'live and write' again ('The Flower,' 37) when his 'Killing and quickning' (17) God returns. Without it, nothing has value; and everything is dull, idle, dead.

Thus, this sense of 'life' is faithful experience of the living God. In Reformed thought the gulf perceived between human and divine is crossed by faith strengthened by the moving Spirit. Human powers once corrupted and deadened by sin are renewed and quickened by finding the Spirit's motions imparted within. The heart can 'get wing, and flie away with thee' ('Whitsunday,' 4). The burgeoning theology of the Spirit in Protestant thought formalizes the attempt to understand the Spirit's imparted motions, both in forming a 'true and lively faith' and also in revealing the nature of a 'living ' God.

This faith moved by the Spirit is the live nerve in what Lewalski calls the 'Protestant paradigm of salvation.'[24] The Pauline formulation (election, calling, justification, adoption, sanctification, glorification),[25] on which it is based, takes faith for granted. Richard Sibbes states the obvious when he says that man lives by faith in these 'several grand passages of this life.'[26] We see more clearly how the spirit animates faith throughout these 'passages' when we bear two factors in mind. The first is that calling, justification, and sanctification, which are the primary 'passages' of the believer's earthly experience, can be viewed as a history of the Spirit's motions in the human heart. Only the Spirit can enable the believer to respond to these motions. The second is that these passages of calling, justification, and sanctification are all continuous conditions in a 'true and lively faith.' By continuing to answer the Spirit's call, the believer is justified before God through his now forgiven sins against God's justice. Yet the inner battle against the 'law of sin ... in my members' (Romans 7:23), as Paul puts it, still rages. The believer still sins, requiring justification, which paradoxically continues, but is not repeated anew. Justification remains the necessary foundation for developing holiness, which is the sanctification that is Christian life aided by the indwelling Spirit. Thus, faith enlivened by the Spirit continues to answer the call that justifies the believer and supports his sanctification. The 'life' of faith is moved by the living God, by the indwelling Spirit.

The elements cited by Lewalski are merged together in the sanctification of daily life. Put simply, a true Christian's whole life is increasing sanctification; its essentials are a living faith sustained by the indwelling and quickening Spirit. It assumes calling, election, justification, and adoption; and it participates in glorification through hope. More important, the standard division of sanctification, into mortification and vivification, formalizes the opposition between death and life. This division derives from Calvin's view that life is a long conversion through repentance, which 'consists of two parts: namely, mortification of the flesh and vivification of the spirit.'[27] Calvin's conception was absorbed into more precisely articulated notions of sanctification later.[28] In any event, the practical consequences for daily spiritual life are that sanctified life is a habitual tension between mortification and vivification.

The Spirit who quickens sanctified life is the Spirit of Christ. And the relationship between that Spirit and the Person Christ is the moving centre of Christian spirituality. Fundamental truths operate in full force here. There is life in his death, and it is his Spirit who applies that paradoxical life to the believer. To 'get a wing and flie away' with the Spirit is, therefore, to 'imp' a 'wing' on the resurrected Christ ('Easter-wings,' 19). Life imparted by the indwelling Spirit is simultaneously trusting in the Person of Christ; it is laying hold of him to rest in him, selflessly surrendering to the power of his Person, while feeling his powers directly enlivening one's own. In that conformity there is quickness and motion in the faculties now doing what they were created to do. That is, there is a 'true and lively' faith quickened by the Spirit.

In Protestant spirituality that fuller truth everywhere admits Paul's inspiration and the botanical turns in his thought. Old Testament 'planting' and 'building' the House of Israel merge naturally in Paul's thought into the living temple and the Body of Christ. These notions are ready at hand to express how individuals communally share life in the Spirit of Christ. In Puritan thought John Coolidge finds the source of this union of the botanical and the architectural, of planting and building the House of Israel, in Jeremiah. When facing a destroyed Jerusalem and its physical temple, he speaks for God:

> See, I have this day set thee over the nations and over the king-
> doms, to root out, and to pull down, and to destroy, and to throw
> down, to build, and to plant.   (Jeremiah 1:10)[29]

Later, in telling the Corinthians that 'ye are God's husbandry, ye are
God's building' (1 Corinthians 3:9), Paul repeats these received
botanical and architectural notions of live growth, of planting and
building the living temple of believers.[30] Coolidge points to the heart
of Paul's conception of communal life: 'For if we have been planted
together in the likeness of his death, we shall be also in the likeness of
his resurrection' (Romans 6:5). But for Paul the shared communal life
through conformity to Christ is, as Coolidge suggests, best expressed
in the one communal Body which, having been planted, now grows,
being continuously edified through Christ's love:

> That body ... is the ultimate form of humanity. The edification of
> the individual and that of the collectivity are one and the same
> process, which comes about by virtue of the death and resurrec-
> tion of Christ. In both it is identification with Christ that changes
> dead and disordered materials into something that lives and grows
> towards its perfect form.[31]

To live is to be planted and built in the living temple most fully
understood as the Body of Christ.

How Herbert draws on the popular stock of botanical figures from
Paul and from other biblical writers is revealing. The living temple,
which typologically fulfils the House of Israel, is both an individual
and a communal reality defining much in *The Temple*. Similarly,
plants represent both realities. It is hard not to hear Jeremiah
contributing to Herbert's conception of the human tree:

> Blessed is the man that trusteth in the Lord, and whose hope the
> Lord is. For he shall be as a tree planted by the waters, and that
> spreadeth out her roots by the river, and shall not see when heat
> cometh, but her leaf shall be green; and shall not be careful in the
> year of drought, neither shall cease from yielding fruit.
>   (Jeremiah 17:7–8)

What the tree and the flower can say about life in the individual, the
vine can say about the church, which is planted by God and given its
life in Christ:

> Early didst thou arise to plant this vine,
> Which might the more indeare it to be thine.
> Spices come from the East; so did thy Spouse,
> Trimme as the light, sweet as the laden boughs
> Of *Noahs* shadie vine, chaste as the dove;
> Prepar'd and fitted to receive thy love.
>
>   ('The Church Militant,' 11–16)

Thus, both the architectural and the botanical represent Herbert's notion of communal life; but, in contrast to Paul and many contemporary writers like Donne,[32] for whom the communal Body best represented the shared life in Christ, he shows no great interest in this important notion. By no means does he reject it, as his reference to Christ's suffering in his 'members' reveals ('Affliction (III),' 16). Nonetheless, it is the vine and the temple, not the body and its members, that comprehend communal life most fully for Herbert.

The communal vine centres in Christ, himself the 'true vine.' Visibly and powerfully biblical, Herbert's notion can be densely typological. Noah's 'shadie vine' to be planted after the Flood (Genesis 9:20) prefigures the Church as well as Christ. The several dimensions in this typology of the vine are more clearly revealed in 'The Sacrifice':

> Then on my head a crown of thorns I wear:
> For these are all the grapes *Sion* doth bear,
> Though I my vine planted and watred there:
>   Was ever grief like mine?   (161–4)

In Isaiah's allegory, the vineyard of Sion is the House of Israel (Isaiah 5:7); more broadly it is a type for the church, in which Christ the true vine is planted. But the vineyard of Sion produced wild grapes, sinful actions typologically like the murder of Christ or the failure of any believer to conform to the 'vine planted and watered there.' This 'true vine' ('Good Friday,' 12), the Christ of John's allegory, seen to 'drop grapes ... Of *Joy* and *Charitie*' ('Love-joy,' 2, 7), is Christ viewed inseparably from his branches, the believers quickened together in his church.

The garden complements the vine, adding to Herbert's characterization of shared life in the community. Whereas a branch is subordinate to the main vine, the garden flower or tree preserves its individual space in a larger shared plot planned and tended by the husbandman. Apparent contradiction between the vine and garden is resolved in a complex whole, for Christ is both the main vine and the husbandman. The garden can embrace all that Herbert has told us about life in the individual flower or tree while keeping it in a communal context. That experience of life in the garden includes both heaven and earth. There is the heavenly garden ('The Flower,' 46) for those flowers quickened by God. Its earthly precursor is a garden made by Christ 'for those / Who want herbs for their wound' ('Sunday,' 41–2). He is the husbandman healing all believers together, even though the communal garden idea allows the identities of individual plants. The communal 'trees ... in a ROW,' which owe both 'fruit and order' to God ('Paradise,' 2–3), can earn their heavenly paradise in relation to one another, subject together to pruning at God's hand. Yet the garden notion itself, like the temple, speaks to both individual and community. In Adam, a 'garden in a Paradise' ('Miserie,' 70), there is the fruitfulness and order of undamaged faculties in the soul. Only in the heavenly garden, in communal life with other elect believers, can sinful man know that original condition.

However suggestively the garden adds to our understanding of Herbert's sense of communal life, the true vine, with its background in John's theology that God is life, tells us more. A central New Testament truth, that God's life is translated to man through Christ, is self-consciously explicated by both John and Paul. Both assume a mutual participation between the believer and the incarnate Christ and other believers. Christ lives 'in' believers; and together they live 'in' Christ. For John this participation in God involves the apostle's Old Testament notion that God is life and that the 'Word of life' is incarnate in Christ.[33] The believer who identifies with Christ can participate in that life through faith, by 'believing ye might have life through his name' (John 20:31).[34] This new life through Christ is a 'seed'[35] that gradually grows into a plant in the believer as he comes to know the Word, conforming himself to the teaching and life of the incarnate Word. So doing, the believer eats of the bread of life,[36] which then dwells within him.

The true vine draws together many of the crucial elements in John's theology of participation. All turns on Christ's injunction: 'Abide in me, and I in you. As the branch cannot bear fruit of itself, except it abide in the vine; no more can ye, except ye abide in me' (John 15:4). Christ, the main stem, quickens together those who conform to his pattern of love that involves God the Father, himself, and the human believer: 'If ye keep my commandments, ye shall abide in my love; even as I have kept my Father's commandments, and abide in his love' (John 15:10). To 'abide' in him, they must conform to his love, obeying in turn: 'This is my commandment. That ye love one another as I have loved you' (v 12). Love for others and obedience characterize the life that the 'branches' have in the true vine. And, as we have already noted, the vine, in configuring a unity with other believers, further distinguishes 'life' as a love relationship to other believers who likewise conform to Christ. For John as for Herbert after him, the life known in a God who is love (1 John 4:9) is necessarily love.

That life is shared with others in the true vine says much about Herbert's relationship to his audience. It follows that the individual voices in *The Temple* prayerfully express Herbert's own direct love of God while they also represent the experience of a participating branch alive in the communal vine. In *The Temple* Herbert can modulate from the communal vine to the individual tree that harbours other creatures and to trees together in an orchard; in each case the individual is conceived in relationship to others. For Herbert, the vine simply makes more explicit how individuals as branches live by participating in the shared whole, through conformity to Christ, the main stem. The Christian lives when faith works by love, both directly to God and also to other men. Life lies not just in faith or in love, but in their necessary connection that implicates man in the lives of both man and God. For Herbert the vine configures this communal life most fully.

For a final word on a life in *The Temple*, we need to look through the apparent contradiction in Herbert's use of the plant. To view man as a flower or a tree would seem to run counter to Herbert's sense of heightened life, for neither quickness nor motion distinguishes plant life. Herbert's love of the mind's intuitive speed and the heart's unimpeded grasp of its object are not immediately suggested by the live plant. The live orange tree, though solid and useful in its given space, harbouring birds and bearing fruit, is a far cry from the glittering motions surrounding Christ's heavenly face and suggesting the mind's own heavenly likeness to a living God. But there is a way to comprehend this apparent contradiction, especially when we first note that the biblical true vine does not deny brightened consciousness in its members while representing other elements in spiritual experience. Nor does Jeremiah's tree. Rather, with its roots spread out by the water like the blessed man who trusts in God, it points the way to understanding Herbert's attraction to the plant. For him the tree, stationary though extending in its place, captures the life of faithful trust in Christ that frees the soul's quickened motions. In that faithful surrender to Christ's person lies earthly life at its deepest, beyond reason's full grasp, but dependent upon it, neither obviating nor contradicting it, nor alien to it. Rooted and stationary, the plant carries this truth of faith. The motions of Herbert's flower carry the further truth. Killed and quickened by God, the heart recovers 'greennesse' and 'in age' the poet can 'bud' again to 'relish versing.' And, significantly, the mind has been quickened, brightened to 'see' the full truth of human experience ('The Flower,' 9, 36, 39, 44).

For Herbert such apparently simple realities as plants embody truth, as do more complex realities. To say *My God, My King* ('Jordan (I),' 15) expresses an essence of adoration for which no other words may seem necessary. At the same time the whirling motions that comprehend divine life are not simple, nor is Herbert's complex poetic form, which is constantly revised, 'reinvented'[37] to embrace the living soul's experience of praising a living God. But just as the light and joy that are the life of heaven are supported by 'Leisure' ('Heaven,' 18), so, too, are the quickness and motion that are the truth of human 'life' supported by faithful resting in Christ. The full truth includes both the simple and the complex.

Conclusion:
The Presence of the Self

A study of Herbert's spirituality leads inevitably to his notion of the self. The quickening self reveals its created likeness to the living God through a commerce centred in mutual presence. Individual lyrics that capture separate but related moments in this prayerful commerce examine the ways in which God's living presence edifies the human temple. These related moments also reveal how the presence of the quickening self ensures a sense of continuity in *The Temple*.

The necessary role of scriptural truths in the edifying commerce with God contributes indelibly to this sense of continuity. In turn, Herbert's poetic temple, which captures the mutual presence between God and the self, imitates the Bible. What Herbert says about the Bible applies also to *The Temple*: one verse 'marks' or illuminates another verse distant from it; and 'both do make a motion / Unto a third' lying 'ten leaves off' ('The H. Scriptures (II),' 5–6). Individual verses, which contribute to minutely crafted lyric frames, also break the containment of these individual frames when completed 'ten leaves off.' That is, discrete frames are broken to build new ones, which in turn are broken to build the architecture of *The Temple*. Paradoxically, these breaking motions build the interconnections in the prayerful dialogue with God in the poem. Herbert would emphasize that such continuities this dialogue require not only God's living presence, but also man's.

It is useful to recall briefly how meaning accrues through Herbert's use of interconnections to express the mutual presence of God and the self. For example, the love moving man's prayer and praise to the God of love requires a language of sweetness that is fully achieved in the sweet communion of speaking and eating in 'Love (III).' Manifest earlier in honey and gall, in love and suffering, Christ's sacrifice later informs the Eucharistic 'sweet and sacred cheer,' with its 'broken' bread, which the speaker prays will elevate both his 'lines and life' ('The Banquet,' 1, 30, 51). But the dialogue itself in 'Love (III)' completes the earlier language of sweetness. So, too, it is in that dialogue and meal with the 'quick-eyed' Love, the Living God, to whom the reluctant speaker entrusts himself, that his faith is fully quickened. The *new, tender, quick* soul motivated by love ('Love unknown,' 70), after experiencing that contritional 'grones are quick, and full of wings' ('Sion,' 21), now comes fully alive in the dialogue with Love. For the believer the faith expressed in love enlivens the self deadened by sin, but quickened through prayer and praise. In these interconnections, which express sweetness and quickened life, important qualities in the spirituality of *The Temple* are expressed.

This literary technique of interconnecting lines in *The Temple*, as Chana Bloch has taught us, reveals an 'exegetical' habit of reading the Bible by collating texts.[1] And 'The H. Scriptures (I) and (II)' leave little doubt that this habit conveys explicitly a conception of biblical truth. Where one verse leads on to another, truth can be found by collating one with the other. As we have already seen, the theology behind this method is received doctrine in which God is here expressed in the 'hony' of the Scriptures pointing to the truth of Christ.[2] That truth is tasted, consumed by sucking 'ev'ry letter' ('The H. Scriptures (I),' 2) for its sweetness. To collate verses is to suck love's truth informing the part and the whole, and converging in Christ. Bloch cleanly singles out the method designed to taste that sweetened truth.

Herbert's reader must also learn to collate. Not only is the sweetness of biblical verses embedded in Herbert's own verses, such as the possessive *My God, My King* ('Jordan (I),' 15) that prepares for the variously biblical 'my Way, my Truth, my Life' ('The Call,' 1). The collating reader can also taste how biblical truth sweetens and enlivens the spiritual experience of individual lyrics which, more broadly, contribute to the prayerful dialogue of love with God in *The Temple*. Most broadly, the reader must collate all these poetic interconnections that build the spiritual temple of the poem.

Both objects of collation, biblical and 'poetic,' embody the stable truth of God present in the dialogue with man. Eugene Veith rightly points to a ritualized stance in this dialogue that expresses constants in Reformation theology and contributes to the interconnected parts in the whole. On one side is the 'active partner' God, who initiates all spiritual action in his Elect; on the other side is the Elect believer, who responds faithfully to God's initiatives, secure in his conviction of his salvation even when complaining about his own sinfulness or about God's actions.[3] This dialogue of persons, with God descending to man, who rises to God, provides the basic frame for interconnections in *The Temple*. The Father-King, who baits the believer with delight and grief, appears as the sacrificial Son, befriending the believer and speaking to him through the Spirit. Throughout, there is a communion of persons: either directly through God's intervention in his own voice, as in 'The Collar' or 'Dialogue,' or in that of a 'friend' in 'Jordan (II)'; or indirectly through intervention, as in the return of Grace in 'The Flower.' In turn, Herbert's prayer to God, which Ellrodt contrasts with Donne's 'egocentrique' devotions,[4] is always a dialogue with a divine listener. That sweetened dialogue is between identifiable persons. The dimensions of these divine persons have given readers fewer problems than the dimensions of the human 'self.'

We must ask if there is a real or merely a supposed problem created by Stanley Fish's notion that the 'self' is 'consumed' in the movement of Herbert's poetry.[5] This seminal argument in recent Herbert criticism has generated Barbara Harman's argument in *Costly Monuments*. Similarly, Fish's claims exert a kind of genetic influence on important 'Protestant' ingredients in Richard Strier's *Love Known*. Fish's troublesome argument lies in wait for any counter-claim about Herbert's conception of the self. For Fish an all-powerful God leaves no initiative to his sinful creature. All initiative and merit for action belong to God and not man, who can claim no credit for his own salvation. Instead, man must 'let go,' humbling the 'self'[6] in order to merge with God. In consequence, the lyrics in *The Temple* enact the dismantling of the self. And the reader's experience must necessarily imitate the inability of the dismantled persona to act independently in achieving his own salvation. Like the self, the speaker's purposive movement in the poems runs aground in the discovery that God and not man is in control. Any independent gestures of the self are exhausted in this discovery.

Barbara Harman's argument is the mildly rebellious offspring of Fish's. She justifiably regrets his 'dark vision'[7] of the self, since for her the impotent self is not consumed in all the poems, but is 'represented'[8] variously. Thus, in some poems neither the self nor the poem is consumed; what remains is an embodiment of the self. Harman's argument necessarily corrects Fish's parent argument, but it is no less dark in its conception of a constricted, sinful 'self.' Like Fish, she cannot account for those lyrics in *The Temple* that embody a much less meagre notion.

For both Fish and Harman, the 'self' is the sinful soul, perverted in its overweening conviction that man, not God, can take the initiative in salvation. Although this claim is happily congenial to Calvin's habit of speaking of the 'self' as the perversion of man's nature, neither Fish nor Harman enlists this historical ally, whose conception of man's relationship to God is assumed in 'Protestant' readings of Herbert. For Calvin all religion is knowledge of the self and God. In knowing the 'self,' the believer finds 'ignorance, vanity, poverty, infirmity, and — what is more — depravity and corruption'; this knowledge leads to the recognition that the 'true light of wisdom, sound virtue, full abundance of every good, and purity of righteousness rest in the Lord alone.'[9] Some knowledge of the 'self' allows no justifiable self-love or self-confidence. This dismal 'self' is denuded of all natural goodness and capacity. Fish's version of Herbert's 'self' lacks Calvin's extreme sense of disgust, but it stresses the same unrelieved incapacity.

This 'self' is admittedly present in some poems of *The Temple*. The long catalogue of human foolishness and pollution in 'Miserie' ends abruptly with an incriminating self-indictment:

> But sinne hath fool'd him. Now he is
> A lump of flesh, without a foot or wing
> To raise him to a glimpse of blisse:
> A sick toss'd vessel, dashing on each thing;
> Nay, his own shelf:
> My God, I mean my self.   (73–8)

Throughout *The Temple*, too, the incapacitated self discovers that God's initiative is never absent in salvation. Fish's argument about this 'self' as Herbert's target throughout *The Temple* is compelling, at least for some poems. Here is the spirit of Calvin's argument, with all good necessarily coming from God to a human nature thoroughly disabled and weakened. Any goodness in man comes from Christ, as the speakers of these poems consistently discover.[10]

But just as Fish ignores those other energies of the self in Herbert that strain against this profound sense of incapacity, Calvin's argument gets reduced by its own emphases. His argument seeks to erase all human strength or goodness, while praising God's gracious salvation of man. Fallen man's weakness and corruption are his essential nature. In this regard Calvin differs substantially from Bernard of Clairvaux and Donne, his disciple, who emphasize that the human Image of God was indelible even in Hell, and hence recognizable as God's creature.[11] Thus, the essential person is the created faculties, whatever the damage done by the law of sin in one's members. The thrust of Calvin's argument, and of Fish's, is that the damage *is* the self, not just its accidental condition. However, even a perverted desire, in expressing a created power, can be said to be a creature of God, hence not totally without its goodness. Calvin's argument wilfully underplays this fact, and so does Fish's. The fuller meaning of the 'self' governing *The Temple* is introduced early in 'Superliminare':

> Thou, whom the former precepts have
> Sprinkled and taught, how to behave
> Thy self in church; approach, and taste
> The churches mysticall repast.   (1–4)

The 'self' comprises not just the perversion of the Old Man, but also the created self indelible in spite of its perverseness. That 'self' is more present in *The Temple* than either Fish or Harman would have us believe. And it is in just those elements of sweetness, fitness, delight, and quickened life examined in this study that the soul reveals the more positive elements in its created nature.

Before looking at that fuller 'self' in any detail, we need to investigate further some entangling implications of Calvin's conception of the 'self.' In granting no good to the damaged 'self,' he concedes all value to Christ's righteousness imputed to man.[12] This is the covering of righteousness that overlays sin's damage and protects man against God's wrath and judgment.[13] The goodness is not man's, but Christ's acting through man by initiating, guiding, raising, strengthening. It is not the 'self,' relentlessly abused by Calvin for its incapacity and depravity, which enables the actions of the regenerate Christian life, but the righteousness of Christ. Calvin's sense of truth cannot allow any merit to the human medium for its experience of goodness.

But the logic of Creation inherently strains against such an argument. One implication of the Genesis account is that rational consciousness, the culminating achievement of the sixth day, is good in itself. And delight in rational self-consciousness necessarily follows. To admit pleasure in the very motions of self-reflexiveness is to admit an essential goodness, however misshapen later by sin. Arguments for total depravity must underplay this delight. Herbert's delight in 'sparkling notions,' the business of the quickened brain, clings to the goodness in rational consciousness. By contrast, Calvin's argument ignores the natural and simple pleasure in self-consciousness itself; instead, he shifts his gaze from the self to the not-self, to God's saving righteousness. But by its very nature the rational soul finds pleasurable motions inherent within.

More than one reader has noted that Herbert does not regard man as depraved. The poet's delight in the created world climaxes in man its highest creature. His request that God 'dwell' in man, a 'stately habitation' and a 'brave ... Palace' ('Man,' 2, 50), affirms the goodness of man's created being. A splendid frame, man is served by a 'cabinet of pleasure,' the universe and its lesser creatures, both a *delight* and a *treasure* (28–30). Hardly depraved, the speaker petitions the Spirit to dwell within that splendid frame. Calvin's notion of total depravity seems alien here.

Herbert's 'self,' which is clearly more than its sinful infection and weakness, derives from his conviction of its created distinctness. Made in God's image and likeness, the human creature nonetheless remains a being distinct from his Creator, however dependent for his well-being. Fish's believer must 'let go' confidence in his own power until 'absorbed into the deity.'[14] Such absorption would erase the distinctness indelibly marking Herbert's several figures for the self. But the 'habitation' or 'palace' is a created frame which does not disappear when God is within, but remains identifiably distinct. Similarly, the human flower is a form identifiably objective, extended in space and time. This form remains distinct and separate, whether punished by God's storms or warmed by his sun; so, too, the tree even when standing among others in an orchard.

One wing imped on another ('Easter-wings,' 19) makes the point most compellingly. For Herbert the conformed soul rising with Christ preserves its separate identity, whatever its sinful weakness. This remarkable image says much about Herbert's understanding of the soul's experience of imputed righteousness. In his hands the received notion of the winged soul, here justified by Christ's righteousness, does 'make a motion' to the indwelling and sanctifying 'golden wings' of the Holy Spirit, 'with' whom the conformed soul can 'get wing, and flie away' ('Whitsunday,' 2–4). Herbert's 'imp' points to a central truth of such conformity:

> Let me combine
> And feel this day thy victorie:
> For, if I imp my wing on thine,
> Affliction shall advance the flight in me.
>
> ('Easter-wings,' 17–20)

Herbert's preciseness affirms the distinctness of the human creature when combined with Christ; for he will 'imp' his wing 'on' Christ – not 'into' or 'in.' Hutchinson gives us the wrong help from the *OED*: 'to engraft feathers in a damaged wing so as to restore or improve the power of flight.' But Herbert says 'on,' not 'in.' Another *OED* meaning comes closer to Herbert's intention: 'to imp wings on or to a person.' For Herbert the difference is essential. In the first case, feathers are dispersed into the wing, surrendering their separateness.[15] The substitute feathers would merge with the wing's remaining feathers, whereas in the second case a full wing imped on a person maintains its own discrete identity. The two wings 'combine' differently than would feathers merged into another wing. The important point is that, as elsewhere, Herbert is underlining the distinctness of the human person, however dependent upon Christ's strength for salvation.[16]

Herbert insists on this distinctness when characterizing the self. There is the temple, an existing spatial frame in which God dwells. And the 'child' of 'The Collar' is distinct from the calling Father, as is the servant speaking in a 'commerce' with the master in 'The Odour.' So, too, the lute is distinct from the divine musician. Even the heavenly dinner guest united with God maintains his distinctness as a person when speaking with Love and sitting to eat his meat in 'Love (III).' The believer who assimilates God's truth still preserves his distinctness as a person. But it is the dialogue of persons in 'Love (III)' that frames the profounder implications of this distinctness and relates to the prayerfulness of *The Temple*. At stake are both prayer as a dialogue of persons and also God's manifestation as a living person. Ellrodt's point that Herbert's lyrics in *The Temple* assume a divine listener can be sharpened by emphasizing that the dialogue is prayerful. Veith's observation that Election invested the individual with a sense of worth has point here, if we keep one eye trained on its paradoxical, rough collision with the sense of total depravity. What emerges in Herbert, in whom sinfulness generally lacks a sense of self-disgust, is the distinct person justified in talking directly with a living God. The very idea of dialogue captures the living presence of two beings talking to one another, both distinct and worthy, however radically different in power and comprehension.

The mutual presence of man and God in prayerful dialogue expresses the divine purpose in creating a rational creature. Through rational man, who offers praise to God 'for me and all my fellows,' the other earthly creatures ('Providence,' 26), God communes with the created world. The believer may anguish that God frequently seems absent, while simultaneously believing that God can never be so. But Herbert never doubts his own presence. This simple truth reminds us that motions of consciousness guarantee a sense of presence – and of worth. The self may seem sorely threatened when 'Broken in pieces all asunder,' its thoughts a 'case of knives' and the faculties and their powers like 'attendants' at strife, 'Quitting their place.' However, the abiding power to identify broken parts and rebellious attendants paradoxically expresses the conscious self, whose petition for God's help in 'building' its own broken frame asserts its presence further ('Affliction (IV),' 1, 7, 13–14, 29). The law of sin inheres in this frame, but so does the presence of the God who created it. And in the living presence of the rational self is the centre of its created likeness to this living God, with whom man combines in prayer.

Helen Vendler has sensitively examined this mutual presence between man and God. Whereas Fish's 'consumed' self is 'absorbed' into the deity, Vendler works to trace Herbert's fine line between preserving individuality and conforming the human will to the divine. In its best moments the self unites with God through 'states of reciprocity and identity.'[17] The fulfilled self preserves its individuality even when 'indistinguishable from God.'[18] This oxymoron succeeds in capturing those moments when God dwells in the sufferer's groan 'O God!' ('Affliction (III),' 1) and 'the human self and the crucified Jesus' can be seen 'as one.'[19] It also captures God's active contribution in composing some poems. However, Vendler's tendency to speak of several selves, depending upon the soul's various spiritual conditions, infringes on Herbert's sense of continuing presence, distinct from God and embodied in the nature of dialogue. Nonetheless, her strong sense that Herbert does not denigrate the self and that his movement toward positive spiritual states dignifies human experience stands firmly against more negative estimates of the self in *The Temple*.

Yet this conviction of the soul's dignity clashes with the powerlessness and aborted initiative described so convincingly by Fish. Herbert finds no easy solution to this problematical clash, which is focused most sharply in the poems of complaint. There a stark, debilitated voice assumes its right to God's comforting presence. In the direct petition that God ease his grief in 'Longing,' frustrated desire for God's favour approaches petulance:

> Lord, didst thou leave thy throne,
> Not to relieve? how can it be,
> That thou art grown
> Thus hard to me?
> Were sinne alive, good cause there were
> To bear.   (61–6)

The razor's edge is treacherous here. The Psalms justify complaint, although its excess – 'murmuring,' as Donne speaking biblically calls it[20] – is sinful. And, in fact, this speaker appears to wield a constricting logic too aggressively, inadvertantly inviting our suspicions of pride. After all, the logic claims, with Christ's sacrifice sin is 'dead' and God's 'promises' alive (66–7); thus, punishing affliction should end. Nonetheless, sin is dead only in ultimate, not immediate terms, and the aggressiveness may be mere pride. The poem finally overlooks the sinfulness of the speaker, whose importunate last petition expresses raw need, not the blindness of self:

> My love, my sweetnesse, heare!
> By these thy feet, at which my heart
> Lies all the yeare,
> Pluck out thy dart,
> And heal my troubled breast which cryes,
> Which dyes.   (79–84)

This voice cannot be accounted for in Fish's sense of the 'self' that needs consuming. Rather, in this desire for comfort in God's presence the self's own continuing presence is represented. Herbert's instinctive objection to suffering here is rooted in a sense of importance for having enjoyed God's presence, favour, comfort, and the promise of more. The poem confesses weakness, 'shames' (28), and the need for humility before God; but at the same time the speaker, whose own presence vivifies the poem, assumes his right to God's attention. The created self knows its worth.

In *The Temple* this conviction of worth emerges in the art that examines the mutual presence of God and man. Strier's claim that Herbert inveighs against overweening ingenuity and craftsmanship[21] must give ground when faced with the splendid variety of Herbert's lyric forms that serve his examination. Arnold Stein finds in the 'personal lyrics' in *The Temple* a Herbert so true to the 'many themes, moments, and feelings' that he 'does not give us a single, consistent attitude toward expression.'[22] This refined truth to his experience demands a minutely flexible adaptation of received forms to express his devotional experience of love and complaint. It is hard to imagine that Herbert, in likeness to his Creator God, the 'perfect Artist,' who 'must needs love ... his owne worke' (*The Country Parson*, p 283), should not love and delight in poetic works that express that likeness. That a proud step sideways can lead to overweening craftsmanship, and sometimes does, cannot invalidate the importance of the created self, which, like the artist God whose presence informs all existence, shows itself present in the refined adaptation of recognizable forms.

Man's art and consciousness have sharp limitations. Nonetheless, Herbert's art in *The Temple* can imitate God's biblical art whereby interconnected truths are revealed progressively in the motions of one verse toward another. And just as *The Temple* imitates the Bible, man's consciousness in its continuing presence imitates the living God, who reveals himself by speaking to prayerful man. In the interconnectedness of Herbert's lyrics lies the presence of both man and God in prayerful commerce with each other, united in growing conformity. Each 'part' of man's broken and contrite heart 'Hath got a tongue' that begs 'Lord Jesu' ('Longing,' 73–6), himself 'broken' for man's sin and 'presented' in love in the Eucharist ('The Banquet,' 30). The same broken God, whose loving presence is invoked throughout *The Temple*, comforts the sinful heart broken by affliction. He will call together the 'broken consort' of saved believers at judgment day ('Dooms-day,' 29). A final word in Herbert's spirituality is that 'broken bones may joy' ('Repentance,' 32). What is broken in man can be rebuilt through the prayerful dialogue with God. Depression, helplessness, powerlessness, frustration – all are constant. But in Herbert's own experience of sweetness, fitness, delight, and quickened life, the self finds the promise of a living communion with God. This promise can be exercised in the arts of spirituality.

Notes
Index

Notes

Introduction

1 James Thorpe 'Prayer as Herbert's Poetic Mode' 3, presented in a
  Modern Language Association Special Session ('Donne and Herbert:
  Their Religious Poetry') 28 December 1982. I have experienced the same
  surprise.

2 Quoted in Izaak Walton 'The Life of Mr. George Herbert' in *The Lives of
  John Donne, Sir Henry Wotton, Richard Hooker, George Herbert and
  Robert Sanderson* with an introduction by George Saintsbury (London:
  Oxford University Press 1966; reprinted from the 1927 edition) 314

3 George Herbert *The Country Parson, The Temple* ed John N. Wall, Jr in
  the Classics of Western Spirituality (New York, Ramsey, Toronto:
  Paulist Press 1981)

4 Competing definitions of 'spirituality' can be exasperating, as Martin
  Thornton complains succinctly: 'Words like "contemplative,"
  "mystical," "spirituality" and "ascetical" still mean very much what
  each individual writer wants them to mean. Every new book begins
  with a chapter of definitions, each slightly different from the others: in
  short, the terminology of the spiritual life is completely out of hand.'
  *English Spirituality: An Outline of Ascetical Theology According to the
  English Pastoral Tradition* (London: SPCK 1963) 16. For a recent development in the study of 'spirituality,' see the useful discussion by Caroline
  Walker Bynum, 'Approaches to the History of Spirituality' in *Jesus as
  Mother: Studies in the Spirituality of the High Middle Ages* (Berkeley, Los Angeles, London: University of California Press 1982) 3–8. As
  she notes, such studies can seem like social history: 'Recently the
  history of spirituality has come to mean something quite different: the
  study of how basic religious attitudes and values are conditioned by
  the society within which they occur. This new definition brings spirituality very close to what the school of French historians known as

annalistes call *mentalité*; the "history of spirituality" becomes almost a branch of social history, deeply influenced by work of structural-functionalist anthropologists and of phenomenologists of religion'(3).

5 John E. Booty *Three Anglican Divines on 'Prayer': Jewel, Andrewes, and Hooker* (Cambridge, Mass: Society of St John the Evangelist 1978) v

6 Gene Edward Veith, Jr *Reformation Spirituality: The Religion of George Herbert* (London and Toronto: Associated University Presses 1985)

7 Louis L. Martz *The Poetry of Meditation: A Study in English Religious Literature of the Seventeenth Century* (New Haven and London: Yale University Press 1965)

8 A.D. Nuttall *Overheard by God: Fiction and Prayer in Herbert, Milton, Dante and St. John* (London and New York: Methuen 1980) 1–82

9 For a brief, useful account of prayer in the household of Magdalene Herbert, see Amy M. Charles *A Life of George Herbert* (Ithaca and London: Cornell University Press 1977) 42. For a portrait of the devotional regimen at Bemerton, see Walton 'The Life of Mr. George Herbert' 302–3.

10 A major recent example is Richard Strier *Love Known: Theology and Experience in George Herbert's Poetry* (Chicago and London: University of Chicago Press 1983).

Chapter One

1 'Take with you words, and turn to the Lord: say unto him, Take away all iniquity, and receive us graciously: so will we render the calves of our lips' (Hosea 14:2). For a good example of British Protestant expression of this idea, see Richard Hooker, *Of the Laws of Ecclesiastical Polity* v, ed W. Speed Hill (Cambridge, Mass and London: The Belknap Press of Harvard University Press 1977) 23.1: 'Prayers are those caulves of mens lippes; those most gracious and sweet odors; those rich presentes and guiftes which beinge carryed up into heaven doe best testifie our dutifull affection, and are for the purchasinge of all favour at the handes of God the most undoubted meanes we can use.' Hereafter cited as *Laws*

2 Quoted in K.J. Healy 'Prayer (Theology of)' *New Catholic Encyclopedia* xi (New York, St Louis, San Francisco, Toronto, London, Sydney: McGraw-Hill Book Co 1967) 671

3 Eg, Healy (ibid) includes praise in 'adoration.'

4 Ibid 671; see Augustine *Sermo LXI* in *Patrologiae Cursus Completus, Series Latina* ed J.P. Migne (Paris 1844–64) 38, 409–14.

5 *The Sermons of John Donne* v, ed George R. Potter and Evelyn M. Simpson (Berkeley and Los Angeles: University of California Press 1962) 270. Hereafter cited as *Sermons*

6 Ibid 272

7 Eg, 'Return, O Lord, deliver my soul: oh save me for thy mercies'

sake' (Psalm 6:4); see Donne's treatment of this text in *Sermons* v, 366–79.

8 Cf 'The sacrifices of God are a broken spirit: a broken and a contrite heart, O God, thou wilt not despise' (Psalm 51:17).

9 'Ask, and it shall be given you; seek, and ye shall find; knock, and it shall be opened unto you: For every one that asketh receiveth; and he that seeketh findeth; and to him that knocketh it shall be opened' (Matthew 7:7–8). Luke 11:9–10 repeats verbatim these words from the Sermon on the Mount. The passage frequently surfaces in standard sixteenth- and seventeenth-century discussions of prayer as in the following passage from Lancelot Andrewes' sermon on Matthew 7:7 in 'Sermon III' in *Nineteen Sermons: Upon Prayer in General, and the Lord's Prayer in Particular* in *Works* v (Oxford: John Henry Parker 1843): 'We must be gone hence, and there is a place whither we desire all to come, which we cannot do except we knock; and because we know not at what door to knock, therefore we must seek the door; but we have no will nor desire to seek, therefore Christ willeth in the first place that we ask it, and the thing that we must ask is the Spirit of grace and of prayer; and if we ask it, then shall we have ability and power not only to seek the door, but when we have found it to knock at it' (325).

10 John Preston *The Saints Daily Exercise. A treatise concerning the whole dutie of prayer* (London 1629) 4

11 John E. Booty 'George Herbert: *The Temple* and *The Book of Common Prayer*' *Mosaic* 12:2 (1979) 75–90

12 Reading modern religious encyclopaedias quickly reveals the arbitrariness in categorizing the kinds of prayer. I am not playing Procrustes here, but just using generally accepted categories. The following have been useful: K.J. Healy 'Prayer (Theology of)' (see n 3 above); E.R. Bernard 'Prayer' in *Dictionary of the Bible* IV (New York: Charles Scribner's Sons 1905) 38–45; Henri Brémond 'Prière' in *Dictionnaire de Théologie Catholique* XIII (Paris: Librairie Letouzey et Ané 1936) 183–4. In regard to the seventeenth-century context, see: Lancelot Andrewes 'Schemes of Prayer' in *Preces Privatae* tr F.E. Brightman (New York: Meridian Books 1961) 11–15; 'Sermon VI' in *Nineteen Sermons upon Prayer in General, and the Lord's Prayer in Particular* in *Sermons* v (Oxford: John Henry Parker 1843) 357–61.

13 Andrewes 'Sermon VI' 358

14 For a discussion of the Augustinian element in this tradition, see Patrick Grant 'Redeeming the Time: The *Confessions* of St. Augustine' in *By Things Seen: Reference and Recognition in Medieval Thought* ed David L. Jeffrey (Ottawa: University of Ottawa Press 1979) 26.

15 Andrewes 'Sermon VI' 358

16 Ibid 354

17 Joseph Hall *The Devout Soul, or Rules of Heavenly Devotion* in *Works* VI, ed Philip Wynter (New York: AMS Press 1969; reprinted from the 1863 Oxford edition) 514

18 Hooker *Laws* v, 48.2
19 Ibid v, 48.4.
20 St Thomas Aquinas *Summa Theologiae* 2a2ae, 83.1 ad 1; English translation is from volume 39, tr Kevin D. O'Rourke (London: Eyre and Spottiswoode 1964). Hereafter cited as *ST*
21 *ST* 2a2ae, 83.1 c & ad 1
22 *ST* 2a2ae, 83.9 c & ad 2
23 Andrewes 'Sermon vi' 351–2
24 Preston's strong Protestant bent did not preclude intimacy with the writings of Aquinas. See *Dictionary of National Biography* xvi (London: Oxford University Press 1917) 308.
25 Preston *The Saints Daily Exercise* 4
26 Ibid
27 For discussions on the relationship between love's desire in prayer and God's will, see Andrewes 'Sermon xi' 398–404; Hooker *Laws* v, 48.9–49.5.
28 Andrewes 'Sermon iv' in *Nineteen Sermons* 337
29 Eg, Thomas Cranmer *An Answer unto a Crafty and Sophistical Cavillation, Devised by Stephen Gardiner* in *Writings and Disputations of Thomas Cranmer Relative to the Sacrament of the Lord's Supper* ed J.E. Cox (Cambridge: The University Press 1844) 346
30 John Calvin *Institutes of the Christian Religion* tr Ford Lewis Battles (Philadelphia: Westminster Press 1973) iv, xviii, 13. Hereafter cited as *Institutes*
31 Ibid iv, xviii, 12
32 Ibid iv, xviii, 13
33 For a useful discussion of this pairing in a Herbertian context, see John E. Booty 'George Herbert: *The Temple* and *The Book of Common Prayer*' 80–1.
34 For a discussion of these traditions, see Rosemond Tuve *A Reading of George Herbert* (Chicago: University of Chicago Press 1952) 32–47.
35 Ronald S. Wallace *Calvin's Doctrine of the Christian Life* (Edinburgh and London: Oliver and Boyd 1959) 31
36 Ibid 209
37 Ibid 57
38 Ibid 62–5
39 Ibid 53
40 Ibid 6–9
41 The notion of 'savour' rising to God derives from Old Testament practices of burnt offering. A representative passage is Leviticus 8:21:
    'and Moses burnt the whole ram upon the altar: it was a burnt sacrifice for a sweet savour, and an offering made by fire unto the Lord; as the Lord commanded Moses.' See F.C.N. Hicks *The Fullness of Sacrifice* (London: Macmillan 1930) 13.
42 Ibid 11

43 See n 29 above.

44 Also, in John 6:31–58 Christ compares manna to himself as bread, making the Eucharistic implications explicit.

45 See C.A. Patrides' note to line 122, p 53 in *The English Poems of George Herbert* (London, Melbourne, and Toronto: J.M. Dent and Sons 1974).

46 John Calvin *Commentary on the Book of Psalms* i, tr James Anderson (Grand Rapids, Mich: William B. Eerdmans 1949; reprinted from Edinburgh: Calvin Society 1845) xx, 3, p 336. Cf Bremond 'Prière' 181–2.

47 'For even Christ our passover is sacrificed for us. ...' (1 Corinthians 5:7). This statement by Paul can refer to the meaning of Christ's full sacrificial experience predicted at the Last Supper and to be assimilated by the believer; it can also refer to him as the Paschal lamb (cf Herbert's 'Paschal Lambe' in 'The Sacrifice,' 58).

48 *The Book of Common Prayer, 1559: The Elizabethan Prayer Book* ed John E. Booty (Washington: Folger Books, Folger Shakespeare Library 1982) 264

49 The term 'Anglican' is merely a useful convenience here and elsewhere in this study to denote a commitment to the established practices of the British church. For a discussion of the term, which came into use well after Herbert's time, see Richard Strier *Love Known: Theology and Experience in George Herbert's Poetry* (Chicago and London: University of Chicago Press 1983) xv; Gene Edward Veith, Jr *Reformation Spirituality: The Religion of George Herbert* (London and Toronto: Associated University Presses 1985) 15–17.

50 The textual history of 'The H. Communion' illustrates my point about Herbert's tendency to merge prayer and the Eucharist. In the Williams manuscript lines 25–40 were a separate poem entitled 'Prayer (ii).' 'Prayer (ii)' of the Bodleian manuscript was then numbered 'Prayer (iii).' The Bodleian manuscript includes a rewritten 'The H. Communion' to which are added lines 25–40, already written but differing in stanzaic form. The form of the new poem subtly distinguishes without strictly demarcating the characterization of the Eucharist from the prayer.

 'Prayer (i),' which immediately precedes 'The H. Communion,' leads us in the same direction. Prayer is 'the Churches banquet' (1) and 'Exalted Manna' (10) that invokes standard Eucharist typology. If to read 'The Church' is to 'taste / The churches mysticall repast' ('Superliminare,' 3–4), that repast is defined by prayer and praise as its necessary ingredients. And by gathering the old 'Prayer (ii)' into the new Eucharist poem and petitioning that God either 'give' him back his 'captive soul' raised to God in the Eucharist or 'take' his body 'thither' and give it a 'life' as well ('The H. Communion,' 25–6), Herbert plays inventively with the psychology of rising, which is inherent in both the Eucharist and prayer.

51 'Unto thee, O Lord, do I lift up my soul' (Psalm 25:1).

52 '... wherefore lift up thy prayer for the remnant that is left' (Isaiah 37:4).
53 'Therefore pray not thou for this people, neither lift up a cry or prayer for them ...' (Jeremiah 11:14).
54 Andrewes 'Sermon vii' 376
55 Hall *The Devout Soul* 514
56 For some useful observations on these matters, see Hicks *The Fullness of Sacrifice* 12, 34, 36–7, 112.
57 Christ offered what has come to be called 'The Lord's Prayer' as a model. In regard to the invocation ('Our Father which art in heaven,' Luke 11:2), Andrewes says, 'this word "heaven" serveth to prepare us to prayer, to the end that we should lift up our hearts and affections from earth to heaven, seeing we speak not to an earthly father but to One That is in heaven' ('Sermon viii' 376).
58 For a discussion of the stringed instrument as a figure for the self in Herbert's works, see John Hollander *The Untuning of the Sky: Ideas of Music in English Poetry, 1500–1700* (Princeton: Princeton University Press 1961) 288–94.
59 See n 11 above.
60 A.D. Nuttall *Overheard by God: Fiction and Prayer in Herbert, Milton, Dante and St. John* (London and New York: Methuen 1980) 9
61 Quoted in Izaak Walton 'The Life of Mr. George Herbert' in *The Lives of John Donne, Sir Henry Wotton, Richard Hooker, George Herbert and Robert Sanderson* with an introduction by George Saintsbury (London: Oxford University Press 1966; reprinted from the 1927 edition) 314
62 Helen Gardner, Introduction in John Donne *The Divine Poems* (Oxford: Clarendon Press 1978) xxxi
63 Nuttall *Overheard by God* 9
64 Henri Bremond *La Prière et les prières de l'Ancien Régime,* vol x in *Histoire Littéraire du sentiment religieux en France* (Paris: Librairie Armand Colin 1968) 224
65 For a useful characterization of this distinction see Kevin D. O'Rourke 'Appendix 3: Prayer' in Thomas Aquinas *Summa Theologiae* 39 (London: Eyre and Spottiswoode 1964) 259: 'St Thomas does not distinguish linguistically two aspects of praying covered by *oratio,* namely a disposition and an activity, corresponding in English to "prayerfulness" and "actual praying" '; 'We cannot and should not always be actually praying. It would be wrong to become absorbed in praying when one is at the wheel in thick traffic: "we must be taken up with other activities", observes St Thomas realistically. All the same, we must keep and nourish constant prayerfulness. This is no optional accomplishment, for it manifests our love for God in one of its essential manifestations and forms an indispensable part of our moral integrity.'
66 Hooker *Laws* v, 23.1
67 Ibid v, 48.2

68 Joseph H. Summers *George Herbert: His Religion and Art* (London: Chatto and Windus 1954) 75
69 Walton 'The Life of Mr. George Herbert' 302
70 Rosemond Tuve 'George Herbert and *Caritas*' in *Essays by Rosemond Tuve: Spenser, Herbert, Milton* ed Thomas P. Roche, Jr (Princeton: Princeton University Press 1970) 189
71 Charles H. and Katherine George *The Protestant Mind of the English Reformation, 1570–1640* (Princeton: Princeton University Press 1961) 129: 'The religious duty and the duty of the calling were seen to be, in fact, inextricably intertwined. The calling thus becomes a kind, and an absolutely essential kind, of Christian worship.' Cf C.J. Stranks *Anglican Devotion: Studies in the Spiritual Life of the Church of England between the Reformation and the Oxford Movement* (London: SCM Press 1961) 26: 'The duty of living continually in the presence of God, and of sanctifying every incident in the day's routine with prayer, had been placed firmly on the shoulders of every Christian. The bed-chamber, the workshop and the common street were to be what the monasteries had been in their best days, places where the work of praise and prayer were carried on continually.'

Chapter Two

1 E.E. Larkin 'Spirituality, Christian' in *New Catholic Encyclopedia*, XIII (New York, et al: McGraw-Hill Book Company 1967) 598
2 John Donne 'The Good-morrow' in *The Elegies and the Songs and Sonnets* ed Helen Gardner (Oxford: Clarendon Press 1965) 70
3 Barbara Kiefer Lewalski *Protestant Poetics and the Seventeenth-Century Religious Lyric* (Princeton: Princeton University Press 1979) 285–6; also, see 13–24.
4 Ibid 16
5 Richard Strier *Love Known: Theology and Experience in George Herbert's Poetry* (Chicago and London: University of Chicago Press 1983) xii–iii
6 See Gene Edward Veith, Jr *Reformation Spirituality: The Religion of George Herbert* (London and Toronto: Associated University Presses 1985) 19: '*Spirituality* I take to mean the religious and mystical life, as distinct from the intellectual and doctrinal formulations of *theology*.'
7 Characterizing faith as 'knowledge' was not uncommon in medieval practice, but not necessarily at the expense of love of God. For discussion of Calvin's faith as 'knowledge,' see my *Fulfilling the Circle: A Study of John Donne's Thought* (Toronto, Buffalo, London: University of Toronto Press 1984) 45–6; R.T. Kendall *Calvin and English Calvinism to 1649* (Oxford: Oxford University Press 1979) 19–20.
8 G. Johnston 'Love in the NT' in *The Interpreter's Dictionary of the Bible* III (New York and Nashville: Abingdon Press 1962) 172

9 Rosemond Tuve 'George Herbert and *Caritas'* in *Essays by Rosemond Tuve: Spenser, Herbert, Milton* ed Thomas P. Roche, Jr (Princeton: Princeton University Press 1970) 167–206; Strier *Love Known* xviii, 1n1, 17, 18n31, 26n50, 27, 52n51, 78, 255

10 Anders Nygren *Agape and Eros: A Study of the Christian Idea of Love* tr A.G. Hebert (London: Society for Promoting Christian Knowledge 1941) pt 1, p 92

11 Ibid 93

12 Martin Luther *Sermons on the Gospel of St. John* tr Martin H. Bertram in *Luther's Works* 24 (St Louis: Concordia Publishing House 1957) 14:21, p 147.

13 Paul Althaus *The Theology of Martin Luther* tr Robert C. Schultz (Philadelphia: Fortress Press 1966) 133

14 John Burnaby *Amor Dei: A Study of the Religion of St. Augustine* (London: Hodder and Stoughton 1960) v

15 John Calvin *Institutes of the Christian Religion* tr Ford Lewis Battles (Philadelphia: Westminster Press 1973) iii, ii, 41, p 589. Hereafter cited as *Institutes*

16 Ibid ii, viii, 53, p 417

17 John Calvin *Commentary on the Gospel According to John* ii, tr William Pringle (Grand Rapids, Mich: William B. Eerdmans 1956; reprinted from Edinburgh: Calvin Society 1847) xvi, 27, p 158

18 Love of God is by no means absent in Calvin's thought, but it is displaced at the centre by justification by faith. The Great Commandment to love God and man continues to exert its Christian force, particularly in a pastoral context. In a sermon on Deuteronomy 5:8–10, he speaks of a true love of God: 'mais il faut que le coeur mache devant, et que Dieu soit servi de nous en vraye affection: et ceste affection-la ne doit point estre contrainte: mais doit proceder d'une vraye amour de Dieu.' Quoted in Ronald S. Wallace *Calvin's Doctrine of the Christian Life* (Edinburgh and London: Oliver and Boyd 1959) 30n3
      Even in the *Institutes*, which is governed by justification by faith, love of God is present. Citing David's experience of prayer, he states that only praises that 'flow from this sweetness of love' can please God (*Institutes* iii, xx, 28, 890).

19 William H. Halewood *The Poetry of Grace: Reformation Themes and Structures in English Seventeenth-Century Poetry* (New Haven, Conn and London: Yale University Press 1970) 88–111

20 Rosemond Tuve *A Reading of George Herbert* (Chicago: University of Chicago Press 1952)

21 Joseph Summers *George Herbert, His Religion and Art* (London: Chatto and Windus 1954)

22 Diana Benet *Secretary of Praise: The Poetic Vocation of George Herbert* (Columbia, Missouri: University of Missouri Press 1984) 39

23 Ibid 26

24 Tuve 'George Herbert and *Caritas*' 171
25 Ibid 168
26 Ibid 175
27 Ibid 168
28 For a brief, useful characterization of the widespread influence of Calvinism, see Lewalski *Protestant Poetics* 13–14. Regarding the emergence of Calvinism at Cambridge, see H.C. Porter *Reformation and Reaction in Tudor Cambridge* (Cambridge: Cambridge University Press 1958).
29 See Lewalski *Protestant Poetics* 484n8; Kendall *Calvin and English Calvinism* 102–9; 117–24.
30 The love of God remained atrophied in Perkins' theological doctrine, though like Calvin's his pastoral works include it. His systematic theology, which was dominated by a Calvinistic preoccupation with sorting out the implications of predestinarian thought, by developing covenant theology, and by investigating the psychology of assurance, did little to redirect the Reformation imbalance away from the medieval love of God centred in Christ. See Ian Breward, Introduction in *The Work of William Perkins* ed Ian Breward (Appleford, Abingdon, Berkshire, England: Sutton Courtenay Press 1970).

   Breward notes in Perkins' theology an 'over-emphasis on God's distance from man and a tendency to subordinate mercy and justice to omnipotence.' Nonetheless, his 'warm and practical piety' (98–9) mollified the harder lines in his thought. Of the 'true professors' of the gospel, Perkins says that 'they have faith which worketh by love (Luke 8:15; Gal. 5:6). And that Christian man which loves God, whatsoever shall befall, yea though it were a thousand deaths, yet his heart can never be severed from the Lord and from his saviour Christ (Cant. 8.6–7)' ('A Treatise Tending unto a Declaration' in *The Work* 360).
31 Martin Luther *Lectures on Galatians – 1535* tr Jaroslav Pelikan in *Luther's Works* vol 27, 5:6, pp 28–9
32 Paul Manns 'Absolute and Incarnate Faith – Luther on Justification in the Galatians Commentary of 1531–35' in *Catholic Scholars Dialogue with Luther* ed Jared Wicks (Chicago: Loyola University Press 1970) 137
33 Martin Luther quoted by Wilhelm Herrmann *The Communion of the Christian with God* tr J.D. Stanyon (London: Williams and Norgate 1930) 277
34 Generally speaking, attention to love for God disappears in Luther's thought. See Paul Hacker 'Martin Luther's Notion of Faith' in *Catholic Scholars Dialogue with Luther* 103: 'It is most impressive to observe how the idea of love of God fades in Luther's works from about 1518 onward ... It is true that the Reformer constantly urges love of one's neighbor. But he did not regard this as an outcome of the primary love of God. For him, brotherly love had no meaning for eternity but was

righteousness confined to this world ... Luther can say, "Love God in his creatures; he does not want you to love him in his majesty." '

35 John's frequent 'knowledge' is a substitute for 'faith,' which he uses just once (1 John 5:4). Although he says much about God's love to man and man's to his fellows, he says little explicitly about direct love to God. Rather, the direct relationship to God is expressed in 'believe,' 'know,' and 'knowledge.' Such knowledge of God precedes love of man.

36 See Kendall *Calvin and English Calvinism* 18–20, 33, 40–1.

37 See my *Fulfilling the Circle* 35–44.

38 John Preston 'Of Faith: the First Sermon' in *The Breast-plate of Faith and Love* (London 1634) 16

39 Ibid 56

40 Eg, 'Fight the good fight of faith, lay hold on eternal life, whereunto thou art also called, and hast professed a good profession before many witnesses' (1 Timothy 6:12).

41 See n 70 below. Luther's Latin *apprehendere* and German *fassen* translate into both 'lay hold of' and 'take hold of.'

42 Eg, see Richard Sibbes 'The Fountain Opened' in *Works* v, ed Alexander Grosart (Edinburgh 1863) 516: 'In the main point of justification and comfort, faith lays hold upon Christ for mercy.'

43 Preston *The Breast-plate* 64

44 Ibid 69–70

45 Ibid 23

46 Sibbes 'The Privileges of the Faithful' in *Works* v (Edinburgh 1863) 276

47 Sibbes 'The Saints Resolution' in *Works* vii (1864) 88

48 Sibbes 'The Fountain Opened' in *Works* v (1863) 514

49 Sibbes 'The Art of Self-Humbling' in *Works* vi (1863) 46

50 Sibbes 'Faith Triumphant' in *Works* vii (1864) 439–40; 443; 'Bowels Opened' in *Works* ii (1862) 6

51 Sibbes 'Faith Triumphant' 443

52 Ibid 422

53 Ibid 441

54 Ibid 440

55 Sibbes 'The Fountain Opened' 514

56 Ibid 515

57 Ibid 515–16

58 Ibid 523

59 Sibbes 'Bowels Opened' 142–3

60 Ibid 174–5

61 Kendall *Calvin and English Calvinism*. In particular, see 79–138.

62 Calvin quoted in ibid 18

63 Calvin quoted in ibid 17

64 Kendall gives two reasons for using the term 'experimental' to describe this religious notion: 'The term "experimental" will be used rather than "experiential" to describe these predestinarians, for two reasons.

First, it is *their* word. Secondly, the word "experimental" contains a useful ambiguity since it refers to experience but also to testing a hypothesis by an experiment. The experimental predestinarians put this proposition to a test: "whether a man be in the state of damnation or in the state of grace" ' (ibid 9).

65 For Sibbes see *Dictionary of National Biography* xviii, 182–3. He was one of the most influential preachers of his day, first at Cambridge University, where he was appointed as a college preacher in 1609, and then at Gray's Inn, where he began preaching in 1617. The publication of his sermons, beginning in 1630, broadened his influence, including his crucial influence on Richard Baxter.

Preston was also influential in both Cambridge and London. He succeeded Donne as preacher at Lincoln's Inn and 'large numbers flocked to hear him' (*DNB* xvi, 309).

66 Tuve 'George Herbert and *Caritas*' 168

67 Ibid 184

68 Lewalski *Protestant Poetics* 292–3

69 Benet *Secretary of Praise* 33, 156

70 The notion of 'confidence' centres in Paul, who says that in Christ 'we have boldness and access with confidence by the faith of him' (Ephesians 3:12). 'Confidence' and 'trust' express the same truth: 'For therefore we both labour and suffer reproach, because we trust in the living God, who is the Saviour of all men, especially of those that believe' (1 Timothy 4:10). This trust or confidence is crucial in Luther: 'Therefore Christ wants to say here: "You have heard that you must trust [vertrauen] in God; but I want to show you furthermore where you will truly find Him, lest your thoughts create an idol bearing the name of God. This means: If you want to believe in God, then believe in Me. If you want to apply your faith and your confidence [vertrauen] properly, that it may not be amiss or false, then direct it toward Me; for in Me the entire Godhead dwells perfectly." And as Christ declares later (John 14:6, 9): "I am the Way, the Truth, and the Life. He who has seen Me has seen the Father. He who hears Me hears the Father. Therefore if you want to be sure to meet God, take hold of Him in Me and through Me" ' (*Sermons on the Gospel of St. John* in *Works* vol 24, 14: 1, p 23). When Luther writes in Latin, the German *vertrauen* becomes *fiducia*. Speaking of love's foundation in faith, he says: 'Perfecta enim seu sincera charitas ex fiducia oritur, quae apprehendit Deum constanter.' See *D. Martin Luthers Werke Kritische Gesamtausgabe* ed J.C.F. Knaake et al (Weimar: Bohlau 1883), xx, 761. Hereafter cited as *WA*

71 Paul Althaus shows the importance of 'holding fast' in Luther's conception of faithful trust: 'God's "yes" to him is hidden in a severe "no." But faith is the art of comprehending God in his opposite and "of holding fast to the deep and hidden 'yes' under and above the 'no' by

firmly trusting in God's word" ' (*The Theology of Martin Luther* 32). See *WA* 17, ɪɪ, 302 for the German 'mit festem glauben auff Gotts wort fassen und hallten.' For the bibilical background of 'holdfast' see G.G. Findlay 'Faith' in *Dictionary of the Bible* ed James Hastings (New York: Charles Scribner's Sons 1947) 255.

72 Cf Strier *Love Known* 65–74.
73 Preston *The Breast-plate* 70
74 Ibid 69
75 See nn 70–1 above.
76 Preston 'Of Love: the First Sermon' in *The Breast-plate* 28–9
77 Sibbes 'The Privileges of the Faithful' 276–7
78 The problem of defining 'sacred love parody' in *The Temple* is posed by Louis L. Martz *The Poetry of Meditation: A Study in English Religious Literature* (New Haven and London: Yale University Press 1965) 186n3; Rosemond Tuve 'Sacred "Parody" of Love Poetry, and Herbert' in *Essays by Rosemond Tuve* 207–49. In assessing Herbert's use of the conventions and of the forms from the tradition of secular love poetry, both Martz and Tuve are careful to empty the term 'parody,' denying that Herbert is mocking his secular sources. Martz says that 'parody' is a 'neutral term' for Herbert, and Tuve denies that Herbert's imitation had to do with ' "turning" another poet's sense and thus obliquely commenting thereon, or with the intention of substituting good love for bad by displacing naughty verses' (212).
    Even though Herbert is not mocking his secular sources, he *is* defining divine love by means of contrast, as he makes clear in 'Love (ɪ)':
    Immortall Love, authour of this great frame,
    Sprung from that beautie which can never fade;
    How hath man parcel'd out thy glorious name,
    And thrown it on that dust which thou hast made,
    While mortall love doth all the title gain!   (1–5)
Herbert's 'sacred love parody,' it seems to me, underlines the contrast.
79 Martz *The Poetry of Meditation* 319
80 Ibid 315
81 Sibbes 'The Privileges of the Faithful' 278
82 Eg, 'Jordan (ɪɪ),' 15; 'The Holdfast,' 11
83 For a useful discussion of this subject, see William V. Nestrick ' "Mine and Thine" in *The Temple*' in *'Too Rich to Clothe the Sunne': Essays on George Herbert* ed Claude J. Summers and Ted-Larry Pebworth (Pittsburgh: University of Pittsburgh Press 1980) 115–27.
84 See Herbert *The Country Parson* 230: 'For every one hath not digested, when it is a sin to take something for mony lent, or when not; when it is a fault to discover anothers fault, or when not; *when the affections of the soul in desiring and procuring increase of means, or honour, be a sin of covetousnes or ambition, and when not. ...*'
85 Sibbes 'The Privileges of the Faithful' 276

86 Tuve 'George Herbert and *Caritas*' 184
87 See John Burnaby *Amor Dei: A Study of the Religion of St. Augustine* (London: Hodder and Stoughton 1960) 106.
88 Cf Sibbes 'Faith Triumphant' 445: 'We embrace not the promises of Christ as man embraceth a dead post, that cannot return embraces to him again. This embracing of Christ and heaven, it is a mutual embracing; and it is a second, reflexive embracing. We embrace God and Christ, because we find God in Christ embracing our souls first in the arms of his love; therefore we embrace him again in the arms of our affections, because we find Christ embracing us in the arms of his affections.' Cf Herbert *The Country Parson* 283: 'And all may certainly conclude, that God loves them, till either they despise that Love, or despaire of his Mercy: not any sin else, but is within his Love; but the despising of Love must needs be without it. The thrusting away of his arme makes us onely not embraced.'
89 Sibbes 'The Art of Self-Humbling' and 'The Art of Mourning' in *Works* VI (1863) 44–75
90 *The Sermons of John Donne* II, ed Evelyn M. Simpson and George R. Potter (Berkeley and Los Angeles: University of California Press 1962) 73
91 Joseph Hall *The Art of Divine Meditation* in *Works* VI, ed Philip Wynter (New York: AMS Press 1969; reprinted from the 1863 edition) 46–88
92 Andrew Marvell 'An Horatian *Ode upon* Cromwel's *Return from* Ireland' in *Poems* I, ed H.M. Margoliouth (Oxford: Clarendon Press 1962) 87, lines 10, 119–20
93 Charles H. and Katherine George *The Protestant Mind of the English Reformation, 1570–1640* (Princeton: Princeton University Press 1961) 129
94 For one useful discussion of the relationship between calling and love, see Karl Holl *The Cultural Significance of the Reformation* tr Karl and Barbara Hertz (New York: Meridian Books 1959) 30–41.
95 Tuve 'George Herbert and *Caritas*' 189
96 See nn 22–3 above.
97 Quoted in Izaak Walton 'The Life of Mr. George Herbert' in *The Lives of John Donne, Sir Henry Wotton, Richard Hooker, George Herbert and Robert Sanderson* with an introduction by George Saintsbury (London: Oxford University Press 1966; reprinted from the 1927 edition) 314.

Chapter Three

1 Jean Chatillon 'Dulcedo, Dulcedo Dei' in *Dictionaire de Spiritualité: Ascétique et Mystique Doctrine et Histoire* III (Paris: Beauchesne 1957) 1777
2 Ibid 1781–3
3 St Francis de Sales *Treatise on the Love of God* tr H.B. Mackey (Westport, Conn: Greenwood Press 1971) I, xvi, p 57

4 Ibid III, iii, p 135

5 Ibid XII, xii, p 553

6 Richard Sibbes 'The Matchless Love and Inbeing' in *Works* VI, ed Alexander Grosart (Edinburgh 1863) 398

7 Sibbes 'The Returning Backslider' in *Works* II (Edinburgh 1862) 68

8 Sibbes 'A Breathing after God' in *Works* II, 232–3

9 Cf Barbara Kiefer Lewalski *Protestant Poetics and the Seventeenth-Century Religious Lyric* (Princeton: Princeton University Press 1979) 296–8. Lewalski's claim that the Song of Songs exerts a strong influence on Herbert, just as it does on other Protestant writers, does not account for the absence of overt references to the Bride and Bridegroom in Herbert's poetry.

10 My discussion is here indebted to Pierre Adnès 'Goût Spirituel' in *Dictionaire de Spiritualité* (Paris: Beauchesne 1967) VI, 642–3.

11 Sibbes 'A Breathing after God' 233

12 Rosemond Tuve *A Reading of George Herbert* (Chicago: University of Chicago Press 1952) 51

13 For a discussion of Calvin, one of the prime sources of this notion, see Ronald S. Wallace *Calvin's Doctrine of the Word and Sacrament* (Edinburgh: Oliver and Boyd 1953) 1-60.

14 Immortall Heat, O let thy greater flame
    Attract the lesser to it: let those fires,
    Which shall consume the world, first make it tame;
And kindle in our hearts such true desires,
As may consume our lusts, and make thee way.
    Then shall our hearts pant thee; then shall our brain
    All her invention on thine Altar lay,
And there in hymnes send back thy fire again: ('Love (II),' 1–8)

15 Then tell me, what is that supreme delight?
                    Echo.   Light.
    Light to the minde: what shall the will enjoy?
                    Echo.   Joy.   ('Heaven,' 13–16)

16 Again, Calvin stands in the background. See *Institutes of the Christian Religion* tr Ford Lewis Battles (Philadelphia: Westminster Press 1973) I, xv, 7.

17 Adnès 'Goût Spirituel' 632

18 St Francis de Sales *Treatise on the Love of God* III, xii, p 158

19 Sibbes 'The Returning Backslider' 260

20 Bernard of Clairvaux *Eighty Six Sermons on the Song of Solomon* in *Life and Works* tr S.J. Eales (London: John Hodges 1896) 62.5, IV, 375

21 Ibid 21.5, p 125

22 Ibid 70.7, p 430

23 Ibid 70.7–9, pp 430–2

24 Ibid 70.9, p 432
25 See 'Herbert' in William H. Halewood *The Poetry of Grace: Reformation Themes and Structures in English Seventeenth-Century Poetry* (New Haven, Conn and London: Yale University Press 1970) 88–111.
26 See 'Repentance,' esp lines 12; 19–30.
27 Herbert is playing with the alternative meaning as well: 'Intercourse or converse with God' (*OED*).
28 'Now thanks be unto God, which always causeth us to triumph in Christ, and maketh manifest the savour of his knowledge by us in every place. For we are unto God a sweet savour of Christ, in them that are saved, and in them that perish: To the one we are the savour of death unto death; and to the other the savour of life unto life. And who is sufficient for these things? For we are not as many, which corrupt the word of God: but as of sincerity, but as of God, in the sight of God speak we in Christ' (2 Corinthians 2:14–17).
29 Christ dwells 'in' the believer through the Spirit (Romans 8:9–11); the believer, in turn, is 'complete in' Christ (Colossians 2:10); and is baptized as a member 'in' Christ's Body the church (1 Corinthians 12:13). Also, John's formulation of man's participation in Christ, the bread of life, is to the point: 'He that eateth my flesh, and drinketh my blood, dwelleth in me, and I in him' (John 6:56).
30 1 Corinthians 11:3; Colossians 1:18
31 C.A. Patrides 'A Crown of Praise: The Poetry of Herbert' in *The English Poems of George Herbert* (London, Melbourne, and Toronto: J.M. Dent and Sons 1974) 17
32 See Tuve *A Reading of George Herbert* 37–9.
33 See Lewalski *Protestant Poetics and the Seventeenth-Century Religious Lyric* 312–13. She distils Tuve's comments on typology in 'The Bunch of Grapes' as follows: 'the poem depends for its meaning upon our recognition of the traditional typological relationship between the grapes hanging from the pole carried by the spies and Christ on the cross, the true vine pressed in the winepress on the Passion (Isa. 63:3) to become the wine of the New Covenant.'

Chapter Four

1 See pp 30–1.
2 Robert Sanderson 'Ad Populum,' the Fourth Sermon, in St Paul's Church London, 4 Nov 1621 in *XXXVI Sermons* (London 1689) 205
3 William Perkins *A Clowd of Faithfull Witnesses, Leading to the heavenly Canaan* or *A Commentarie upon the 11. Chapter to the Hebrewes* in *Workes* III (London 1613) 106
4 Perkins *A Treatise of the Vocations, or Callings of men* in *Workes* I (London 1612) 752
5 Ibid 756

6 Sanderson 'Ad Populum,' the Fourth Sermon, 224

7 Sanderson 'Sermon *Ad Clerum*' on 1 Corinthians 12:7, 13 March 1620 in *XXXVI Sermons* 45

8 Perkins *A Commentarie or Exposition upon the Five First Chapters of the Epistle to the Galatians* in *Workes* II, 271–2

9 Sibbes 'Bowels Opened' in *Works* II, ed Alexander Grosart (Edinburgh 1862) 25

10 Ibid 13; cf Sibbes 'The Saint's Happiness' in *Works* VII (Edinburgh 1864) 71: 'God is a goodness *that is proportionable and fitting to our souls*, which is the best part in a man.'

11 Both notions are biblical commonplaces. About deeds as works, David says, 'One generation shall praise thy works to another, and shall declare thy mighty acts' (Psalm 145:4). Elsewhere, talking about man's dominion over things made at creation, he says, 'Thou madest him to have dominion over the works of thy hands; thou hast put all things under his feet' (Psalm 8:6).

12 Perkins *A Golden Chaine: The Description of Theologie, Containing the order of the causes of Salvation and Damnation* in *Workes* I, 15

13 Thomas Adams *Meditations upon Some Part of the Creed* in *Workes* (London 1629) 1129

14 For an informative discussion of employment and business in *The Temple*, see Diana Benet *The Secretary of Praise* (Columbia, Missouri: University of Missouri Press 1984) 101–32.

15 For a useful discussion of the relationship of business imagery to the ideas of ransom, sale, and debt in the relationship between man and God, see Bernard Knieger 'The Purchase-Sale: Patterns of Business Imagery in the Poetry of George Herbert' *SEL* 6 (1966) 111–24.

16 Perkins *A Treatise of the Vocations* 751

17 Sibbes 'Bowels Opened' 10

18 See ibid 11: 'God prunes us by crosses and afflictions.'

19 The general call to salvation is applied specifically by the Holy Spirit to each individual. For a useful discussion of this distinction, see Robert B. Shaw *The Call of God: The Theme of Vocation in the Poetry of Donne and Herbert* (Cambridge, Mass: Cowley Publications 1981) 13.

20 Barbar Kiefer Lewalski *Protestant Poetics and the Seventeenth-Century Religious Lyric* (Princeton: Princeton University Press 1979) 16

21 Ben Jonson *Discoveries or Timber* in *The Poems; The Prose Works* ed C.H. Herford and E. Simpson (Oxford: Clarendon Press 1947) 635

22 Jonson *Horace: Of the Art of Poetrie* in ibid 311, line 149

23 Ibid 325, line 452

24 Herbert's contemporary reader would have detected allusions to Seneca in 'Jordan (II)': '*There is in love a sweetnesse readie penn'd: / Copie out onely that, and save expense*' (17–18). In his 'Epistle LXXXIV' Seneca examines how borrowed literary sources are absorbed when imitated. Does the bee collect honey ready-made from flowers or does it transform

what it has already collected? By analogy Seneca is asking which is
the case when literary sources are borrowed: 'We also, I say, ought to
copy these bees, and sift whatever we have gathered from a varied
course of reading, for such things are better preserved if they are kept
separate; then, by applying the supervising care with which our nature
has endowed us, – in other words, our natural gifts, – we should so
blend those several flavours into one delicious compound that, even
though it betrays its origin, yet it nevertheless is clearly a different thing
from that whence it came.' Like food, borrowings must be digested
and assimilated; as a result, determining the source is sometimes difficult: 'I think that sometimes it is impossible for it to be seen who is
being imitated if the copy is a true one; for a true copy stamps its own
form upon all the features which it has drawn from what we may call
the original, in such a say that they are combined into a unity.'

Herbert's point in recalling this passage in 'Jordan (ıı)' is that the
sweetness of the indwelling God is 'readie penn'd' and allows no question about its origin. But Herbert leaves the ironies to the perceptive
reader, since God's inspiration, even in the sweetness of the divine
'friend' (15), must be translated by the human mind receiving it. And
even biblical verses, God's 'hony' ('The H. Scriptures (ı),' 2), may
become digested in the poems which contain them.

For the above quotations from Seneca see *Epistulae Morales* ıı, tr R.M.
Gummere, Loeb Classical Library (London: William Heinemann 1930)
276–84.

25 Stanley E. Fish *The Living Temple: George Herbert and Catechizing*
   (Berkeley, Los Angeles, London: University of California Press 1978)
   58–63
26 'Let us therefore follow after the things which make for peace, and things
   wherewith one may edify another' (Romans 14:19).
27 'And he gave some, apostles; and some, prophets; and some, evangelists;
   and some, pastors and teachers; For the perfecting of the saints, for
   the work of the ministry, for the edifying of the body of Christ'
   (Ephesians 4:11–12).
28 'Let no corrupt communication proceed out of your mouth, but that
   which is good to the use of edifying, that it may minister grace unto
   the hearers' (Ephesians 4:29).
29 For discussion of Protestant conceptions of the Holy Spirit, see Geoffrey
   F. Nuttall *The Holy Spirit in Puritan Faith and Experience* (Oxford:
   Blackwell 1947).
30 Heather A.R. Asals *Equivocal Predication: George Herbert's Way to
   God* (Toronto, Buffalo, London: University of Toronto Press 1981) 18
31 For a discussion of Calvin's contribution to Protestant conceptions that
   all of Scripture expresses Christ and that the Holy Spirit moves the
   reader of Scripture, see Ronald S. Wallace *Calvin's Doctrine of the Word
   and Sacrament* (Edinburgh: Oliver and Boyd 1953).

32 The notion of 're-edifying,' which considerably antedated early
seventeenth-century restoration activities like Herbert's, applied most
specifically to rebuilding and restoring actual structures. More broadly,
it also referred to re-establishing or rebuilding less physical entities such
as human social bodies. In any event, Paul's notion of edifying church
members is often in the near background.

33 Izaak Walton 'The Life of Mr. George Herbert' in *The Lives of John
Donne, Sir Henry Wotton, Richard Hooker, George Herbert and Robert
Sanderson* with an introduction by George Saintsbury (London: Oxford
University Press 1966; reprinted from the 1927 edition) 279

34 Quoted in Amy M. Charles *A Life of George Herbert* (Ithaca and London:
Cornell University Press 1977) 151

35 The term 'Anglican' here distinguishes those liturgists who wanted to
maintain and restore many traditional physical elements in the
established church from those who in varying ways wanted to do the
opposite. See 161n49 for more on the use of the term 'Anglican.'

36 G.W.O. Addleshaw *The High Church Tradition: A Study in the Liturgical Thought of the Seventeenth Century* (London: Faber and Faber
1941) 40–1

37 One example of such Pauline argument can be found in Herbert Thorn-
dike's 1642 discussion, *Of Religious Assemblies, and the Publick
Service of God* in *Theological Works* I (Oxford 1845) 222–3.

38 Quoted in Walton 'The Life of Mr. George Herbert' 278

39 John E. Booty 'George Herbert: *The Temple* and *The Book of Common
Prayer*' *Mosaic* 12:2 (1979) 76–7

40 Addleshaw *The High Church Tradition* 75

41 Lancelot Andrewes quoted in ibid 78

Chapter Five

1 'And this is an admirable way of teaching, wherein the Catechized will
at length finde delight, and by which the Catechizer, if he once get
the skill of it, will draw out of ignorant and silly souls, even the dark and
deep points of Religion. *Socrates* did thus in Philosophy, who held
that the seeds of all truths lay in every body, and accordingly by questions well ordered he found Philosophy in silly Trades-men. That
position will not hold in Christianity, because it contains things above
nature: but after that the Catechisme is once learn'd, that which nature is towards Philosophy, the Catechism is towards Divinity. To this
purpose, some dialogues in *Plato* were worth the reading, where the
singular dexterity of Socrates in this kind may be observed, and imitated'
(*The Country Parson* 256).

2 Herbert possessed Augustine's works, which he mentions in his will.
See Joseph Summers *George Herbert: His Religion and Art* (London:
Chatto and Windus 1954) 76.

3 One of the fundamental themes of the Psalms is the delight experienced in the search for God.

4 For a useful discussion of Plato's attitude to pleasure, see G.M.A. Grube *Plato's Thought* (London: Methuen and Co 1935) 51–86.

5 See Edward Surtz *The Praise of Pleasure: Philosophy, Education and Communism in More's Utopia* (Cambridge, Mass: Harvard University Press 1957) 23–35.

6 For an informative discussion of this factor, see Phillips Salman 'Instruction and Delight in Medieval Renaissance Criticism' *RQ* 32 (1979) 310–11.

7 St Augustine *Exposition on the Book of Psalms* tr A.W. Haddan in A Selected Library of Nicene and Post-Nicene Fathers, gen ed Philip Schaff (Grand Rapids, Mich: Wm. B. Eerdmans 1956; reprinted from New York: Christian Literature Co 1888) cxix, 62, p 570

8 Heather A.R. Asals *Equivocal Predication: George Herbert's Way to God* (Toronto, Buffalo, London: University of Toronto Press 1981) 57

9 Augustine *On Christian Doctrine* i, xxxiii, 37

10 Helen Vendler *The Poetry of George Herbert* (Cambridge, Mass and London: Harvard University Press 1975) 226

11 In 'The Pulley' the drawing rope or line is implicit. The notion of the pulley is expressed in the title and in the hieroglyphic stanza. The experience of restlessness in the form of suffering is the pulley by which God draws man.

12 Paul saw himself fulfilled in Christly suffering for the church: 'Who now rejoice in my sufferings for you, and fill up that which is behind of the afflictions of Christ in my flesh for his body's sake, which is the church' (Colossians 1:24). For a discussion of Paul's influence on Donne's joy in suffering, see my *Fulfilling the Circle: A Study of John Donne's Thought* (Toronto, Buffalo, London: University of Toronto Press 1984) 124–9.

13 Salman 'Instruction and Delight' 325

14 Louis L. Martz *The Poetry of Meditation: A Study in English Religious Literature of the Seventeenth Century* (New Haven and London: Yale University Press 1965) 309–20

15 Richard Sibbes 'A Fountain Sealed' *Works* v (Edinburgh 1863) 414–5

16 John Calvin *Commentaries on the Epistles of Paul to the Galatians and Ephesians* tr William Pringle (Grand Rapids, Mich: Wm. B. Eerdmans 1957; reprinted from the 1841 edition) iv, 30, p 301

17 Lancelot Andrewes 'A Sermon Preached Before the Kings Majesty at Whitehall, on the Twenty-Third of May, A.D. MDCXIII, Being Whit-Sunday' in *Ninety-Six Sermons* iii (Oxford: John Henry Parker 1841) 213–14; Joseph Hall 'The Sin and Punishment of Grieving the Holy Spirit' in *Works* v, ed Philip Wynter (New York: AMS Press 1969; reprinted from the 1863 edition) 572

18 Quoted in Izaak Walton 'The Life of Mr. George Herbert' in *The Lives of*

John Donne, Sir Henry Wotton, Richard Hooker, George Herbert and Robert Sanderson, with an introduction by George Saintsbury (London: Oxford University Press 1966; reprinted from the 1927 edition) 314. Cf Amy M. Charles *A Life of George Herbert* (Ithaca and London: Cornell University Press 1977) 174

Chapter Six

1 Richard Sibbes 'The Life of Faith' in *Works* v (Edinburgh 1863) 360
2 John Preston *An Elegant and Lively Description of Spirituall Life and Death* in *Foure Godly and Learned Tretises* (London 1633) 152
3 In Psalm 119 the psalmist repeatedly asks that God 'quicken' him. The transitive 'quicken,' like a refrain, honours God as the giver of life. This quickening life is 'according to thy word' (v 25), 'in thy righteousness' (v 40), 'after thy lovingkindness' (v 88), 'according to thy judgement' (v 149), etc. In affirming his willingness to follow God's precepts, the psalmist conforms himself in a direct personal relationship to these elements in the divine nature. Love and delight in God's law are the effects of this life received through the personal relationship.
      Definition of the 'quick' through sharp opposition to the 'dead' is the work of the New Testament. The judge Christ will not only distinguish the quick from the dead (eg, 2 Timothy 4:1); he is also the revealed God who gives life: 'And you, being dead in your sins and the uncircumcision of your flesh, hath he quickened together with him, having forgiven you all trespasses' (Colossians 2:13). Raised from spiritual death to life, the believer enjoys the living presence of a God whose word is 'quick and powerful' (Hebrews 4:12).
4 William Perkins *A Golden Chaine: The Description of Theologie, Containing the order of the causes of Salvation and Damnation, according to Gods word* in *Workes* I (London 1612) 12
5 For a very useful, brief discussion of the biblical concept of the 'living God,' see P.M. Coyle 'Life, Concept of (in the Bible)' in *New Catholic Encylopedia* VIII (New York, St Louis, San Francisco, Toronto, London, Sydney: McGraw-Hill 1967) 739–40.
6 Preston *An Elegant and Lively Description* 56
7 Ibid
8 Ibid 57
9 Ibid; cf Sibbes 'The Dead Man' in *Works* v, 400: 'What is death? Death is nothing else but a separation from the cause of life, from that whence life springs.'
10 Preston *An Elegant and Lively Description* 58–60
11 See nn 27–8 below.
12 For a useful discussion of this meaning of 'quick,' see Richard Strier *Love Known: Theology and Experience in George Herbert's Poetry* (Chicago and London: University of Chicago Press 1983) 164.

13 John E. Booty 'George Herbert: *The Temple* and *The Book of Common Prayer'* *Mosaic* 12:2 (1979) 81

14 For an assessment of Herbert and motion according to a traditional geometric conception, see Thomas Ramey Watson 'God's Geometry: Motion in the English Poetry of George Herbert' *George Herbert Journal* 9 (1985) 17–25.

15 See Chana Bloch *Spelling the Word: George Herbert and the Bible* (Berkeley, Los Angeles, London: University of California Press 1985) 53–78.

16 Romans 11:16–24

17 John 15:1–7

18 One *OED* meaning for *extend* is 'to write out at full length' some expression in a different form. Herbert's punning 'extend' has subtle layers for a poet who saw all experience prevened by the Spirit and embodying the Word. The poet's own experience is extended in the words of his poetic vocation.

19 The basic grounds for this emphasis are familiar. Faith working by love yields the fruits of charity. Cranmer's official homily says it thus: 'Another faith there is in scripture, which is not ... idle, unfruitfull, and dead, but worketh by charity (as S. Paul declareth, Gal. 5) Which as the other vaine faith is called a dead faith, so may this be called a quick or lively faith' (19; see n 21 below for full entry). Charity is the basis for the fruitful works in one's vocation. Richard Sibbes says: 'Let us then strive and labour to be fruitfull in our Places and Calling: for it is the greatest honour in this world, for God to dignifie us with such a condition, as to make us fruitfull. We must not bring forth fruit to our selves ... Honour, Riches, and the like, are but secondary things, arbitrary at God's pleasure to cast in: but, to have an active heart fruitfull from this ground, that God hath planted us for this purpose, that we may doe good to mankind, this is an excellent consideration not to profane our calling' ('Bowels Opened' in *Works* II, 18–19).

The Augustine *frui* metamorphosed into 'fruit' is not beside the point here. Both good works – the fruits of charity and also the fruitful works in one's calling – give enjoyment to those servants of God performing them.

20 For a discussion of the traditional Tree of Life typology in relation to Herbert, see Rosemond Tuve *A Reading of George Herbert* (Chicago: University of Chicago Press 1952) 81–90. More generally useful are John Erskine Hankins *Source and Meaning in Spenser's Allegory: A Study of 'The Faerie Queene'* (Oxford: Clarendon Press 1971) 117–19; James Nohrnberg *The Analogy of 'The Faerie Queene'* (Princeton: Princeton University Press 1976) 161–70; Stanley Stewart *The Enclosed Garden: The Tradition and the Image in Seventeeth-Century Poetry* (Madison, Milwaukee, and London: University of Wisconsin Press 1966) 75–86. Among the many contemporary works dealing with typology and

specifically useful on the Tree of Life see William Guild *Moses Unvailed* 2nd ed (London 1623) 1.

21 'A Short Declaration of the true, lively, and Christian Faith' in *Certaine Sermons or Homilies appointed to be Read in Churches, In the Time of Queen Elizabeth I (1547–1571)*. A facsimile reproduction of the edition of 1623 with an introduction by Mary Ellen Rickey and Thomas B. Stroup (Gainesville, Florida: Scholars' Facsimiles and Reprints 1968) 20

22 'Article v' quoted in H.C. Porter *Reformation and Reaction in Tudor Cambridge* (Cambridge: Cambridge University Press 1958) 371

23 Eg, Sibbes 'The Life of Faith' 370: 'As we see a lively fountain, the water whereof will sparkle and leap, so there will be living joys, speeches, delights, exhortations, sensible of good and evil. He will trust God, rely on his word and promise, because Christ cannot touch the soul, but we must be lively.'

24 Barbara Kiefer Lewalski *Protestant Poetics and the Seventeenth-Century Religious Lyric* (Princeton: Princeton University Press 1979) 265; 13–24

25 The basic frame is expressed in Romans 8:30–1: 'whom he did predestinate, them he also called: and whom he called, them he also justified: and whom he justified, them he also glorified.' The elect are called by God, justified by Christ's sacrifice, adopted as God's sons, and sanctified throughout their lives by the attendant Spirit.

26 Sibbes 'The Life of Faith' 372

27 John Calvin *Institutes of the Christian Religion* tr Ford Lewis Battles (Philadelphia: Westminster Press 1973) III, iii, 8, p 600

28 Eg, Sibbes 'The Life of Faith' 368: 'Now being brought by faith to live in justification, we must of necessity also live by faith in sanctification. There be two parts of a holy life: 1. *In mortification, dying to sin;* 2. *In vivification, living to righteousness.*'

29 John S. Coolidge *The Pauline Renaissance in England: Puritanism and the Bible* (Oxford: Clarendon Press 1970) 29

30 The temple and the plant intersect in the idea of growth. Paul's building, which 'fitly framed together groweth unto an holy temple in the Lord' (Ephesians 2: 21), fulfils Old Testament configurations of the communal 'house' growing as a plant.

31 Coolidge *The Pauline Renaissance* 39

32 For a discussion of Donne and the Body, see my *Fulfilling the Circle: A Study of John Donne's Thought* (Toronto, Buffalo, London: University of Toronto Press 1984) 93–101.

33 'That which was from the beginning, which we have heard, which we have seen with our eyes, which we have looked upon, and our hands have handled, of the Word of life; (For the life was manifested, and we have seen it, and bear witness, and shew unto you that eternal life, which was with the Father, and was manifested unto us)' (1 John 1:1–2).

34 Cf 'That whosoever believeth in him should not perish, but have eternal

life. For God so loved the world, that he gave his only begotten Son, that whosoever believeth in him should not perish, but have everlasting life' (John 3:15–16).

35 'Whosoever is born of God doth not commit sin; for his seed remaineth in him: and he cannot sin, because he is born of God' (1 John 3:9).

36 'For the bread of God is he which cometh down from heaven, and giveth life unto the world. ... I am the bread of life: he that cometh to me shall never hunger; and he that believeth on me shall never thirst' (John 6:33, 35).

37 Helen Vendler *The Poetry of George Herbert* (Cambridge, Mass and London: Harvard University Press 1975) 25–56

Conclusion

1 Chana Bloch *Spelling the Word: George Herbert and the Bible* (Berkeley, Los Angeles, London: University of California Press 1985) 53–78

2 See chapter three, 170n13.

3 Gene Edward Veith *Reformation Spirituality: The Religion of George Herbert* (London and Toronto: Associated University Presses 1985) 25

4 Robert Ellrodt *L'Inspiration Personelle et l'Esprit du Temps chez Les Poètes Métaphysiques Anglais* (Paris: Librairie Jose Corti 1960) I, 109, 129

5 Stanley E. Fish *Self-Consuming Artifacts: The Experience of Seventeenth-Century Literature* (Berkeley, Los Angeles, London: University of California Press 1972) 156–223

6 Ibid 157

7 Barbara Leah Harman *Costly Monuments: Representations of the Self in George Herbert's Poetry* (Cambridge, Mass and London: Harvard University Press 1982) 20; Harman's first chapter is a history of critical assumptions about the self in Herbert (1–38).

8 Ibid 34–5

9 John Calvin *Institutes of the Christian Religion* I, tr Ford Lewis Battles (Philadelphia: Westminster Press 1973) I, i, 36, p 36

10 Fish *Self-Consuming Artifacts* 173: 'In a world where Christ occupies every position and initiates every action, ambiguity – of place, of person, of agency – is the true literalism. His word is all.'

11 See my *Fulfilling the Circle: A Study of John Donne's Thought* (Toronto, Buffalo, London: University of Toronto Press 1984) 165. For Bernard even the Image of God in Satan cannot be burnt out in Hell.

12 Calvin *Institutes* III, xi, 21–3, pp 751–4

13 Ibid III, xi, 22, p 752; for a discussion of Luther's use of this image, see Barbara Kiefer Lewalski *Donne's 'Anniversaries' and the Poetry of Praise: The Creation of a Symbolic Mode* (Princeton: Princeton University Press 1973) 127–8.

14 Fish *Self-Consuming Artifacts* 157
15 The standard practice of imping is described succinctly as follows: 'In imping, the injured feather is cut obliquely with a razor near its center so as to fit exactly part of a previously chosen plume (collected by the falconer as part of his stock in hand) cut at the same angle. A small metal "imping needle," first dipped in brine, is now carefully adjusted within the shafts of the fragments until a firm union is made of the two, *in situ proprio.*' *The Art of Falconry: being the 'De Arte Venandi Cum Avibus' of Frederick II of Hohenstaufen* tr Casey A. Wood and F. Marjorie Fyfe (Stanford: Stanford University Press 1943) 426. For the more contemporary source commonly cited, see the detailed discussion of the same procedure in George Turbervile *The Booke of Faulconrie or Hauking* (London 1575; reprinted in a facsimile edition, Amsterdam and New York: Da Capo Press 1969) 275–9.
16 Herbert may be alluding ironically to Icarus here. Herbert also was interested in rising through art, at the same time that he was keenly aware that art can be proud and that the only true rising is through conformity to Christ's humility.
17 Helen Vendler *The Poetry of George Herbert* (Cambridge, Mass and London: Harvard University Press 1975) 251
18 Ibid 152
19 Ibid 238
20 John Donne '5. Expostulation' in *Devotions upon Emergent Occasions*. One biblical precedent is the 'murmuring' of the hungry Israelites after Moses leads them out of Egypt. In response, God provides manna and quail (Exodus 16).
21 Richard Strier *Love Known: Theology and Experience in George Herbert's Poetry* (Chicago and London: University of Chicago Press 1983) 31–41
22 Arnold Stein *George Herbert's Lyrics* (Baltimore: Johns Hopkins University Press 1968) 19

Index